open source

Dan Woods · Gautam Guliani

for the enterprise

MANAGING RISKS, REAPING REWARDS

O'REILLY®

Beijing • Cambridge • Farnham • Köln • Paris • Sebastopol • Taipei • Tokyo

Open Source for the Enterprise

by Dan Woods and Gautam Guliani

Copyright © 2005 O'Reilly Media, Inc. All rights reserved.
Printed in the United States of America.

Published by O'Reilly Media, Inc., 1005 Gravenstein Highway North, Sebastopol, CA 95472.

O'Reilly books may be purchased for educational, business, or sales promotional use. Online editions are also available for most titles (*safari.oreilly.com*). For more information, contact our corporate/institutional sales department: (800) 998-9938 or *corporate@oreilly.com*.

Editor:	Andy Oram
Production Editor:	Sarah Sherman
Cover Designer:	Mike Kohnke
Interior Designer:	Phyllis McKee

Printing History:

July 2005:	First Edition.

Nutshell Handbook, the Nutshell Handbook logo, and the O'Reilly logo are registered trademarks of O'Reilly Media, Inc. *Open Source for the Enterprise* and related trade dress are trademarks of O'Reilly Media, Inc.

Many of the designations used by manufacturers and sellers to distinguish their products are claimed as trademarks. Where those designations appear in this book, and O'Reilly Media, Inc. was aware of a trademark claim, the designations have been printed in caps or initial caps.

While every precaution has been taken in the preparation of this book, the publisher and authors assume no responsibility for errors or omissions, or for damages resulting from the use of the information contained herein.

 This book uses RepKover™, a durable and flexible lay-flat binding.

ISBN: 0-596-10119-8

[M]

Table of Contents

Preface ix

1. The Nature of Open Source 1
   The Open Source Debate 3
   Understanding Your Open Source Readiness 4
   The Nature of Open Source 6
   What Is Open Source? 7
   Where Does Open Source Come From? 12
   How Does Open Source Grow? 14
   How Does Open Source Die? 15
   Leadership in the Open Source Life Cycle 16
   Second-Generation Trends in Open Source 18
   The Different Roots of Commercial Software 19
   Productization: The Key to Understanding the Challenge
   of Using Open Source 23
   Comparing the Risks of Commercial and Open Source Software 24

2. Measuring the Maturity of Open Source 29
   Open Source Traps 30
   The Elements of Open Source Maturity 31
   The Open Source Maturity Model 41

3. The Open Source Skill Set. 45
    Preventing an Open Source Nightmare 46
    Open Source Skill Levels 48
    Open Source Skills Inventory 57
    How Maturity Affects Required Skills and Resources 64
    Skills and Risks 64
    Open Source Skill Building 65

4. Making the ROI Case 67
    ROI Fashions 68
    How Open Source Costs Differ from Commercial Software Costs 69
    Making Your Own ROI Model 75
    Skills Versus Money 78

5. Designing an Open Source Strategy 79
    Crafting a Strategy for Open Source Adoption 80
    Crafting a Strategy for Applying Open Source 89
    Crafting a Strategy for Managing Open Source 91

6. Support Models for Open Source. 95
    Open Source Support Offers 96
    When Is Commercial Open Source Support the Right Choice? 101
    Buy Carefully 103

7. Making Open Source Projects Easy to Adopt 105
    One Program for Productization 106
    Basic Information and Community Support 107
    Reducing the Skills Gap for Getting Started 109
    Accelerating Learning 110
    Integration 111
    Benefits of Increased Adoption 114
    Opportunities for Skill Building 115

8. A Comparison of Open Source Licenses 117
    Many Flavors of Licenses 118
    The Classic Licenses 119
    The BSD Licenses: FreeBSD, OpenBSD, and NetBSD 121
    The MIT License 122
    Second-Generation/Single-Project Licenses 122
    Corporate Licenses 123
    Why Pick Just One? The Dual Licensing Option 126

9. Open Source Under Attack 127
    SCO Versus IBM and the Legal Quandary of Open Source 127
    What You Need to Know About SCO 129
    What It All Means: The Implications of the SCO Crisis 131

10. Open Source Empowerment 137
    Two Poles of IT: Buy Versus Build 138
    Where to Buy, Where to Build 139
    Closing the Requirements Gap 140
    Open Source Empowerment 141
    The Vision and Challenge of IT 146

A. The Open Source Platform 147

B. End-User Computing on the Desktop 151

C. Open Source and Email 159

D. Groupware, Portals, and Collaboration. 175

E. Web Publishing and Content Management. 189

F. Application Development. 203

    Index 209

Preface

This book is not a tirade as to why you should use open source. Rather, it is a sober reflection and a pragmatic approach to an ocean of opportunity. Companies that learn how to take advantage of open source software will have an advantage over those that do not. Information Technology (IT) departments that build the skills needed to put open source to work alongside existing systems will serve their companies better than those that do not. This book aims to be a guide to the challenges IT departments will encounter when they undertake this journey.

If this book is successful, it will transform the conversations between programmers and managers, merging the best of both perspectives. No longer will programmers and managers speak at cross purposes and argue for different values. Instead, the techniques and recommendations in this book can help them focus such conversations on the value that software can create, regardless of its origin, and how to manage the risks involved.

The fundamental problem with using open source is that it is so profoundly exciting to everyone involved. Developers see a way to keep learning and to apply their skill and craft using open source projects to build systems that solve problems in creative ways. IT management is thrilled with the possibility of cutting costs, building solutions for less, and gaining power in negotiations with vendors.

But that excitement can too easily blind otherwise sophisticated professionals to hidden costs, unacknowledged responsibilities, and governance challenges inherent in using open source.

If using open source were as easy as just installing Linux and learning to use a few open source tools and applications, the world would have completely converted to open source by now. But it is not that easy.

Organizations with the highest skill levels, such as Google, Yahoo!, and Amazon. com, as well as financial services companies, scientists, and researchers, are all heavy users of open source. But this does not mean that mere mortals cannot succeed with open source. Millions of people around the world at organizations large and small are making open source work for them.

This book will be a guide to making open source work for you. To get it right you have to understand what open source is and what it is not. You must know the problem you are trying to solve and the quality of the tools you are using. You must understand the fully loaded costs of using open source and have a strategy for acquiring and maintaining the needed skills. You must understand how to craft a hybrid stack of open source and commercial software that makes sense for your organization. You must understand open source licensing, the new commercial services for open source, and the ongoing attacks on open source.

This book approaches these problems in the following 10 chapters by Dan Woods, with assistance from Gautam Guliani, along with an additional series of appendixes by Gautam Guliani that identify the most promising open source for various problems facing IT departments:

Chapter 1, *The Nature of Open Source*
    The origins, evolution, and life cycle of open source, and an evaluation of its potential benefits for the enterprise.

Chapter 2, *Measuring the Maturity of Open Source*
    How to determine the quality of an open source project, and whether it is right for your company.

Chapter 3, *The Open Source Skill Set*
    An analysis of the knowledge required to effectively implement open source, and a discussion of how an enterprise can build skills from within.

Chapter 4, *Making the ROI Case*
    How to calculate the return on investment of open source, and make a compelling case to management.

Chapter 5, *Designing an Open Source Strategy*
    A low-risk plan for adopting and applying open source.

Chapter 6, *Support Models for Open Source*
> Where to find help in implementing open source projects, and how to evaluate competing offers.

Chapter 7, *Making Open Source Projects Easy to Adopt*
> Closing the productization gap, and expanding the opportunities for open source deployment.

Chapter 8, *A Comparison of Open Source Licenses*
> The legal underpinnings of open source licensing, with evaluations of GPL, Copyleft, LGPL, BSD, and others.

Chapter 9, *Open Source Under Attack*
> FUD, the legal challenges being mounted against open source, and how an enterprise can manage the risks involved.

Chapter 10, *Open Source Empowerment*
> Build versus buy, the middle road less taken, and how using open source will change your IT department for the better.

Appendix A, *The Open Source Platform*
> Building a platform and assembling the right portfolio of open source software.

Appendix B, *End-User Computing on the Desktop*
> Recommended solutions for replacing commonly used desktop applications.

Appendix C, *Open Source and Email*
> Recommended email application and server solutions.

Appendix D, *Groupware, Portals, and Collaboration*
> Recommended portal, groupware, and collaboration solutions.

Appendix E, *Web Publishing and Content Management*
> Recommended web publishing and content management solutions.

Appendix F, *Application Development*
> Recommended application server solutions.

Perhaps the biggest benefit of using open source is the process of self-improvement that an IT department undergoes in learning how to make open source work. All of the fundamental issues in IT—understanding requirements, finding a focus, building skills, managing scarce resources, and designing a coherent architecture—must be addressed. Solving these issues through pursuing a course of open source adoption can bring new empowerment to an IT department.

This book is not a vitamin pill that will make you a muscled-up open source superhero in one swallow. It is more of a workout routine based on the distilled experience of years of work by IT professionals.

Open source should play some role in most IT departments, including yours. This book will show you how to get it right—not through reckless enthusiasm, but through prudence, patience, and a methodical search for risks and ways to remedy them.

Comments and Questions

Please address comments and questions concerning this book to the publisher:

> O'Reilly Media, Inc.
> 1005 Gravenstein Highway North
> Sebastopol, CA 95472
> (800) 998-9938 (in the United States or Canada)
> (707) 829-0515 (international or local)
> (707) 829-0104 (fax)

We have a web page for this book, where we list errata, examples, and any additional information. You can access this page at:

> *http://www.oreilly.com/catalog/opensourceent*

To comment or ask technical questions about this book, send email to:

> *bookquestions@oreilly.com*

For more information about our books, conferences, Resource Centers, and the O'Reilly Network, see our web site at:

> *http://www.oreilly.com*

Safari Enabled

 When you see a Safari® enabled icon on the cover of your favorite technology book, that means the book is available online through the O'Reilly Network Safari Bookshelf.

Safari offers a solution that's better than e-books. It's a virtual library that lets you easily search thousands of top tech books, cut and paste code samples, download chapters, and find quick answers when you need the most accurate, current information. Try it free at *http://safari.oreilly.com*.

Acknowledgments

The authors would like to thank Dale Dougherty, who first believed in this project and was rewarded for his faith with a Red Sox victory in the World Series. Our editor, Andy Oram, helped us bring it to completion through his gentle yet scorching insights and methodical attention.

This book is a product of several conversations, debates, and other forms of discussion with many people. The authors would like to thank the following people for their help and ideas during the writing of this book. Tim O'Reilly helped move the book along by holding two FOO camps during its writing that allowed the authors to make many valuable contacts. John Castro and Han Lievens researched mature open source projects in various categories. Dan Seltzer and Steve Wainstead provided interesting thoughts on the nature of open source communities. Alan Warren helped review early drafts and added many useful comments on licensing. Moshe Weitzman of Drupal and John Cox of Xaraya explained the history and dynamics of PHP content management systems. Jon Williams, Kevin Bedell, Paul Kavanaugh, and Andrew Cowie provided technical review of the material. Cornelius Willis, Kim Polese, Robert Lefkowitz, and Chet Kapoor provided an invaluable perspective from the commercial end of the open source world. Noah Robischon, Greg Lindsay, and Deb Cameron provided exquisitely valuable assistance with various writing and editing tasks.

Most of all, the authors would like to thank the countless open source developers for their continuous and prolific contributions to the various open source projects. It is your work that made this book worth writing. Thank you.

Dedications

Dan Woods would like to dedicate this book to his wife, Daniele Gerard. Her ferocious desire for justice, boundless energy, miraculous organizational skills, and incomparable talents for life and motherhood make her the most inspiring partner imaginable.

Gautam Guliani would like to dedicate this book to his parents, Naubat Rai and Nirmala Guliani, whose blessings make all good things in life possible, and to his wife, Fatemeh Haghighi, who makes life worth living.

CHAPTER 1

The Nature of Open Source

This book is a long and thorough answer to the question, is open source right for you? The intended audience is the typical Information Technology (IT) department that is charged with supporting a business with appropriate application of technology. This book is written from an IT department's perspective and is organized around the common problems that face those who struggle in the trenches. The goal of *Open Source for the Enterprise* is to help technology and business executives determine whether they can benefit from using open source in their environments.

Open source began as free software built by thousands of volunteers who shared the results of their work without charging any fees. Billions of dollars of value has been created based on this simple structure. The adoption of open source software has become a cultural phenomenon. The basic facts regarding the growth of the open source movement are amazing.

Open source success stories are well known and more arise every week. For instance, the city of Munich chose OpenOffice.org, an open source suite of desktop applications, very publicly sticking a finger in the eye of Microsoft, which aggressively sought the contract. Amazon.com dumped Sun hardware and software in favor of Linux, the most popular open source operating system available. Apache, an open source web server architecture, is the most popular web server in the world. Perl, a robust scripting language, is used to run huge, highly scalable sites such as Ticketmaster. Large financial companies are creating massive clusters of Linux machines for crunching numbers in complex portfolio analysis. This is just the tip of the iceberg. The examples of corporate success for open source would fill a phone book.

Internationally, open source is being adopted by entire governments. Smaller communities are using it to create versions for their specific languages. China, Brazil, Thailand, Peru—are all adopting open source software officially and are spending millions to improve the software and encourage its adoption.

All of this success has changed the nature of open source. No longer can one assume that the typical open source project comprises a small band of programmers toiling away in obscurity. Major technology vendors got open source religion and made broad and long-term commitments to open source software. IBM released as open source its Eclipse platform for creating development tools, a project on which it spent $40 million. IBM has become the largest corporate proponent of Linux, and it spends hundreds of millions of dollars to support and market that platform. Hewlett-Packard uses open source in all sorts of ways, from supporting development of useful projects to releasing device drivers into the marketplace. Novell has purchased several major open source-related companies, and is creating a large and integrated collection of open source applications for enterprise use. Nearly every important enterprise-grade software product has support for Linux. Even commercial web servers based on Apache are available, including Hewlett-Packard's Secure Web Server for OpenVMS.

Companies large and small have taken to open source as a way to increase collaboration, reduce development costs, provide a friendly platform for their products, and sell services.

For an IT department, the stakes can be high. Becoming the sort of IT department that can successfully use open source means empowerment, saving hard dollars and ensuring freedom from captivity to vendors. Other significant benefits include:

- Saving money on license fees
- Reducing support costs
- Reducing integration costs
- Avoiding vendor lock-in and gaining power in negotiations
- Gaining access to the functionality of thousands of programs
- Improving the value of IT to your business

But gaining these benefits comes with responsibilities. Installing open source does not mean all your problems are solved. To use open source and support it in a commercial environment, IT departments must learn to:

- Develop and maintain skills required to install and configure open source
- Increase their software development skills

- Become experts in evaluating the maturity of open source

- Improve their understanding of the technology requirements of the business

- Understand and manage open source licensing issues, especially if their company distributes software applications

The Open Source Debate

One way of looking at this book is as a tour of the benefits and responsibilities of using open source. The opportunity provided by open source is too large to ignore for any organization that seeks to support its operations with software.

The scope of open source has grown beyond basic development tools to become a top-to-bottom infrastructure for computing of all stripes, including development environments, databases, operating systems, web servers, application servers, and utilities for all types of data center management. Open source now encompasses a huge variety of end-user applications, such enterprise applications as Enterprise Resource Planning (ERP) and Customer Relationship Management (CRM), tools such as portals and data warehouses, and integration tools for messaging as well as for web services. All of these can be the foundation of the sort of automation and productivity gains that can lead to a company's competitive advantage.

But in most organizations, discussing open source brings up strong opinions on all sides that obscure pragmatic analysis of the key question: can you use open source profitably at your organization?

There is no simple answer to this question. People on both sides have good points to make and are also protecting their own interests. At its worst, the debate becomes a cartoonish farce.

Programmers, systems administrators, and other technologists who are fascinated by various open source programs might tout the fact that the software is free. While this is true, managers sometimes suspect a hidden agenda of seeking more cool toys to play with, without adequate consideration of the other costs that are incurred when using any piece of software, including the costs of evaluation, testing, installation, configuration, customization, upgrades, operations, and support.

Managers frequently take the opposite position, that open source is not worth considering because it can lack features of commercial software such as support and maintenance services, installation scripts, and documentation. For good reasons, managers like the idea of one throat to choke if something goes wrong. It is a remedy for the finger pointing that characterizes all commercial technology support in multivendor installations. But hiding behind this objection ignores the fact that technologists at tens of thousands of companies have proved that the risks and responsibilities of using open source are manageable.

One ideal that is rarely achieved is to merge the creativity and technical brilliance of the open source world with the operational discipline and process of IT. But the two sides look at each other with disdain. The open source experts look at IT and see a massive skills gap: what is so hard about picking up and maintaining the skills needed to use open source? The IT professionals look at open source software and frequently see a productization gap because of half-finished products: what is so hard about finishing all the administrative interfaces, configuration tools, Application Programming Interfaces (APIs), and documentation to make the software useful?

Both the skills and the productization gaps represent real challenges to wider adoption of open source. Organizations that can learn to overcome the skills and productization gaps and put open source to work will have an edge in terms of cost and flexibility over those that cannot.

Fortunately, the debate has moved out of the cartoonish phase, and many organizations are now taking up the real job of analyzing what kind of company they want to be, what their long-term needs are, and whether open source can play some sort of role.

The prudent course is to choose carefully when to use open source, based on a thorough understanding of what is involved. This book won't answer every question for every different type of project. But it will show you how to evaluate open source software for common scenarios, and it will teach you how to get the answers to commonly asked questions and communicate them to others.

Understanding Your Open Source Readiness

Whether open source will work at any company depends on both the capabilities of the company and the maturity of the open source software. The fact is that some open source is so rickety that it isn't useful to anyone except the most highly skilled. If you browse the popular directories of open source software, it doesn't take long to find dormant projects that have not been updated for years. For example, Cheetah, a Python-powered template engine, was posted on the *www.freshmeat.net* site on July 15, 2001, was updated July 16, 2001, and hasn't been touched since. Other open source software, such as the Apache Web Server, is at the other end of the quality spectrum; it is widely considered better in every way than all the commercial alternatives, and it is as easy to use. Thousands of projects occupy the space in between these two extremes.

Not all users of open source are equal. Given the IT budget of Amazon, Google, Yahoo!, or Ticketmaster and the pedigree of their engineering staff, it is no wonder that they can make open source work. They could write their systems in assembly language. But when you look far from the gurus of Silicon Valley and focus instead on the city of Houston, or on the Ernie Ball Company, a guitar-string maker that's run entirely on open source software, you must realize that there is some middle ground. You don't have to be an MIT Ph.D. to make open source work for your business or organization.

Getting It Right

The difference between the successful open source implementation, in which the value of open source is realized for a company, and the unsuccessful one, in which the struggle to use open source is not worth the effort, amounts to knowing your problem, knowing the software, and knowing yourself.

The key to a successful outcome in applying open source is a thorough understanding of answers to the following questions:

- What problem are you trying to solve?

- How would open source software help in providing the solution?

- Does any open source software provide all or part of the solution?

- How can the maturity and stability of relevant open source software be determined?

- What skills are required to install, configure, customize, integrate, operate, and maintain the open source software?

- Does your organization have the needed skills? If not, how can they be acquired and institutionalized?

- In which cases does the value provided by the open source software exceed the cost of using and maintaining it, compared with other solutions?

This book approaches these questions in terms of skills, risks, and fully loaded costs. An IT department that intends to adopt open source must have not only the resources to do so, but also a belief in skills building and an inclination to take increased responsibility for its IT infrastructure. In Chapters 1 through 5 of this book, we analyze the nature of open source and describe three different models that can help companies evaluate the vast world of open source in a manner that is consistent and enables them to understand their own capabilities.

The models presented are:

Open Source Maturity model
> A set of questions that help determine the stability and maturity of an open source project, the responsibilities involved in using a particular piece of open source, and the skills needed to manage those risks

Open Source Skills and Risk Tolerance model
> A set of questions that help determine the ability of an organization to handle various risks and the tolerance of risk for a specific project

Software Cost and Risk model
> A set of questions that help determine the total costs and risks of using open source as a solution for a project

With the information collected in using these models, half of the problem—knowing what you are getting yourself into—is solved. An IT department will be able to avoid choosing open source projects that are immature or ill-suited to its skills. The other half of the problem is finding the right open source project for a particular task, which can be vexing.

Finding and Evaluating Open Source

Finding open source that you can relate to your needs is all too easy. Go to *http://www.sourceforge.net/* and you will find an uncharted jungle of more than 70,000 projects. At *http://freshmeat.net/* more than 30,000 projects are listed. Finding the right open source for your needs and evaluating its maturity can be exhausting and time consuming. Most open source projects are useless to organizations and businesses focused on solving problems, but a small number are incredibly valuable.

Also available are more organized and higher-quality sources of open source software, such as the Apache Software Foundation and Tigris.org (supported by Collab-Net). Although these sources offer a significantly smaller set of open source applications, they are relatively mature, stable, and useful.

And don't be fooled into thinking that using open source requires you to master Linux. Plenty of open source programs work perfectly well on the Microsoft platform, including Apache, MySQL, and Perl.

Once you find an open source program that might fit your needs, a host of questions arise: how do you know how stable it is? How can you find out if someone will be around to help if you have a problem? How can you find others who are using it? None of these questions has a simple answer.

The bottom line is that if you set out to use open source, you must learn to evaluate the software's maturity and the level of support provided by the community that surrounds the project so that you can understand the risks. That is what the Open Source Maturity model is all about.

The Nature of Open Source

The way that open source comes to life, evolves, and finds its way to new groups of users is a profoundly democratic, decentralized, and somewhat chaotic process. For commercial software, investors demand a plan reflecting what the software will do and who will buy it. Vendors pay for sales staff, marketing and advertising departments, and conferences and events to let potential buyers know about their products. The trade press offers a steady stream of product reviews. Analysts write reports on new types of products.

Open source is a grass-roots effort. Open source developers create code to meet their own needs, and throw it up on the Internet so that others can interact with it and make it better. Nobody buys you lunch. Nobody is going to call you on the phone and suggest that using open source is a good idea. In most cases, you will have to find out about open source software yourself. It will not come to you. This is slightly less true now than it used to be (see the upcoming sidebar, "Open Source Sales and Marketing"). IBM will call you about Linux, but the conversation will quickly get to hardware and services. Newly formed support companies are also encouraging use of open source, but none of this changes the fact that open source means taking responsibility.

The way that open source grows is an amazing demonstration of community evolution. It turns out that communities are not interested in documentation until late in the cycle, and even then the documentation does not tell you what you need to know about the project's health and how well the software works.

So, when you go looking for open source to fill your needs, it can be difficult to understand what is happening with a particular project. For the most popular and widely used projects, a lot of information is available, including books, magazines, conferences, and even consultants offering services. But leaving the most popular products aside, there are many sources of raw data but a dearth of useful information.

If finding and evaluating open source is this difficult, one might ask, why bother? The reason is that open source has grown to such an extent that huge opportunities are waiting for IT departments. Many of the newly formed open source support companies are focused on drawing IT's attention to these opportunities.

A clear model of how open source software comes to life and grows is crucial for the IT community to understand what they will find when they go looking for open source. This chapter explains the life cycle of open source: how open source is created, how it evolves, what you will find when you look at an open source project, and how to make sense of this evidence. Being able to evaluate open source is particularly important for projects outside the realm of usual suspects, where much value lies waiting.

To explore the nature of open source, we will present several definitions of open source, followed by a review of the life cycle most open source projects go through. Then, the differences in the life cycle of commercial software and the end product will be analyzed and compared to that of open source software.

What Is Open Source?

We've been sharing software since computers were invented. Significant portions of the early IBM operating systems, such as HASP (a print spooler), were developed in the field by users sharing and improving the software. IBM happily accepted that informally shared software, called it "field development," and then included it in the operating system that helped run the huge mainframes that were the company's vehicle for making money.

Open Source Sales and Marketing

While most open source products have no sales staff, companies are cropping up that sell services and products based on the most popular open source software. This arrival of commercial interests means that some open source is marketed and advertised. IBM is personifying Linux as a cute little blond boy when advertising its Linux services. Red Hat and other companies sell subscriptions to their distributions of Linux. SugarCRM and Compiere have fully developed CRM and ERP packages, respectively. Start-ups such as SpikeSource and SourceLabs are offering support services.

Commercial software vendors are increasingly using the open source licensing model for various reasons, but none of this activity has fundamentally changed how open source is born and evolves. And for the most part, after Linux, Apache, and perhaps MySQL, plus a small handful of others, few open source projects have received such attention. For most open source, if you want it, you must hunt it down yourself.

Today, this would not even be considered open source by its strictest definition. Many believe that software can be defined as open source only if it meets the 10 criteria in the "Open Source Definition" that is published and maintained by the Open Source Initiative (OSI; *http://www.opensource.org/*).

In the academic and scientific community, sharing software has always been a routine part of research and teaching activities. Many books tell the story of Arpanet, and how the Internet was developed and improved by sharing code over the network, with hardly a thought about licensing.

When PCs proliferated, starting in the early 1980s, a thriving exchange of software developed. This evolved into *freeware*, software that was available for use at no charge, and *shareware*, software that was available to try, but with the proviso that if you used it regularly, you should send in a small licensing fee. Extremely popular programs such as PKZIP, a file compression program created by Phil Katz, grew at amazing rates under this model.

Here we get to the key difference between open source and all other forms of software sharing. Open source is not just about giving away useful tools. It is about sharing source code and keeping it sharable. Remember that in open source, unlike in shareware or freeware, all of the source code used to build an application is shared, not just the executable version that allows you to run the program but not see how it works or be able to improve it. At its core, open source is about a cycle of innovation in which those who have the skills share ideas and build on each other's work.

Richard Stallman originally defined *free software* as software that protected Four Freedoms for its users:

- The freedom to run the program, for any purpose (freedom 0).

- The freedom to study how the program works and adapt it to your needs (freedom 1). Access to the source code is a precondition for this.

- The freedom to redistribute copies so that you can help your neighbor (freedom 2).

- The freedom to improve the program and release your improvements to the public, so that the whole community benefits (freedom 3). Access to the source code is a precondition for this.

It takes a lot of work to create software, and programmers, while eager to share, are not generally eager to share and then have someone else decide to take their work and sell it. One key innovation that contributed significantly to the growth of open source software was the development of software licenses that prevented corporations from simply taking open source software and embedding it into their products. These *open source licenses* ensure that software developers can control the terms under which others can reuse the software they contribute to open source projects. Richard Stallman published the first open source license, known as the GNU *General Public License* (GPL). The GPL is a software license in which Richard specified licensing terms that he believed embodied the spirit of his Four Freedoms. Linux, among many other open source applications, is distributed under the GNU GPL.

The innovation of open source is the creation of the legal structures that were first used to define a way to share software, and to keep contributions to it shareable as well. This avoids what is known as the *Free Rider Problem*, whereby freely shared work is appropriated for commercial gain.

So, the first definition of open source has to do with licensing:

> Open source software is distributed under a type of license that promotes sharing by preserving public availability of source code and preventing restrictions on the software's use and distribution.

Literally hundreds of licenses are now considered to be open source in some form or another. The OSI, as mentioned earlier, approves licenses as "open source" based on conformance to a set of criteria known as the Open Source Definition (OSD). Currently, more than 50 licenses are approved as open source by the OSI.

The Free Software Foundation, founded in 1985 to promote the development of the GNU operating system and free software in general, administers the GNU GPL, which is also known as *Copyleft*:

> Copyleft is a license that permits people to freely copy, modify, and redistribute software so long as they do not keep others from also having the right to freely

copy, modify, and redistribute the software. Copyleft provisions in a license require that anyone modifying the software can distribute only their modified versions under the terms of the open source license they originally received with the software. You can actually sell Copyleft software (haven't you seen box sets of Linux at the computer store?), but you must also offer the source for free, either with the product or available for free (or for the cost of copying/shipping) to anyone on request. Not all open source licenses contain Copyleft provisions (from *http://c2.com/cgi/wiki?CopyLeft*).

The zeal with which some people have taken up the cause of open source has created another definition of open source:

> Open source is a social and political movement that promotes the idea that all software should be made available under terms that embody the Four Freedoms initially defined by Richard Stallman.

Richard Stallman is famous for saying that the word *free* in *Free Software Foundation* is meant to be like free speech, not like free beer. But one can make excellent use of open source without joining this movement and adopting its attitude toward information and private property.

The term *open source* itself is an attempt to remove the emphasis from *free*—as in "no cost"—and also to draw a distinction between Stallman's orthodoxy and those who were less strident politically but wanted to promote the idea of collaborative development with guaranteed access to source code. The term was coined in January 1998 by Christine Peterson, then president of the Foresight Institute in Santa Clara, California, in the wake of Netscape's announcement that it would publish the source code of its browser. Eric Raymond's essay, "The Cathedral and the Bazaar," which later became a book (see upcoming sidebar), about the power of collaborative, community-based development, was mentioned by Netscape as having influenced its decision.

For the user of open source in the enterprise, it is important to understand how open source evolves, sometimes in a lurching manner, through a collaborative process that is long on communication and short on planning.

The Cathedral and the Bazaar

We scratch only the surface of open source's origins in this book. For a more thorough, firsthand account of the history of the movement, read *The Cathedral and the Bazaar* (O'Reilly, 2001). The book explores in detail such topics as scratching a personal itch, people and communication skills, Linus's Law, and the historic Netscape announcement.

As the number of open source projects has grown, and higher-quality software projects have emerged and have had a significant impact on the market, engineers have noticed the benefits of the loosely structured way in which open source software is created. This leads to the third definition of open source:

> Open source is a community-based, iterative, incremental, and evolutionary software development methodology that emphasizes experimentation and experience over planning and formal design.

As we will discuss later in this chapter, little centralized planning governs the development of open source software, yet the result is frequently profoundly better than approaches that emphasize up-front design. In this sense, open source can be thought of as evidence in favor of some of the principles behind so-called "Agile" development methodologies such as eXtreme Programming, which emphasizes rapid iterations. For the purposes of this book, understanding the nature of how open source development takes place is key to making effective use of open source software.

Companies such as VA Software and CollabNet have sprung up to provide this open source development methodology to enterprises, packaged as a set of services.

The final definition of open source is one that arrived only after open source became a successful way of forming communities and creating a safe environment for cooperation:

> Open source is a collaboration and marketing technique that can bring people and organizations together.

The Python-based Zope application server, which was initially commercial software but found more success as an open source project, is one example of this trend. MySQL, a popular database program, is marketed as open source and as commercial software simultaneously. IBM's Eclipse project is perhaps the most prominent example of this aspect of open source. After pouring more than $40 million into the development of the Eclipse framework for creating software development tools, IBM decided to convert the project to open source. This meant that anyone could copy the source code it had cost IBM so many millions of dollars to create. Why would IBM do such a thing?

Here is one analysis that explains IBM's behavior: IBM needs a development environment to support its Java™-based development platform. That's why the Eclipse project was started in the first place. But IBM realized that it was never going to make any money by selling development tools. IBM also saw that it would benefit greatly if other companies used its development tools and joined the development of Eclipse. There were two reasons for this. First, the more companies that signed on, the more credibility Eclipse would have. Second, having outside companies work on improving Eclipse would lower the cost of development. Finally, making Eclipse open source had a devastating effect on everyone else—including IBM's competitors—who was trying to sell the same tools.

IBM explains the decision as an attempt to build trust in the Eclipse project among vendors, partners, and users, improve code quality, and encourage innovation. (Visit *http://www.ibm.com/developerworks/linux/library/l-erick.html* for details.)

As it turns out, releasing Eclipse as an open source project achieved all the goals mentioned earlier. The Eclipse Foundation (*http://www.eclipse.org/*) now governs Eclipse development, many companies have joined the project to help with development, and the platform is rapidly becoming one of the most popular integrated development environments, excelling not only at Java (which it was originally created for) but also across a diverse range of languages—an awesome example of the power of open source collaboration at work.

These definitions help describe the context in which open source exists. Now, let's examine the way in which open source projects get started and how they grow.

Where Does Open Source Come From?

Most of the time, open source is born out of a need that leads to inspiration. Somebody somewhere who is frustrated, bored, or in some other state of creative readiness starts with an initial thought that begins with one of these phrases: "Wouldn't it be cool if" or "I am sick of having to put up with…" or "I bet a lot of people would like…". The end of these statements is a description of some sort of software. In open source parlance, this is called *scratching a developer's personal itch.*

Linus Torvalds thought it would be cool to have a full Unix implementation that ran on the Intel chip set, and he created Linux. Larry Wall was interested in a language to help him with system programming tasks, and he created the Perl language. A group of people building their own web sites were frustrated with the NCSA web server and started sharing patches to it; these patches became the Apache web server (a-patch-y server; get it?).

The key thing to remember is that at first the designers and builders of open source applications were the primary users as well. This is the first principle of open source:

> Open source software is most frequently built by programmers for other programmers.

So, what follows inspiration? Well, hard work, of course. The inspired developer now sets to work, creating the masterpiece that will solve the problem at hand. There is no formal requirements-gathering process. There is no market research. There is nothing but a smart, driven person thinking about what he wants to do and then setting about doing it.

After toiling alone at a keyboard, the inspired developer creates something that he is proud of and then shares it with others. This is the real birth of an open source project. If other programmers are captivated by the way the software meets a need they also have, they will join the project as either users or developers of the software. If such a community forms, the open source project is on its way to faster development and wider recognition. The second principle of open source, then, is as follows:

> Open source projects are communities of developers and users organized around software that meets a common need.

Where does open source come from? It comes from inspiration about a solution to a problem that is compelling and common enough to attract other people to join a community and work on the project for free. In addition, many companies allow developers to work on open source as a part of their jobs if the project is important to that company.

The implications of this are that open source projects usually form around needs that programmers have. The first generation of open source programs are almost all focused on programmers' needs and ways of working.

So, if not money, what are the rewards of a successful open source project, besides scratching that itch? One major reward is status and peer recognition. Doing good and helping others is another factor that keeps many a programmer working late into the night. There is a strong ethic of community service in many developers, and a great sense of satisfaction is frequently derived from the knowledge that thousands of lives have been improved as a result of an open source project.

Developers are also motivated by rational self-interest. Aside from improving skills in general, thus becoming increasingly marketable, the developer becomes part of a great team. By releasing code as open source, a programmer can get significant help improving his software if a community forms around it. Bug fixes and enhancements in areas outside of a developer's area of interest are benefits of a successful open source project. Even Microsoft, which is not at all friendly to open source, understands the value of community involvement and released millions of lines of code for inspection under its Shared Source Initiative. (It is important to note that when Microsoft says *Shared Source* it does not mean *open source*.)

As the use of open source becomes more widespread, and more tools are developed, open source projects grow larger as well, resulting in new uses and motivations that we describe in the section "Second-Generation Trends in Open Source," later in this chapter. More projects are focusing on meeting needs outside of the programming community, but even those projects, such as a server that can stream MP3 files, are usually close to the hearts of developers. Where is the open source software for creating knitting and crochet patterns? It hasn't yet caught the imagination of a developer.

How Does Open Source Grow?

So, there the inspired developer sits, with a handful of competent developers contributing to the project, all of them working away to make the software better. How does this work? The inspired developer is now the acknowledged leader of the project, but the position doesn't come with much authority. Frequently, no legal agreements of any kind define the relationships in the community, except for the open source software license used to declare the software's terms of use. Usually there is a shared source code repository, perhaps a web site that is used to organize the work of the project, and an email list that is used for communication. Any rules or structure are informal and are a matter of community acceptance and voluntary compliance. Very few projects have stated these rules in writing. The Apache Software Foundation's community process is a rare example of a formal process, but even this process must be voluntarily accepted.

Because of this loose structure, an open source project is usually more like a high school rock band in a garage than the orderly and planned engineering process used in designing complex products such as automobiles. Rock bands break up and re-form quite often before (and after) they become successful. Open source projects are the same.

As a result, an informal community culture forms. Generally, the project leader—who is usually the inspired developer, but sometimes is someone else who is more suited to the task—starts setting the agenda and making a few rules. For example, is testing important? Is backward compatibility important? Are users welcome to participate or are they an annoyance? Are decisions made by a group vote or by one person?

The structure of open source communities can be all over the map. Some have a project leader and others have a community of developers. For example, the Apache Software Foundation is a meritocracy. There are no project leaders per se, but natural leaders emerge as they gain respect from peers working on the project.

One measure of a programmer's status in the community is the level of access he is given to the source code repository. Some developers must submit source code to the group for approval. But others are allowed to make changes to the source code on their own. This is known as being a *committer*, and it usually carries a high degree of status. Any programmer who is a committer on the Apache Web Server project is hot stuff among his peers.

The focus of all this community activity is on improving the software. Is there a plan or a roadmap for how the software will evolve? In most cases, the answer is no. Even in mature products used by millions of people, such as Apache, there is no written roadmap explaining what functionality will be developed in the current version and what will be added in later versions. There are just programmers writing code to make the software better.

Open source software, then, can be thought of as evolving, pulled along by the vision of the project leader, the core group of developers, and feedback from users. If the need is focused, well defined, and well understood, the software usually reflects that. If the need is unclear and vague, the software reflects that, too. This leads us to the third principle of open source:

> Open source software is not planned, but evolves according to the changing values and goals of the community.

For IT developers and managers, this point is significant. It means that to understand how an open source project is likely to grow, one must first understand the shared values of the community.

It is not uncommon for an open source community to change after the initial needs are met. The pace of change and the addition of new features might slow down dramatically once the project leader and developer community have achieved their goal. At that point, one project leader might step down and new leadership might emerge to take the project in a different direction.

How Does Open Source Die?

In some respects, most open source projects never really die. Even if the original developers abandon the project, the source code usually remains available so that it's possible for someone interested in the code to pick it up at a later date and bring it back to life. This lowered risk of losing access to an application, in fact, is one of the advantages that comes from using open source. If a proprietary company builds a product and then goes out of business, the source code might be gone forever; with open source, there's always an opportunity for a user to pick up development himself (or fund some other party to continue development).

That being said, many open source projects do "die" in the sense that they become dormant or are abandoned by their developers. Many open source projects die, because a community never forms around the need. In the early days, such deaths were invisible. But now, thanks to the rise of public web sites such as SourceForge (*http://sourceforge. net/index.php*), where open source projects can be started and shared, many stillborn projects are there for all to see. For example, not much has been happening with the Skydiver's Online Logbook project (*http://skydivelogbook.sourceforge.net/*).

The second way that open source projects die is that they never reach completion. The inspired developer creates some software that partially meets the original need, and then for one of many potential reasons he loses interest in the project. The inspired developer gets married, has a baby, gets a new job, has a big project at work, gets bored, starts learning guitar, whatever. For some reason, he is no longer compelled to work on the project, so there it sits, in a half-completed state. Sometimes, at some point another developer picks up where the inspired developer left off, but usually the project just languishes and the source code collects digital dust.

One common reason that open source projects die is that the community behind the project has a schism and some of the developers copy the source code to a new repository and start doing things their own way. This is known as *forking* the project. This story is told over and over in the open source world. The PHP Nuke project is a typical example.

With this project, developers of PHP Nuke forked into two camps. One camp wanted to make some radical changes to fix the things they didn't like, and the other camp wanted to take a more incremental approach. The radical-change camp took a copy of the source code and started an open source project called Post Nuke. This was developed for a while and then another schism formed and a set of developers took the source code and started a project called Xaraya. All three projects are in the same area of Web Publishing and Content Management, and we cover Xaraya in detail in Appendix E. To an outsider the differences might not seem too significant, but to those involved they can be important.

Sometimes the community that creates a new project is the one that keeps the momentum going, while other times the community from the original project takes this responsibility. Sometimes both communities continue their involvement. But frequently, such community problems kill off all progress in all branches of a project. Forking is actually rare in open source circles, perhaps because of the associated trauma and risk (for more details, visit *http://www.infoworld.com/article/03/10/24/42OPstrategic_1.html*).

Frequently the project leader, or core group, is the one who sets the tone that either causes or prevents such problems. The dependence on the community for any meaningful progress leads us to the final principle of open source:

> The health, maturity, and stability of an open source project is a direct reflection of the health, maturity, and stability of the community that surrounds it.

But remember, there is no authority declaring the life, death, or health of an open source project. If a project dies, its web site can live on. It just might be hard to tell what is happening with it.

Figure 1-1 summarizes the steps in the open source life cycle that we have described in this chapter so far.

Leadership in the Open Source Life Cycle

You can define success for an open source project as a community of developers making steady progress creating software to meet a need. Greg Stein, the chairman of the Apache Software Foundation, who has been deeply involved in many different open source projects, observes that there are two keys to the success of an open source project:

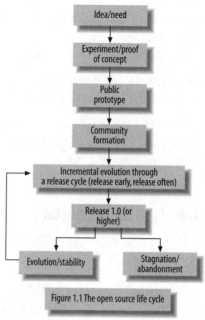

Figure 1-1. *The open source life cycle*

- A clear, shared focus for the project's vision among the developer community (i.e., strong shared values among the developer and user communities)
- A project lead who encourages and rewards community participation

From the perspective of an IT department using open source, evaluating leadership quality is crucial, because it is such an important factor in the long-term viability of an open source project.

It is much easier to understand the concept of leadership in the commercial world than in the world of open source. In the commercial world, somebody is writing payroll checks, a formal corporate structure is in place, and people are assigned authority. People come and go, but who is in charge is not really at issue most of the time. Staff generally is motivated by getting paid, the challenge of the work, and the status and rewards of building a successful business.

Take out the formal authority and the getting paid part, and you are left with the motivation for most open source developers. They are working for the love of the craft and for the rewards of creating a successful open source project.

When a project leader is rigid, doesn't accept and acknowledge the contributions of others, and is hostile to new directions for a project, it is much harder for a community to form.

"When someone comes to a project lead with an idea, the right attitude is to respond 'Cool idea, why don't you run with it' in most cases," says Stein. "Reconciling differences of opinion and at the same time keeping people motivated requires diplomacy, an inclusive attitude, and a generous, secure personality."

This can be hard to achieve, given that people are working for the love of it and to fulfill their particular vision of what the software can do.

For the purposes of this book, the important point is that when evaluating open source projects, a key thing to look for is the presence of an open, accepting, community-oriented project leader. In Chapter 2, we will discuss in greater detail what specific evidence to look for.

Second-Generation Trends in Open Source

Some of the characteristics that governed the early days of open source have changed now that open source has become popular. Today, open source software is often being created not just for programmers, but also for end users. The OpenOffice project has created versions of nearly all popular desktop applications for word processing, spreadsheets, presentations, and email. Today's open source projects are starting to compete with successful commercial projects, by developers who want to create a better solution or by commercial companies seeking to create open source alternatives for their own purposes.

It is also becoming more common for large and small companies to use open source code as the basis of applications they have built, either as products or for internal use. Sun Microsystems has been a strong sponsor of the development of open source solutions including OpenOffice, which has become an increasingly credible alternative to Microsoft Office. SAP released a version of a database it bought from another company as open source to provide a database alternative to power its enterprise applications.

The early days of open source focused on creating infrastructure that could be used to create programs. The GNU C compiler enabled the creation of languages such as Perl and development tools such as Emacs so that they could run on a wide variety of platforms. The Linux kernel itself, Apache, databases including MySQL and Postgres, graphical user interface toolkits such as GTK (which led to the GNOME desktop) and Qt (which is the basis of the KDE desktop), and hundreds of other programs have resulted in a top-to-bottom application stack that helps developers create the tools they need, from the bare metal operating system right up to the user interface layer.

The existence of this complete stack has resulted in a proliferation of applications aimed at specific groups of users. Open source has become a new way to start a software business. A developer creates an open source product, gets help from a community of developers who are interested in the area, and runs a consulting business selling services to put the open source software to work. Open source content management systems such as Bricolage and Plone (both of which are covered in detail in Appendix E) have consulting firms operating on this model. Open source products exist for ERP software, portals, data warehouses, and enterprise application integration. The maturity of the stack has created a huge opportunity for IT. Learning how to take advantage of it is the point of this book.

The Different Roots of Commercial Software

Commercial software comes into existence in a completely different way. At the core of the creative process for commercial software is a vision that many people will pay for the software being created. For open source software, the intended audience and the developer are usually the same. So there is no mystery about what the audience wants. The requirements process consists of developers deciding among themselves what they want the software to do.

Commercial software companies must somehow determine what the intended customers want. This introduces a large amount of risk into the process, because determining requirements means making lots of assumptions about whom the audience is. The economics of commercial software resemble those of a health club. Customers pay to join the club, because they can get access to a much better facility than if they built it themselves. But the club has to have the exercise machines the customers want. In commercial software, costs are shared across all customers and the company must create software that is powerful and configurable enough to solve business problems in all sorts of different environments.

Figuring out the needs of the market is a key skill for a commercial software company, and many people are involved in the process. Investors in the company, or the product marketing department, might conduct research to understand what customers want. Prototypes might be built and put in front of the target audience.

The problem for most commercial software companies is that it is fiendishly difficult to tell if they are getting it right. The ultimate test is if the software sells, and the sales staff frequently plays a key role in requirements gathering. But even if they get the first version right, the same issues of what the customers want must be revisited with every new version.

The Commercial Software Life Cycle

What generally happens with a successful software company is that the first version of the product is released, a few initial sales are made, and these customers start providing more and more information about what they like about the product.

Requirements gathering and the product roadmap

At most software companies the product management department keeps the list of potential features to be added to the product and crafts the definition of what each version will include. The product marketing department focuses on understanding what customers need (inbound requirements gathering) and then sending the message about why the product is of value to customers (outbound marketing).

The challenge in this process is that 10 or 20 segments of customers and potential customers might be providing information. The potential feature list is gathered from the developers, sales staff, product management, and product marketing. In most cases, even before the first release, the feature list contains years of work and hundreds of potential features. Each customer has his own opinion about what is most important.

The process of deciding what to do next involves several factors, among them balancing the features desired by the customers currently buying the software; adding features that might be attractive to new buyers; adding features that allow integration with other software in the marketplace; and adding features desired by other software companies that are using the software as part of their product or helping sell the software in combination with their product. In performing this balancing act, a company must ensure backward compatibility, which means that new features must not break old ones or force customers to redo work to configure or customize the product.

One way companies communicate their decisions to potential customers is through a product roadmap, which shows which features are coming along in the next version and what can be planned for future versions.

Notice how different this is from the open source requirements process. In the commercial process a group of people—engineers, product managers, product marketers, sales staff, senior managers—is trying to figure out what another group of people—customers and partners—want from the software. In the open source process there is only one group, the open source community. The community decides which features to include in each release of an open source project. And the developers decide what each individual feature should do based on their understanding of the need.

The odd shape of the commercial software feature set is caused by that attempt to balance the perceived needs of the current and future customer base, requests from important customers, recommendations from the sales staff, and features announced by competing companies. Open source features sometimes have an odd shape, because the competing and conflicting needs of developers are being balanced in a strange compromise.

Productization

One of the most challenging aspects of creating commercial software is taking a program that provides certain features and functionality, and turning it into a product. Many promising software companies fail, because they underestimate the difficulty and importance of this step.

Productization means making software work for the general case and making it as easy as possible to use. For a custom program written by an IT department, it might be fine to have an XML properties file that controls the program. For a commercial product, users will probably expect a simple administrative interface to help set the parameters. For an open source product, installation might mean unzipping the source code, compiling the program, and then figuring out how to fit it into your production or development environment. Commercial products generally have an installation program that does a lot of this automatically.

Productization requires a huge amount of work. It can take double or triple the amount of work it took to complete the original features and turn a program into a product. Here is some of the work that takes place during productization:

- Creating administrative interfaces
- Writing installation scripts
- Testing features
- Testing on different platforms
- Performance tuning
- Runtime monitoring through SNMP
- Creating engineering documentation
- Creating end-user documentation
- Developing adapters to other programs, such as reporting software
- Developing support for different databases and operating systems
- Creating graphical configuration tools
- Developing APIs
- Developing web services

It is not crazy to think of an original development team of 5 requiring a productization team of 50 or more with various specialized skills to complete a product. What happens in most start-up software companies is that the original development team becomes the productization team, which causes two problems. First, the engineering team doesn't like the work of productization and is not good at it. Second, it slows down development of later features.

Early in a company's life, highly skilled customers oriented toward innovation will do without many aspects of productization as long as the functionality provided by the software is compelling (these people fall into the innovators category of customers we will discuss when we talk about the Open Source Skills and Risk Tolerance model in Chapter 3). This happens because the companies that are most likely to buy new versions of commercial products are composed of innovators and early adopters, and they have the skills to overcome the lack of productization.

But if a company does not learn how to productize its software, it is doomed when it comes time to sell to a broader market.

Maintenance and support

Once a commercial software product has been released, it is supported with patches and bug fixes as needed. It is also supported by a technical support department that answers questions, and perhaps a training and education staff. Support services can be delivered through online resources such as email, or through discussion forums or telephone support.

Customers must usually pay between 15% and 25% of the original licensing fee in annual support costs.

The presence of a support team to help solve problems is one of the most popular aspects of commercial software. It is also required, because users don't have access to enough information about how the product works to solve problems on their own. But even if all such information were available down to the source code, IT users of software still want support. Later in this book, we will analyze the emerging category of companies that provide support services for open source software.

End-of-life

When a commercial product goes into end-of-life, it means it will no longer be improved. Bug fixes and support might be provided for a limited period, but after that, commercial software companies will stop fixing bugs and answering questions about the software.

End-of-life happens for many reasons. Perhaps the product did not succeed, or it was superseded by a newer product. Companies can afford to support only a few versions of a software product. If Version 4 is just coming out, Version 1 that was released five years ago is no longer as important to customers or to the company. Version 1 might go into end-of-life so that resources can be focused on recent versions.

Sometimes, companies put versions into practical end-of-life by raising support and maintenance fees.

Productization: The Key to Understanding the Challenge of Using Open Source

Perhaps the simplest way to understand what you are getting into by using open source is to think of it in terms of the productization idea introduced earlier in this chapter:

> Using open source software means taking on the burden of overcoming the lack of productization.

Most open source projects are only partially productized. But all of the information required for you to work around the lack of productization is available.

The key questions are:

- How large of a burden will it be to overcome the lack of productization?
- Will it be easy or difficult for you to overcome?
- Are the risks worth the benefit derived from the software?

The models described in the next chapters are aimed at answering those questions:

- The Open Source Maturity model helps define the size of the productization gap.
- The Open Source Skills and Risk Tolerance model helps gauge how hard it will be for an IT organization to overcome the productization gap.
- The Software Cost and Risk model provides a framework for understanding the total costs, the risks, and the benefits of using an open source product.

It is no accident that the most skilled engineering teams in the country are also the largest users of open source. For them, the cost of overcoming the productization gap is small. The rest of this book will help IT departments understand the size of the gap for them.

In fairness to the open source community, we should mention another interpretation. From the perspective of a person with the required open source skills, the lack of productization is not a problem. Productization might even get in the way of a developer's needs. From this perspective, the barrier to wider adoption is not the lack of productization, but the lack of skills in those who desire to use open source—the skills gap mentioned earlier.

Remember, productization in a commercial product is not black and white. Some companies do a better job of it than others. There will always be problems to overcome with any software, and commercial software also comes with a productization gap most of the time. In the rest of this chapter, we will look at commercial software and open source software side by side.

Comparing the Risks of Commercial and Open Source Software

The episodic, sporadic, incremental evolution of open source is in sharp contrast to the more methodical design process that most commercial projects go through. This chapter has pointed out that IT technologists and executives who are seeking to understand the opportunity open source provides must understand the nature of commercial software, which is born out of a completely different process and has different strengths and weaknesses.

But the different processes can easily obscure the nature and quality of the end product. Whether open source or commercial software is better for a particular company or a particular purpose is a complex decision that is a function of the quality of the software, how well it fits to a particular task, and the skills present in the development team. The models that we describe in subsequent chapters provide a framework for understanding these issues.

The fact is that most software, open source and commercial, has problems that must be overcome for it to be useful. Figure 1-2 shows how the best software from the open source world shares certain characteristics, as does the worst. But most software is not located at the extremes of this scale. Most software falls into a gray area, meaning it has significant problems that might or might not be showstoppers, depending on the context.

Commercial software vendors would have you think their software is perfect and without blemish. However, anyone who has bought commercial software and used it extensively finds all sorts of rough edges. This is true even for the best software from the best companies. The closer you get to a commercial software product, the uglier it looks. Most software is in the gray area, which means that in the evaluation process the nature of the software's defects must be revealed to determine whether a program is suitable for your company. In the following discussion, we will examine some important differences between open source and commercial software that affect the evaluation process, and differences in the risk of owning and operating each type of software.

The Sales Process

As we have pointed out repeatedly, open source software generally doesn't come with a salesperson to guide you through the process of learning how the software might help you. While salespeople can be a tremendous help in gathering information about a piece of software, even the most naïve among us knows that all the information comes with a strong positive bias. Whitepapers, references, case studies, and so on, all paint a rosy picture. Software companies spend millions of dollars to influence the opinions of third-party analysts. Much of the most useful information, such as product support databases, is not available until after purchase. Sales staff is seldom rewarded for providing reasons not to buy the software. The sales process is generally of little help in getting to the key problems of software in the gray area.

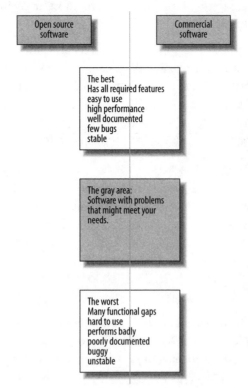

Figure 1-2. *Shared characteristics of open source and commercial software*

With open source, much more information about the software is available on the product's frequently asked question (FAQ) lists and bulletin boards. Much of the discussion on these forums actually concerns the problems of keeping an open source project in the gray area. The information will not come to you, but in most cases it is there for you to find. And you must be careful about accepting such information as authoritative. Some open source project participants have anonymously and systematically posted negative information about competing projects.

Transparency

With a commercial product, the company controls most of the information. The claims for product features might or might not be backed up by solid code, especially when it comes to new features. Customers who have run into problems usually don't post this information for public display, to avoid harming their relationship with the company or to avoid legal retribution. Independent user groups also usually want to keep good relations with the company. And user-group information is frequently available only after you are a customer anyhow.

In an open source project, the entire sausage factory is there for you to see, in all its complexity and ugliness, from day one. The chief barrier to getting the information is the time it takes to rummage through source code, bulletin boards, and so on. Search engines have made this process much easier. The most annoying and controversial bugs are usually not hard to find.

The ultimate test of whether an open source software product will work for your company is to install it and try it out. With commercial software, this is not always an option, and one that frequently costs money when it is an option. In open source, the costs are measured in terms of time and effort, but the opportunity to test the software is always available. While it might require effort, with an open source project there are no barriers to finding the problems in the gray areas.

Flexibility

There are well-defined ways to extend a commercial product. APIs are defined to allow users to write programs using the functionality of the applications. If the APIs allow everything you need, all is well. But if the product doesn't expose some deep, inside functionality in the right way, it can be years before a requested change becomes part of the product. The company's view of how many other customers want the same type of feature determines its decision to incorporate the requested change.

In open source, there is no such barrier. If you want to use deep, inside functionality of the software, you can write your own APIs to get access to it. Of course, this requires time, effort, and expertise, and for a large program it is hard to know if such deep surgery will have unintended side effects. But you have nobody to ask. You must simply do the work.

Risk of Quality

It is not uncommon for a commercial product to be interesting because of a new feature. That is why new features are created—to attract customers. But how well does that new feature work? With a commercial product, it is hard to tell until you buy it, mostly because of the issues mentioned already. And if you encounter any problems, you can't fix them.

In an open source project, a new feature might be implemented to spur discussion. The problems with the new feature might be announced on the project web site, without shame. The idea, of course, is that the developer might not have the time or skill to get the feature right. In an open source project, everything is open to improvement, if you have the time and skill. Figuring out what skill level you possess and what kind of tasks you can handle is the goal of the Open Source Skills and Risk Tolerance model.

In an open source project, it is generally possible to access the knowledge of senior programmers. In healthy open source projects, intelligent questions that are crucial to determining the product's future, or fixing new bugs, are addressed by the most senior developers on the project. With commercial software, access to senior engineers is difficult for an external company to get.

Risk of Productization

As a general rule, commercial software is more productized than open source software. Installation scripts, administrative interfaces, and documentation are usually better for a commercial product than for an open source product of the same age.

This chapter argues that to succeed with open source software, it is wise to plan for overcoming the lack of productization. It is the fundamental argument of this book that developing such skills can pay great benefits.

Risk of Failure

Both commercial software vendors and open source projects can crash and burn. Commercial software companies almost always try to protect customers by putting their source code in escrow, so it will be available should the vendor go out of business. The problem is that escrows can become out-of-date. It requires a lot of effort to keep an escrow current, along with everything needed to create the software. Does the escrow match the software at every customer site? How can it be made to match? Who would do this work?

In an open source project, a working copy of the source code is in the possession of the company using the software, from day one. This copy of the software is not out of sync, and it has everything needed to change, recompile, and assemble the working program. If an open source project tails off, those using the software are at a much lower risk.

Risk of Takeover

In the world of commercial software, a takeover can change everything. If a larger company buys a smaller competitor, the customers of the smaller company might eventually face a forced migration to the larger company's product. In a recent series of shocks to the IT industry, PeopleSoft bought J.D. Edwards, only to be acquired in a hostile takeover by Oracle. It's not hard to imagine how worried the original J.D. Edwards customers are. Sometimes, an acquiring company bends over backward so as not to alienate its new customers. But in this case, we've heard horror stories concerning loss of support and forced migration.

Open source projects are similar to takeovers in that both have forks, whereby a group of developers takes the source code and moves it in a different direction. A fork can take people's attention away from coding or hurt morale. But unlike what happens in some takeovers, nobody is forcing work to stop.

Support

Support is perhaps the biggest advantage of commercial software. The 15% to 25% of the license fee paid every year funds a staff of engineers and support technicians who are on call to help when you have a problem. This is of great value to most companies and is a great comfort if the support is well organized and of high quality.

Some open source projects provide excellent support to their users; sometimes the quality of that support exceeds that of commercial products. But in a broad sense, while commercial software has clear channels of support, open source support comprises figuring things out on your own.

With open source projects, large collections of information can help with some elements of support, but for the most part, you are on your own. This is a scary prospect for all but the most skilled programmers. Some companies have stepped into this gap and are offering support services for popular open source products. One of the fundamental arguments of this book is that companies who become skilled enough to be able to support open source have much to gain.

Looking back on this list of risks, we can see many risks and responsibilities for both commercial and open source software. With commercial software, the customer pays the vendor to manage the risks. In the world of open source, you must manage the risks yourself. By the end of Chapter 5 of this book, you will be an expert at determining and comparing these risks.

CHAPTER 2

Measuring the Maturity of Open Source

The difference between evaluating open source and commercial software is that in open source it is all up to you. Nobody teaches you how the product works. No experts call to explain everything. No whitepapers provide summaries of features and functionality. Nobody buys you lunch. You have to spend time gathering information and understanding the software. In other words, evaluating open source thoroughly enough to reduce risk is real work.

This chapter is a guide to doing that work.

Measuring the maturity of any software, commercial or open source, is far more an art than a science. This chapter will focus on the specific elements of an open source project, and those elements will serve as a guide to determining its maturity. Maturity, for the purposes of this chapter, is an indicator not only of age, but also of various dimensions of quality. It is also a proxy for the question, How much work is really required to use this software?

If some of the key elements of maturity are lacking—if information is difficult to find, if code is poorly structured and difficult to read, if forums are inactive and documentation is scant, if the project in general is of low quality—it translates into more work for those who would use the software. Problems will be hard to address. Help will be hard to find. Customization and configuration will be difficult. If the elements of maturity are present, the software will be much easier to use.

As the last chapter illustrated, most software, commercial or otherwise, exists in the gray area between mature and ill-formed. Almost every potentially valuable program also comes with significant drawbacks. The key to the successful deployment of software of any kind is to understand how the software will provide value and how you will avoid or compensate for the drawbacks inherent in using the software. The larger picture of whether a particular open source project will work for a particular purpose goes beyond issues of maturity, of course. Determining how the software will be used, who will be using it, and what it will fully cost are important factors that must be taken into account.

The purpose of this chapter, and the two that follow, is to lay out a comprehensive program to help you avoid the most common mistakes IT departments make when they decide to use open source software.

This chapter begins with a look at the traps an IT department can fall into if it does not take a comprehensive approach to evaluating open source, followed by a discussion of the elements of an open source project that determine maturity. The chapter ends with the formulation of an Open Source Maturity model that will be used later in the book to evaluate the open source projects in the chapters on specific areas of interest to IT departments.

Open Source Traps

All of the open source traps we identify in this section can be avoided if careful research and sober thinking of the type described in this and the following two chapters precede commitment to the use of open source. Let's face it: many IT departments gravitate toward open source without adequately considering the issues involved, simply because it is exciting. It represents an interesting opportunity for the technologist and a way to save money for the business. The pitfalls outlined in this section occur because of overconfidence on the part of technologists, lack of due diligence, and poor communication.

Getting burned while selecting open source is usually the result of mistakes made in one of these broad categories:

- It requires more work than expected.
- It does not work well with existing systems.
- It is harder to extend than anticipated.
- Getting answers from the open source development team is impossible.

The good news is that most of the time it is easy to determine in advance whether these problems are likely to occur. And even if they are unavoidable, there is no barrier to overcoming them. Figuring out what an open source program does, and fixing it, is always possible.

The danger lies in rushing into using an open source program just because it is easy to get something running. Avoiding traps requires discipline. Here are six common ways of getting burned:

- Selecting a product that is ill-suited for the technical skill set of the people responsible for running it. Ill-suited in this case can mean it uses a technology stack that the company's IT department has little or no experience with.

- Selecting a product that has withering community support. This means you have no support, and almost every question will have to be answered the hard way— by experimenting with the product or reading the code.

- Selecting a product based on the buzz it is getting. Sometimes the buzz is about factors that have nothing to do with the software's quality. A hot product can have gaping holes in terms of functionality.

- Selecting a product that is being pushed out of the market because of commercial conflicts (trademark, copyright, etc.). Sometimes open source projects run afoul of commercial products. When an open source product emulates or extends a commercial product, it makes a huge difference whether the commercial firm ignores the effort, supports it, or seeks to shut it down.

- Selecting a product that does not have momentum. Products with slow momentum lie dormant for a long period of time between releases. A bug reported to be fixed in the next release might not become available for quite a while.

- Taking a product out of its natural home. If a product is most often used with Apache, MySQL, and Linux, and you want to use it with IIS, Oracle, and Solaris, integration problems might soar.

Some of these traps, of course, are not unique to open source. But paying careful attention to the methods in this book will help you to avoid all the problems just listed.

The Elements of Open Source Maturity

As mentioned previously, the elements of open source maturity are direct indicators of the potential difficulties you can encounter when using open source. The specific elements of open source maturity we will discuss are:

- Leadership and culture

- Vitality of community

- Quality of end-user support

- Extent and scope of documentation

- Quality of packaging

- Momentum

- Quality of code and design
- Quality of architecture
- Testing practices
- Integration with other products
- Support for standards
- Quality of project site
- License type
- Potential for commercial conflicts
- Corporate commitment

Each of these strengths is directly related to the difficulty an IT department will encounter when using the software. These criteria are not absolute. Some are fuzzy, some are matters of taste and judgment, and many overlap in different ways.

As an IT department becomes more adept at using open source, the weaknesses that are difficult to overcome during an open source deployment will become easier to understand and identify.

Leadership and Culture

One of the most important factors in evaluating the maturity of an open source project is the quality of its leadership. Are they serious developers with a strong understanding of technology and the kinds of problems that you, with a business at risk, are facing? What previous successes do they have to show for their work?

Unlike a commercial software company, open source projects don't rely on CEOs or directors—individuals, that is, whose reputations, associations with other companies and organizations, and previous executive positions are typically described on a web site for all to see. But that hardly means the official leaders of an open source project cannot, or should not, be assessed before one commits to that project's code and its community of fellow users and developers. Indeed, precisely because the open source movement is open, with most of its participants' activities and exchanges recorded on various Internet mailing lists and web forums, more valuable information might actually be available about those people than what is available about executives at private and public companies. Far more than its commercial counterparts, the open source community and process are self-documenting.

The first question to ask about a potential project is simply this: is the leadership identified? Unfortunately, a number of open source projects get started by individuals who hack together a piece of code that works, more or less, and then leave it there, unfinished, unpolished, and unworkable for any serious applications. What's worse in terms of evaluating leadership is that beyond an out-of-date "About Me" statement on the project's web page, there is no indication that anyone is in charge of moving the project forward. Clearly, no enterprise wants to start depending on what is essentially an abandoned project, no matter how good its founders' original intentions were or how hard they once might have worked to realize an initial vision. Like all software, open source evolves; it's more a process than a static, deliverable object. It is practically a living thing that needs ongoing nourishment, encouragement, and care. And without leadership of some kind, an open source program will wither and eventually die.

One good indicator of serious, devoted, and informed leadership specific to the open source realm is the degree to which a project leader or other team member participates in the many forums that have sprung up to facilitate the open source movement. Not every project leader will be as prolific and active a contributor to these forums as Gavin King of JBoss fame, for instance, or Scott Ferguson of Resin. They have distinguished themselves by speaking regularly at major open source conferences and participating in numerous online forums and mailing lists. All of this shows a level of personal, emotional, and perhaps even financial investment in not only leading their specific projects, but also furthering the progress of the open source concept as a whole.

But even individuals who don't demonstrate exemplary participation can be evaluated just the same. You can review their contributions to online forums and their appearances at important conferences. Most of the significant online forums get archived for a period of several years or more, which makes it possible to see how often an individual has contributed and how favorably his peers have responded to his comments. Is he articulate? Is he technologically savvy? Has he made a significant contribution to the public knowledge base for the product?

It should be noted, however, that sheer celebrity is not a perfect measure of leadership skills. Due diligence analysis is still required, even if a project has received a lot of press or is backed by a large company, such as Sun or IBM. Neither fame nor sponsorship is a guarantee of quality.

Besides personal ability to lead, another crucial measure of an open source project is its culture. What is the project's attitude? How does it respond to questions or suggestions for changes or new features? Are the people who represent the project publicly defensive? A prickly attitude, for instance, is not likely to help engender warm feelings among the users, developers, and respected industry analysts who might contribute to the project's long-term success. To a large extent, open source projects live or die by word-of-mouth, by the Net's myriad grapevines, where anyone can evaluate a developer's attitude and expertise. By the same token, an excessively fawning attitude can be detrimental, too. There is such a thing as using open source forums to draw too much attention to a particular body of work or using them as outlets for a tacit form of advertising.

Good leaders spend their time wisely, but with generosity. Highly knowledgeable individuals, such as Scott Ferguson, have made themselves available to the community and have demonstrated a remarkable responsiveness, without capitulating to the many naïve and downright lazy questions that his exposure inevitably invites. Ferguson doesn't bother to respond when he's asked, for the 50th time, "How do I configure security restraints?" But when a substantial issue arises, he's there with useful questions and answers that help the community. And those who have followed his activities over the years say Ferguson gives credit where credit is due.

In the end, a strong, professional, respectful culture leads to a healthy project. If people feel they are part of something good, if developers and users aren't put off by bad attitudes among a project's leaders, there is a better chance that they will remain committed to the project—and even throw themselves into it.

Superior culture also attracts superior people. It is a self-sustaining process.

A developer's time and energy are limited, and the best won't waste their resources contributing to projects that don't provide the kind of payback they are seeking, whether it is monetary gain or just the satisfaction of knowing they've made the world a better place.

Vitality of Community

There is a huge correlation between leadership and the vitality of the community. Leadership breeds a healthy culture that will spawn an active community. In such communities, everyone finds something useful to do, and one of the key indicators of this is a division of labor between the project's developers and users. Evidence of this can include separate lists for users and developers, and subprojects dedicated to productization activities such as creating easy-to-use installation packages or user documentation.

Healthy open source communities also tread a fine line between disciplining lazy behavior, such as using curt replies to direct people who have simple questions to locations where the answers can be easily found, and welcoming new people into the project.

The size of the community is also a good indicator of a project's viability. How active are forums? How many downloads happen, and how often? How frequently is the project referred to on Google? What is the project's rating on sites such as OSDIR (*http://www.osdir.com/*)?

Quality of End-User Support

End-user support is a key element of a project's maturity, and it's one of the most crucial elements in terms of saving time when using an open source project. Active forums, well-maintained FAQs, and documentation that are available through a search engine are generally the biggest time-saving feature of an open source project. Such mechanisms identify not only answers, but also members of the community who are fellow travelers, who are using the software in the same way you are. Contacting such community members directly can often be a huge timesaver if both sides of the conversation have something to offer to each other.

As discussed earlier in this chapter, one of the most compelling aspects of open source projects are the very public and free-ranging discussions that take place among the lead developers, far-flung contributors, and end users. These discussions serve a variety of purposes, not the least of which is providing general advice, tips, and specific answers to end users' problems. Most open source projects rely on these open forums as low-overhead substitutes for the kind of profitable annual support contracts for which commercial software companies typically charge a handsome price.

Not surprisingly, the most popular open source applications and programs tend to have the most active forums—and the most seasoned and helpful experts participating in those forums. Under the best of circumstances, answers to a technical question might show up within minutes or hours of the original post. Overnight is more typical. Usually, the answer is entirely satisfactory. But on some lists and boards, questions simply go unanswered.

Two extremely helpful features of the best online forums are a searchable archive of questions and answers, and well-maintained FAQs. Both arrangements make it easier for developers to find out if their particular problem has been addressed already. Ideally, an archive is organized according to topic, but a free-text search can be enormously helpful, too. Likewise, the best FAQs address the most recent issues that have been important to developers and users. This requires a certain amount of attention from someone on the project in question and is often neglected as other tasks get priority. But an up-to-date FAQ is usually a sign of a healthy, actively supported project.

Extent and Scope of Documentation

Another good clue about a project's work process and code quality is the quality of its documentation. Sloppy documentation can well reflect sloppy coding practices or, at the very least, an arrogance or even disrespect for the final user of the code. Perhaps it's too much to expect that every line of source code should have a comment attached to it, as some textbooks would prescribe. But it's not out of line to expect that the instructions for installing, running, and fine-tuning a piece of enterprise software be written in reasonably clear English. Moreover, the historical milestones in the code's development ought to be available for all to see. Transparency is a must.

Tomcat, an open source, Java-based servlet container, is a good example of how this documentation should be done. Better than most open source projects, documentation for the Tomcat site is organized by major version release, in reverse order: Release 5.x, Release 4.1, and so forth, back to the original Release 3.0. The original documentation for each release is kept available, just as they were when each release was current. This comprehensiveness is essential to using Tomcat, because many users are still using older releases of the program. Easy, direct access to older documentation, without the trouble of having to search for and unpack the relevant files, makes it much easier for consultants, say, to reconfigure, tweak, or debug any particular Tomcat installation they happen to stumble across.

Something else to look for in a project's documentation is a comprehensive user manual or reference guide. This manual should provide complete instructions for installing the software in question, and not just simplistic *README* files. Particularly important, and too often completely missing, is information about how to configure the software. Configuring a new program can be enormously time consuming, even *with* good documentation at hand. But working without a manual clearly outlining the common configuration scenarios can add significantly to the integration costs. Now, if you're working with a very well-known and widely used piece of open source, such as the Apache Web Server or its frequent companion, Tomcat, you might be in luck. These especially popular programs have spawned their own commercial books, written by expert users or by the developers themselves. Like all third-party computer and software manuals, the quality and comprehensiveness can vary. But the fact that such a book is available at all is a good indication of a program's usefulness and reputation in the marketplace. In most cases, a project's web site will offer pointers to such books, perhaps with commentary. Likewise, by scanning online forums you might find mention of relevant titles. Several technical publishers, including O'Reilly Media, have published manuals on open source programs and books concerning the movement in general.

Quality of Installation Packaging

It behooves prospective users to evaluate how an open source program is packaged. Some programs are available only as source code, thus requiring users to undertake the somewhat difficult task of compiling that code into binary, executable form. Other projects provide both source and binaries, and still others come complete with installers designed for specific operating systems.

Perhaps the highest state of evolution for an open source project is when someone has had time to write an installation package that can install the software easily on many different platforms and configurations. This usually is not fun work, and for a project to have attracted a community that is large enough for this to be accomplished is a sign of the project's maturity and strength. Sometimes, one of the senior developers will actually take the time to do this sort of work himself, and much earlier than it would have happened otherwise. This is not uncommon when the open source effort is fueled by a core team that is also interested in selling consulting services related to the project.

Momentum (or Frequency of Releases)

Like all software, open source tends to undergo constant updating. New features, new extensions, bug fixes, and other changes get worked into each new release. How often new releases of a program become available might help or hinder its effective use. Clearly, if updates are not released often enough, users will be forced to wait too long to use the latest code and won't be able to use the program as effectively as possible. And if an important bug is discovered, the fix for it ought to be made available as quickly as possible.

Veterans of the open source world know how frustrating it can be to discover in the archives of a project's mailing list that an important problem has been addressed with new code but that the code is not yet available in an official release of the program. Until the official release is available, the only option users have is to undertake a new build of the program on their own, using the prerelease version of the software—a difficult undertaking that many developers wish to avoid.

On the other hand, there is such a thing as a too-frequent release schedule. Ideally, new releases should be put forth only when substantial additions and changes have been made to a program, and not simply with every sprinkling of not-so-important changes.

The right release schedule depends largely on how stable and mature a project is. Many programs reach a stage where they are not receiving many updates and the rate of new releases slows down to one or two a year, if that. On the other hand, a lack of updates can be an indication of abandonment or stalled development activity, so look carefully at other clues on the project's web site. In the past, stalled open source projects have been resurrected as business conditions and related technologies changed. A less mature product that is in high demand and wide use can be updated as often as once a month.

Check out the release history, though, to see if the new releases are mainly significant or more trivial. A well-managed release cycle indicates the presence of experienced technologists at work. Well managed can mean different things depending on the culture of the open source project. For example, Drupal and Tikiwiki, two excellent LAMP-based content management systems, have well-managed release cycles. But Drupal favors longer beta periods and multiple release candidates, because that project favors stability over new features.

Quality of Code and Design

Exceeding the importance of almost every other factor, of course, is the quality of the actual code that is produced for others to use. In contrast to commercial software, open source code is just that: open to direct inspection at the source-code level by anyone and everyone, including potential users, developers, competing development teams, and yes, even nefarious hackers. Few people have the knowledge or time, however, to evaluate the software's quality fully, by inspecting its source code line by line, module by module. But it is possible to glean some meaningful insight into the thinking that has shaped the code—into the mind or minds that have produced what you see.

The clues are primarily visual. Take the code layout, for example. Have the authors organized the code in a way that invites understanding, and that reveals at least some organization? Is the code modularized? How are the modules grouped together? Has a naming convention been rigorously adhered to? Anyone with a modicum of experience in writing and working with enterprise-level software should be able to "read" this high-level structure and the labels being used and get at least a partial feel for the software's functions and the quality of its coding.

The deeper the inspection of a program, of course, the more fully its quality will be revealed. Many open source programs are the result of team efforts, with some modules, functions, and Java classes, for instance, of much higher quality than others.

Quality of Architecture

The quality of an open source program's architecture is difficult to assess, but for obvious reasons, it tends to be an important measure of the code's maturity. By architecture, we mean system components (such as classes in J2EE and PHP systems, modules in Perl), use of design patterns, OO techniques, and naming conventions. To evaluate this kind of architecture fully, it's necessary to understand the program's requirements to some degree. And even then, it can take a fair amount of investment and time to fully determine and understand a program's internal architecture.

Fortunately, a small industry of open source-focused support companies—essentially consultancies specializing in helping users to employ selected open source projects—has been spawned by open source's growing popularity. Maintaining a critical understanding of the architectures of open source programs is the bread-and-butter work of these firms. It can be extremely helpful in the early stages of evaluating an open source project to call on such firms for help in understanding the project and code, and how it stacks up against commercial alternatives.

Testing Practices

Some open source code comes with automated, built-in testing facilities as standard features. In particular, the developers of many mature Java projects have gotten the testing religion and have begun to make test routines a significant portion of the code they develop and make available for public use. As much as 70% of some code is devoted to this kind of testing, which can be especially important when building, say, a public web site whose servers will have to deal with high volumes of visitor traffic and transactions. The presence of unit tests is a key indicator of good design.

Integration with Other Products

All software in the enterprise operates as part of what developers often refer to as an *ecology*, meaning that a set of interdependencies cause programs to call on each other, vie for shared resources, and exchange transactions and information. As users evolve their computing setups, they might swap out one program for another or install a new system, and such changes can disrupt the ecological balance, as it were, by altering or ignoring certain dependencies between the previous set of applications and subsystems. Release 3.4 of Program A might work fine with Release 7.8 of Program B, but when the user upgrades A to 3.5, the long-existing compatibility between the two programs might break down. Much as what happens within a desktop PC, conflicts can arise as programs are added to and removed from a working system.

Frequently, open source projects are aware of such dependencies and new releases are proactively tested with other open source software. The Zope application server, for example, has been used frequently with the Squid reverse proxy cache. It is likely that when a new release of either comes out, it will be tested with the other. Pay attention to and take advantage of such nests of compatibility.

Support for Standards

Closely related to the question of dependencies is the need for programs to use standards-based APIs. For various reasons, open source projects sometimes trail the standardization being pushed forward by the still-dominant commercial marketplace. In other cases, two or more open source projects focused on the same area of technology might be competing to set the standard for a certain brand-new API. The situation can get particularly confusing and difficult for users to negotiate if a project that is pioneering a new category of software advertises itself as adhering to a standard API, but in fact ends up implementing an API that diverges from the standard.

The problem of dependencies and nonstandard APIs is sometimes addressed in open source projects by having a program download with a preselected set of other programs—the programs that make up its local ecology, that is. By predetermining this collection of applications, subsystems, and drivers, perhaps supplied by a number of different projects or authors, it is possible to make sure all the pieces work together correctly. In short, someone else is managing dependencies for the user.

Quality of Project Site

Open source project web sites are usually masterpieces of brevity and clarity when it comes to site design. That said, some are more concise and well organized than others, and this can matter a lot when a large team with different skills and relationships to the open source project are involved in a deployment. A great site can make it easy for everyone to educate himself and find what he needs.

License Type

Open source projects employ a variety of different licenses. In some cases, there might be no restriction on the use of the software for developing a new system that is based on a certain open source program. But when it comes time to distribute those applications and the underlying program in a commercial application, or to make the applications available through a public web site, users must pay a fee—perhaps determined by how many servers are executing the software. Some licenses give the user freedom not only to work with the program to develop new applications, but also to distribute it at no charge. Still another level of license permits users to modify the software themselves, perhaps requiring that they contribute their improvements back to the open source project.

One of the great attractions of open source is that users get direct access to the program's source code. This can be of great comfort when problems arise. One of the worst disasters to hit a corporate IT environment is when a piece of commercial software breaks down and the code's supplier has gone out of business. When this happens, an enterprise's entire investment in a piece of software can be lost, and there is no way to save it. With an open source program, users can get at the source code and change it if need be. This is a vital form of insurance, with advantages that many corporations are now waking up to. Not every company will bother to modify open source code, but just knowing that it is an option can be a major comfort.

Potential for Commercial Conflicts

Unfortunately, software of all sorts, open source and commercial, sometimes has a dubious legal status. Code might infringe—or simply appear to infringe—on the intellectual property of a commercial company. This puts developers as well as users at risk of potential legal action by those commercial suppliers. A software company's decision about whether to sue to protect its product can depend more on how well the competing open source project is faring in the marketplace than on actual infringements. The Open AMF project, for example, implements a proprietary protocol created by Macromedia. While the Open AMF software does some very interesting things, if Macromedia frowns on the effort, it might have the power to shut down the project.

This sort of conflict is a rare occurrence, however, given that open source projects focus mostly on integration with other open source projects. It is also a risk that is inherent in the use of any software, open source or commercial.

Corporate Commitment

Several open source projects, such as the Linux operating system and Apache Web Server, have enjoyed tremendous support from large, established computer companies, including IBM, Sun, HP, and Dell. IBM, in particular, has helped the Apache server effort with people and valuable source code, not to mention its name and reputation.

Corporations also lend their support to open source projects by adopting them on a massive scale. Nothing brings an open source project to maturity like a deployment on 50,000 desktops by a highly professional IT organization.

Putting It All Together

The elements of open source maturity are stepping-stones on the path to realizing what you are getting yourself into. Understanding an open source project means being able to estimate how much work will be required, and how hard that work will be based on a department's assessment of its skills and how it intends to use the software. The result of a maturity analysis, then, should be a list of worries.

The next section of this chapter boils down the Open Source Maturity model into a concise set of factors that will be used later in the book to put the recommended open source projects on the same simplified scale. Readers might find in the model an easy way to organize the results of their research.

The Open Source Maturity Model

The Open Source Maturity model attempts to quantify the maturity of an open source product. This should help an enterprise decide whether to adopt the product for long-term use.

This model assumes the following:

- A functional specification of requirements exists
- A functional specification has been matched to a product functionality list, and a short list of products that match has been created

The IT department uses the results of these two steps to determine which product from the short list is *suitable* for adoption. It should be noted that this evaluation process might be too resource intensive for the short-term use of an open source product but is a very wise investment for medium to long-term use.

We assess maturity in three major areas:

Product criteria
    Product criteria are specifics about the product itself. Since open source software (OSS) products are often under rapid development, with major advances made in a few weeks to a few months, we list momentum as a criterion to offset the age criterion. This helps us spot products that aren't mature enough today but are worthy of keeping an eye on.

Use criteria
    Use criteria are specifics about what it takes to use the product from day to day, from the effort of initial installation and configuration to the work required for daily upkeep and support mechanisms available to help in tailoring the product to an enterprise's needs and fixing defects encountered.

Integration criteria

> Integration criteria are specifics about what it takes to make the product work in the enterprise's environment. This is often overlooked during evaluations and is a critical factor to consider if you want to win with open source in the enterprise.

For each criterion we assign a score of 1, 2, or 3:

1 (Immature)

> The product is lacking in several critical areas. It would be dangerous for an enterprise to use it in a business-critical function. Some projects remain in this state until the first major release.

2 (Reasonably mature)

> The product has a sufficiently long history of stable deployments, a loyal user base, and a bright future. For example, while MySQL is lacking many features for certain types of high-performance enterprise use, most everyone agrees that it is well on its way to being a mature open source product fit for most requirements.

3 (Very mature)

> The product has a long and stable history, a broad and vibrant user community, etc. Apache Web Server is a good example of a level 3 open source program.

While useful, this numerical categorization should not be used as a categorical measure. You can ignore the difference of a single point in scoring. We provide the scoring as a suggestion, mostly for convenience and as a way to organize the analysis and comparison of many open source projects. Table 2-1 shows the Open Source Maturity model.

Table 2-1. *The Open Source Maturity model*

Maturity criteria	Score = 1	Score = 2	Score = 3	Criteria description
Product criteria				
Age	< 6 months	6 months–2 years	> 2 years	OSS efforts that are just getting underway are risky for enterprises.
Multiple supported platforms	One platform	Many related platforms	Multiple heterogeneous platforms	Products that work on both Windows and Unix are more desirable.

Table 2-1. *The Open Source Maturity model (continued)*

Maturity criteria	Score = 1	Score = 2	Score = 3	Criteria description
Momentum	No release in last 6 months	< two releases in past year	Regular releases	This is key to helping separate vital products from ones that are withering.
Popularity	Unknown product	Viable alternative	Category leader	Popular OSS products are well tested and therefore more mature. They are also likely to be interoperable with a large number of other products.
Design quality	Monolithic application	Multiple components	Well-defined API	This criterion is key in determining the effort required to extend and adapt the product for enterprise use.
Use criteria				
Setup cost	Poorly documented install process; poor documentation; help available from developers	Well-documented install process; reasonable documentation; help available from developers; help available in support forums	Well-documented install process; install wizards/scripts available; reasonable documentation; help available from developers; help available in support forums; third-party install services	Most products should require a setup effort of hours or days, not weeks or months.

Table 2-1. *The Open Source Maturity model (continued)*

Maturity criteria	Score = 1	Score = 2	Score = 3	Criteria description
Usage cost	Poor or non-existent documentation; help available only through direct contact with developers	User manuals available; help available in support forums	Third-party training services available	This criterion is often overlooked when evaluating a product.
End-user support	No forums or mailing lists	Some forums or mailing lists	Well-run forums and mailing lists, with archives and search; third-party support options	User community (forums, mailing lists) and third-party support are vital to a product's success.
Integration criteria				
Modularity	Monolithic structure; possible but hard to extend	Multiple modules; possible to extend	Multiple modules, well-defined API; possible and easy to extend	
Collaboration with other products	Unknown	Known cases of integration	Lots of integration documented	
Standards compliance	Unknown or proprietary	Outdated	Current industry standards	
Developer support	No forums or mailing lists	Some forums or mailing lists	Well-run forums and mailing lists with archives and search; third-party support options	

Armed with the information in this chapter, most IT departments will be able to do a first-rate job of evaluating open source projects. The next most important factor is whether an IT department properly understands its skills, which is the subject of the next chapter.

CHAPTER 3

The Open Source Skill Set

In Chapter 2, we determined how to evaluate the maturity of an open source project. In this chapter, we look at what an IT department must bring to the task of using open source. Making open source a key part of an IT infrastructure involves a commitment to acquiring and maintaining a certain set of skills. The exact skill set for any open source project depends on the maturity of the technology used to build it, how well it matches the needs of an application, and the importance of the application in an organization.

The last chapter showed clearly that all open source projects are not created equal. At the most mature end of the spectrum, using open source is pretty much exactly like using commercial software. Mature open source projects offer everything commercial products do, plus the benefits of a thriving community, online resources, and a fully developed ecosystem. At the least mature end of the spectrum, open source projects can be little more than an idea, and some code that partially implements that idea. Using this sort of open source means, in effect, that you've joined the development team.

Choosing the right open source to use in an enterprise depends on the skill level of the company's IT department. Beginners will be able to use only the most mature open source. As an IT department's skill level increases, more and more value can be found in all sorts of open source projects.

The way that open source will be used is also key to understanding the commitment required. Trying open source in an experimental or low-performance context requires much less of an investment in terms of acquiring knowledge and skill building than choosing to use open source for a mission-critical function. The skills required of an IT department to handle each type of project are vastly different. In a low-performance context, you might have days to fix a problem, whereas mission-critical systems might need to be fixed in minutes.

This chapter explores the skills needed to handle open source of varying maturities and examines the risks companies take by using open source. When properly planned and executed, open source adoption can be a rewarding adventure that increases the power of an IT department.

The approach in this chapter will be as follows:

- First, we'll examine the relationship between an IT department's skills and its ability to use open source.

- Then, we'll provide a proposed taxonomy of increasing skill levels of companies, inspired by Geoffrey Moore's analysis of the high-tech industry, first published in his book, *Crossing the Chasm* (HarperBusiness, 1991).

- Next, we'll offer a description of the specific skills needed to be able to handle open source of varying maturities.

- We'll follow that with an analysis of the way the operational risk profile of a particular system affects the suitability of open source.

- We'll end the chapter with a discussion of how to progress from one level to the next, and how to transform individual skills into institutional skills.

Before proceeding further, we should mention the two most important skills of all: communication and sales. Persuading most organizations to use open source is a difficult task. By the end of this chapter, advocates will be able to make their case and detail not only the benefits of using open source, but also the responsibilities involved.

The ultimate goal of this chapter is to help managers and technologists in IT departments construct a realistic plan for creating and improving institutional skills, so they can unlock more value from open source projects and avoid the open source nightmare that occurs when open source adoption is not pursued carefully.

Preventing an Open Source Nightmare

IT departments end up creating open source nightmares, because they don't ask the right questions and they don't prepare for the responsibilities and risks involved. Of course, implementation of commercial technology often ends in a nightmare, too, but that is a different story.

The typical open source nightmare begins when a lead architect or a development team approaches management and suggests using open source for a particular project. In many ways, such requests resemble a child asking a parent if she can have a puppy. The parent generally replies, "Yes, if you promise to take care of it." The child promises to do so, not knowing anything about housebreaking a puppy, what it will take to feed and groom it, and how often it needs to go for a walk. After a while, the child just plays with the puppy and the parent is left to clean up the mess.

While this is a cruel analogy for technologists, it does accurately illustrate one of the major problems with using open source in the enterprise: the difficulty of understanding an IT department's skills. One major cause of open source failure is that the business staff doesn't know the IT department's skill level, and the IT department has an unrealistic view of its own skill level. The amount of work involved in evaluating and deploying open source is also frequently underestimated by IT teams with little open source experience.

The most common open source nightmare involves using open source in a project and having implementation take three or four times as long as expected, because so much needed to be learned to get the job done. A worse situation occurs when the implementation goes smoothly, and the difficulty of supporting or changing an open source project is discovered after the software is in production.

Then, of course, there is the problem of having the person who championed the use of open source leave the company after implementation but before any institutional skills have been built. This is known as a *key-person problem*.

It is important to note that commercial software is not immune to any of these problems.

A broad oversimplification about open source versus commercial software is that open source represents primarily an investment of time, and commercial software represents primarily an investment of money. Any organization setting out to use open source must set aside some time for research and experimentation. There is no way to skirt this time commitment.

This same sort of work must be done for commercial software as well, but in those cases at almost every turn a vendor or consultant is ready to help exchange time for money.

One implication of this is that anything that systematically reduces the time required to effectively use open source projects increases its value to an organization. In the end, the higher the skills and the more experience an organization has with open source, the more potential value it has. Higher skills reduce the time investment and the cost of using open source, and that increases the promise of using more open source projects. It has been shown over and over again that the most highly skilled organizations are the first to adopt open source, and are the most aggressive in exploiting it. Amazon.com, Google, Yahoo!, Ticketmaster, NASA, academic research labs, and most Wall Street financial firms are heavy users of open source.

This chapter will provide a framework for sober analysis of the biggest factor that eats up time in an open source implementation—building skills. Your understanding of the skills and risks involved is the most important factor in determining whether using open source will be a valuable step forward, or a nightmare.

Open Source Skill Levels

It is impossible to capture precisely and on a simple scale a detailed assessment of an IT department's open source skills. What's more, the skills required for any particular implementation can vary widely, depending on the maturity of the open source project. The goal of this model, then, is not to create an authoritative aptitude test, but rather, to help an IT department understand what skills are required to use open source projects in different situations.

The Open Source Skills and Risk Tolerance model will serve four purposes:

- It is a guide to self-assessment that can combat the frequent over-optimism of IT departments and technologists in general. All technologists feel in their hearts like highly skilled innovators. The descriptions presented of the specific skills an IT department has to have at each level can assist in making a sober judgment about what sort of open source is appropriate.

- It gives the authors a quick way to talk about what sort of skill level will be needed in the later chapters that review specific open source projects.

- In understanding the skills required at each level, an IT department will be able to create an organized plan for creating and improving institutional skills so that the cost of using open source drops and the potential value created from using open source grows.

- If an IT department chooses to use consultants to help in evaluating and implementing open source, the model provides a framework for evaluating the skills of a consultant or consulting firm, or other service providers.

Skill Levels Defined

The skill levels presented here are intended to imitate the stages of technology adoption made famous by Geoffrey Moore in his book, *Crossing the Chasm*. In the book, Moore presents a model for how technology is adopted based on a diffusion model that was first created to explain the adoption of technology in agriculture.

In Moore's model, users of technology are split into the categories shown in Figure 3-1. Note how the size of the area under the bell curve illustrates the number of people in each category.

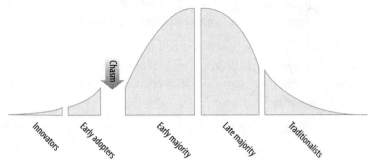

Figure 3-1. *Geoffrey Moore's categories for technology adoption*

Moore's analysis is that between the early adopters and the early majority exists a chasm that companies selling technology have to cross over. The difficulty in crossing the chasm is that the way technology is adopted by innovators and early adopters is completely different from the way the early majority and late majority adopt technology.

Moore has written several books explaining and expanding on this analysis, but here are his views in simplified form:

*   Innovators and early adopters have a high tolerance for risk and for the defects of new technology, because they are highly skilled. Innovators and early adopters are attracted primarily to technology because of the power of its raw functionality.

*   The early and late majority have low tolerance for risk and are interested not in raw functionality but in the acquisition of technology to solve specific business problems.

*   Most high-technology companies start out selling to innovators and early adopters, emphasizing functional strengths and how innovative their technology is. This approach turns off the early and late majority. To "cross the chasm," companies must learn how to change their tune and package their product to solve specific business problems in a predictable, low-risk fashion.

Much the same chasm exists in open source technology. But unlike commercial technology, few open source developers are attempting to push their projects across the chasm. This is changing as open source is used as a business model for consulting firms, and open source developers start to understand the benefits of wider adoption. (Chapters 6 and 7 address some of these issues.)

Open source projects do not have marketing departments, sales staff, and product managers thinking about how to gain a wider audience. They have developers creating great technology to meet their own goals. For open source projects to cross the chasm, they must be either pulled across by IT departments that realize the benefits of increasing institutional skills to unlock the value of open source, or pushed by a person, group, or organization that is interested in wider adoption.

This does not mean that to use open source an IT department has to become an innovator such as Google, Amazon.com, or Ticketmaster. It does mean that an IT department has to develop enough skill to recognize and implement mature open source that is ready to cross the chasm.

This chapter will explain the kind of skills needed, using levels that are parallel to those in Moore's analysis:

- Beginner (late majority/traditionalist)
- Intermediate (early majority)
- Advanced (early adopter)
- Expert (innovator)

Each skill level enables an IT department to handle open source of different degrees of maturity.

To be precise about our definition, each level of expertise will be described along each of the following dimensions:

Open source development tools
   What knowledge of open source development tools will be required?

Hosting
   What hosting capabilities will be needed?

System administration
   What system administration skills will be required?

Operations
   What operations capabilities and skills will be needed?

Open source infrastructure
   What open source infrastructure—programs such as Apache, MySQL, etc.— must be understood?

Programming languages
   What programming language skills will be required?

Open source community skills
   What sort of skills for getting help through open source community channels will be needed?

The following definitions summarize the skills at each level, and how this enables open source to be employed.

Beginner

The beginner level is defined by the minimum amount of skill needed to use the most mature open source products and infrastructure. IT departments at the beginner level are defined by the following abilities:

Open source development tools
> These users understand at a superficial level the packaging and development tools involved in downloading and unpacking the binary versions appropriate for an existing operating system.

Hosting
> They use a hosting operation for servers and networks provided to them by the IT department.

System administration
> Beginners perform basic system administration involved in installing and executing the operating-system-level configuration of the open source software, such as specifying where log files will be written, what ports the software will use, and other such fundamental settings.

Operations
> These users gain basic operational skills to monitor servers and determine the use of resources by the open source program, such as whether log files are filling up, whether software is starting and/or stopping, and whether the software is running.

Open source infrastructure
> They understand the functionality of the open source project they intend to use, and they perform basic program configuration. If multiple open source projects are working together, they understand the connections between the programs so that they can configure them properly.

Open source community skills
> They use open source community assets such as mailing lists and bulletin boards in a way that elicits a positive response from the community.

The beginner level for an IT department goes far beyond the skills and knowledge required just to get an open source project running. For the most part, it is possible to get an open source program running with very little knowledge. But for an IT department the minimum knowledge is of greater scope because the program must be operating in a stable manner.

To an IT department at the beginner level, then, open source is a black box with a few simple knobs that control its functionality. If the black box plays a helpful role as is, it might be appropriate for use in a production environment. All of the normal operational and performance testing can take place on such a product without the IT department having to know much about its internal workings.

Stable infrastructure such as the Linux operating system, Apache Web Server, and MySQL database, or products such as the Mozilla browser, can be used by beginners. Toolkits and frameworks that require more configuration and programming are not appropriate for beginners.

Intermediate

At the intermediate level, open source is still a fundamentally black box, but one with many more dimensions of configurability. Those with intermediate skill levels should be able to grasp not only advanced configurations of open source, but also basic uses of programming languages. The intermediate skill level is defined by the following abilities:

Open source development tools
> These skills are the same as those at the beginner level, except compilation might be required or other packaging tools might be needed to put templates and simple programs into production.

Hosting
> These skills are the same as those at the beginner level.

System administration
> These skills are the same as those at the beginner level, but these users also can handle any additional configuration needed when using templates.

Operations
> These skills are the same as those at the beginner level, but these users also are capable of monitoring the operations of templates or simple programs added to configure open source projects.

Open source infrastructure
> Intermediate-level users must be able to understand all the configurations possible for an open source project or group of projects working together. They must be able to read the programming language of the project to understand how configuration parameters are used, and they must have ready knowledge of certain common open source infrastructures, such as the Apache Web Server or MySQL database. They must be able to compile simple templates or entry-level programs into executable programs, or promote the templates and programs into production. Templates are reusable structures designed for easy configuration.

Programming languages
> These users must have a basic ability to read the programming languages of the open source projects in use. They also must be able to write simple code for templates or other such elements used to configure and control the behavior of open source programs, frameworks, and toolkits.

Open source community skills

Building on the beginners' understanding of how to interact with an open source community, users at the intermediate level must be able to find and engage other users and developers who are interested in using the open source software in the same way. They can find these other users, because the intermediate users ask and answer questions in an intelligent way that helps others traveling the same path.

Much more of the world of open source is available to users at the intermediate level. Toolkits and frameworks can be employed, because the intermediate user can write simple templates or other entry-level programs. While the intermediate user is not going to push any open source project in a new direction, she will be able to adapt open source projects that are relevant to the needs of her organization. If an open source project has add-on components, the intermediate user has the skill to use those components. An intermediate-level user is akin to a superuser of a desktop program.

At the intermediate level, programs such as simple content management frameworks, weblog publishing systems, or Wiki implementations become useful, because their behavior is controlled by templates and other configuration mechanisms that are easy to use. Such programs can be agents of huge productivity and cost savings that can affect thousands of users. The mature implementations run in a stable manner, without much care and feeding. The most mature operational infrastructures—spam management, intrusion detection, email list managers—can also be deployed.

A danger that users experience at the intermediate level concerns getting too far ahead of their skill set. Of course, this is a danger at all skill levels, but one that intermediates are especially prone to because the excitement of expanding knowledge is so seductive. It is important to make sure that any open source project used is adequately tested and that provisions are made to handle failures through either failover or some other means that informs the system's users that a problem exists. The most common mistake at this level is to push open source too far into mission-critical systems without adequate analysis of how to provide operational support.

If there is a chasm in open source, beginners and intermediate-level users are on one side, the side that represents the majority, and advanced and expert users are on the other side, in the domain of the innovators and early adopters.

Advanced

At the advanced skill level, open source projects are no longer a black box. Advanced users have the ability to look inside the open source project and understand how it works in great detail, and how it can be pushed to the limit and fully exploited through integration with other technology. Advanced users are capable of performance-tuning open source projects, which opens the door to high-performance applications. The advanced skill level is defined by the following capabilities:

Open source development tools

While beginner and intermediate-level users depend on precompiled binary versions, or perhaps can run a script to perform a simple compilation, advanced users are capable of recompiling an entire open source project and handling all the difficulties that might arise. For simple projects, this is trivial. But for larger projects, such as the Linux kernel, more knowledge is required. Advanced users have ready knowledge of development tools used in all the platforms in which they have expertise.

Hosting

Advanced users can specify the machines and the configuration needed to run open source projects.

System administration

These users understand the way an open source project consumes operating system and network resources and can configure the open source project, operating system, infrastructure, and network to achieve maximum performance.

Operations

They can harness all the tools of the operating system to examine and diagnose the resource usage of an open source program and are thus able to analyze and diagnose performance problems. Advanced users create monitoring and failover systems for open source projects to make them as stable and easy to operate as possible.

Open source infrastructure

Advanced users know, inside and out, the open source infrastructure of the projects they have deployed. They understand which toolkits and frameworks were used in constructing the projects, and how they were used. Advanced users are able to change the projects to integrate common IT infrastructure such as single sign-on or SNMP monitoring hooks inside the applications. Integration with other applications can also be added if needed.

Programming languages

These users have excellent coding skills. They can read code and understand a program well enough to fix simple bugs or to adjust the code's behavior. They can write code to support any desired integration, or rewrite code and redesign parts of an application to improve performance. Advanced users can choose to not wait for releases, and are able to apply patches for fixing bugs or introducing enhancements into their implementation.

Open source community skills

> Advanced users are significant players in open source communities. They might be part of the core development team committed to the master open source repository. They might play a leading role in implementing important features. They might be active on projects in which they are participants, and are able to ask penetrating questions about other projects in a manner that catches the attention of the core group of other projects. Advanced-level users have huge networks of experts of all sorts and can assemble, in a matter of hours, information on advanced topics that would take intermediate- or beginner-level users weeks to collect.

People at an advanced skill level are extremely powerful forces in an organization. They enable any and all open source projects to be put to use according to the highest enterprise-grade operational standards.

Among the things advanced skill levels make possible are recompiling the Linux kernel with advanced intrusion protection features; integrating into open source projects parts of the IT infrastructure, such as single sign-on, logging, business activity monitoring, failover, and so forth; solving performance problems by changing the code; and extending an open source project in simple ways.

The danger of having a member of an IT department with advanced skills is that the technology that is created can easily creep ahead of the institutional skill set of the IT department and can result in a serious key-person problem. Advanced-level use of open source must be accompanied by documentation and training so that staff at lower levels can support what has been done. Skill building must be a part of rising to the advanced level if an IT department expects to stay at an advanced level. Of course, managing creative technologists can be a challenge, but one that is usually worth the reward because talented technologists tend to like to work with other talented technologists.

While an advanced-level skill is wonderful to have in-house, it is increasingly possible to rent this level of skill for open source projects from consulting firms and other service providers. The emerging models for third-party support of open source are explored in Chapter 6.

Expert

Both the companies and the individuals who are the stars of the open source world operate at an expert level. Experts are active leaders who create new open source projects and lead projects in new directions. Experts improve the work of others by providing direction and an inspiring example. People we think of as hackers in the most positive sense of the word are experts. If it can be done with open source, experts can do it. The expert skill level is defined by the following abilities:

Open source development tools

Expert users can create reusable packages for organizations. Needless to say, they are experts at using a wide range of open source development tools.

Hosting

They can understand the entire application, from the user interface to the hardware implementation, and they insist that projects be written to optimize performance at all levels. For hosting, they are likely to be extremely well-educated consumers and will probably improve the performance of any hosting organization with their suggestions.

System administration

Experts are demanding customers for system administration staff and will likely push the team to analyze the configuration more carefully to optimize performance.

Operations

Experts love data and will push an operations team to make sure that appropriate data is collected so that application performance can be analyzed and improved. Experts love to anticipate problems so that they can be dealt with automatically, and they love to challenge a data center's operations staff to higher levels of performance.

Open source infrastructure

Experts can create open source infrastructure. One or two expert-level players have been the driving force behind each major innovation or platform in open source. When experts see an unfulfilled need, they frequently become obsessed by it and work fiendishly to fill it. Experts have a thorough knowledge of open source infrastructure and can quickly become skilled in virtually any area of open source.

Programming languages

Experts are virtuoso coders and can create mountains of code in days that would take people with less skill weeks or months to create. Experts can easily extend the functionality of an open source project, solve performance problems, or fix difficult bugs.

Open source community skills

Experts can lead the creation of open source projects or act as the driving force for moving a project in a new direction. Experts inspire other technologists to buy into their vision, and in doing so they create the kernels of what can become much larger open source communities. Experts command the respect of their peers and are frequently able to get significant help from other members of the community when they face problems. Experts are also frequently generous with their time and are helpful to others who share their goals and ethics, if approached properly.

Richard Stallman (GNU Emacs, Free Software Foundation), Linus Torvalds (Linux), Larry Wall (Perl), Brian Bellendorf (Apache), Greg Stein (Apache, Subversion), and hundreds of others are the experts who created open source as we know it today. Institutions also have become players at the expert level. For instance, IBM created and released the Eclipse platform to the open source community. Sun picked up and carried on StarOffice. MySQL created the leading open source database.

Experts are stars. Experts are the favorite teacher we all want to make happy. That said, IT departments can be extremely successful without ever becoming an expert institution or interacting with an expert-level player.

Any individual cannot be advanced and expert in more than a few projects. There is too much to know. Institutions have to choose what they will be experts in. Luckily, open source expertise is increasingly for sale. The open source world is changing rapidly, and for the most popular open source projects it is becoming possible to buy expertise from consulting firms and various service providers.

As we will explain in Chapter 5, the biggest payoff for an IT department is probably to build an intermediate level of institutional skills, and then to rent advanced and expert skills selectively to help solve difficult problems or accelerate skills development.

Open Source Skills Inventory

This section provides a precise definition of what is meant by each category of skills in each level, so an IT department can understand exactly the sort of skills it will need to succeed using open source. (In Chapter 5, a program on skill improvement will be proposed.)

Open Source Development Tools

Open source started as primitive fundamental elements, languages, and operating systems that were combined and recombined to create the incredible trove of software available today. Appendix A examines the different sorts of platforms that can be constructed with open source.

One of the earliest and still most active areas of open source is the creation of tools for developers. The keyboard mappings of Emacs and vi editors are deeply embedded in the brains of millions of developers. Other tools such as Ant are used widely to compile and assemble programs. Open source is bundled together with its own set of tools, such as tar.

The fact is, when you start digging into an open source project, you might encounter 5, 10, or 15 open source or Linux development tools or commands that are crucial to understanding how to compile and construct the project on your computer. The first few times you wade through this it can be slow going. But eventually you become one of the informed, and a process that started out taking 6 to 8 hours now takes 15 minutes.

The most important tools to understand are:

Utilities for dealing with distribution archives (tar, gzip, bzip, zip, unzip, etc.)
Almost all open source projects are distributed as downloadable "tarballs."

The GNU configure and build system (autoconf, automake, libtool, gettext, m4, and perl)
This system is the most popular among open source projects written in C, C++, and other low-level languages. It uses the three-step process of *configure*, *make*, and *make install* to install software from source by determining your system's setup (*configure* step), compiling the source and linking it to your existing libraries (*make* step), and then installing the source according to your system's conventions (*make install* step).

Perl-centric systems
These follow a high-level process that is built on top of the GNU configure and build system. It involves generating a system-specific makefile based upon your Perl installation parameters. For most Perl module installations, Perl provides a very simple interface to the Comprehensive Perl Archive Network (CPAN) that takes care of all the low-level details.

Java-centric systems
These have started to unite in their use of Apache Ant. More comprehensive build and configure systems such as Apache Maven are also ready for prime time.

PHP systems
These are more informal in their packaging. Since most PHP systems are accessed through a web server, installation normally involves unpacking the source in the web server's document space. Larger PHP systems use the GNU configure and build system.

Python-based systems
These are a mixed bag when it comes to build and configure methods. The more popular and mature systems come with sophisticated installers for each major platform, since Python is portable and works on Windows, Mac OS X, and Unix systems equally well. Less mature systems fall back to GNU autoconf or tarballs.

Hosting

Open source software has to run somewhere, and the hosting environment must be friendly to the installation, operation, and support of open source if it is to ever go into production. Here we describe the difference between beginner/intermediate hosting, which is focused on running open source reliably as a black box, and advanced/expert hosting, which is focused on optimization for the highest possible performance:

- Beginner/intermediate hosting
  - Manage domain registration information (setting up domains).
  - Manage bandwidth and disk-space quota issues (control space used by installed open source software and log files).
- Advanced/expert hosting
  - Manage web server configuration (set up virtual hosts).
  - Manage runtime configurations (tune PHP or Java runtime settings to help the open source software run better).
  - Manage DNS records (redirect traffic to a test site, for example).

System Administration and Operations

System administration and operations skills can be a significant problem when open source is introduced into departments that lack Unix skills. Many of the tools used in open source, and the way the programs interact with the operating system, are Unix oriented, and if an IT department already has Unix skills, adoption is easier. Certain skills are needed for running open source as a black box, and other skills are needed for running it in a more high-performance mode for optimization. System administration and operations work for open source projects is largely similar to that performed for commercial software. There is just more of it because of lack of productization. These are the skills required at each level:

- Beginner/intermediate system administration and operations skills
  - File management: if you are trying out a few open source projects (or one large one) you might need to manage space issues by recompressing tar files. You might also need to tweak the install process by setting up symbolic links and deleting unwanted files. From time to time you might also need to distribute files securely, as well as manage file permissions and ownership.
  - Execute commands and scripts: often the open source project is available as a tarball, and the *README* or *INSTALL* file describes the series of steps needed to get it running.
  - Starting, stopping, and monitoring applications: on Unix systems, the init scripts are not usually provided by the installation process and have to be configured manually.
  - Testing: open source projects typically have a wide installed base, and the installation and configuration process does not anticipate all the environments it is going to be installed in. So, the process of installing and configuring an OSS project is filled with incremental testing steps. Upon encountering an error, one often has to check the project's community documentation (FAQs, mailing lists, etc.) to find similar situations and possible solutions.

- Advanced/expert system administration and operations
  — Patches: apply security-related patches and associated corrections.
  — Monitoring: perform monitoring and intrusion detection.
  — Manage process resource usage: control the resource usage of long-running processes.
  — Manage configurations: sometimes the configuration for your system might not match the assumptions made by the install process of the open source project you are trying to install, and you might need to edit system configuration files.
  — Network interface configuration: in general, when dealing with web-based systems you might need to tweak the configuration of your network interface.
  — Change control: since living with open source software means changing the source or configuration, it is vital that you manage these changes via change control.

Open Source Infrastructure

An understanding of the infrastructure components that form the open source stack is crucial to rapid evaluation and successful deployment of open source. Most of the time, open source projects are constructed from top to bottom using open source components. Linux is the most common operating system, although it is not a requirement. Most mature open source runs well on Windows operating systems and other flavors of Unix. MySQL or Postgres can be used as the database, and Apache is usually the default web server. Other common components can also be included, depending on the programming language used to create the project.

Each component is a world unto itself that usually must be configured in a way that allows the open source program to work correctly. It is not uncommon for the configuration of one or more of these components to have to be adjusted to make an open source project work in a particular environment. For example, making open source work with single sign-on systems can be challenging. If an IT team is not familiar with a particular component, it can take a while to understand how to adjust the component to the required configuration. Familiarity with components can reduce this time period to a matter of minutes. Here is a list of the sort of knowledge that is helpful to have about each of the most prominent components of the open source stack:

- Linux
  — Knowing which configuration settings are commonly in need of adjustment
  — Associated package management functions
    Red Hat Package Manager (RPM)
    BSD has ports

- Apache
  - Virtual hosts
  - Apache module management
  - Access control issues
- MySQL
  - Basic database administration
  - Backup/restore

Programming Languages

To really understand an open source project and be able to analyze and fix bugs, it is important to be able to read and understand the programming language in which the project is written.

Understanding the programming language of all but the most mature open source software should be a requirement for mission-critical use of all but the most mature category of open source projects. Using Linux, Apache, MySQL, and other programs seldom requires knowledge of source code.

But imagine how hard it would be to track down a problem in a less mature project if you had to learn the language and try to understand the program at the same time. Of course, if the use of the software is not mission critical, an IT department has more time. But when faced with a severe operational crisis, all the skills required for diagnosis and debugging should be available.

This is not to say that you must be an expert in every language, or that it is impossible to use an open source project without knowing the language. But the more deeply you become involved with, and dependent on, an open source product, the more likely it is that you will need to interact with some level of the source code.

The source code can be useful for several different reasons:

- During evaluation of an open source project, the source code could be inspected as a way to evaluate the quality and maturity of a project.

- If the project must be extended to add new functionality or to support integration with other software, the source code must be consulted.

- If a bug is encountered that nobody else has discovered, the source code is required.

- For security audits, the source code is required.

- For performance tuning, it is often necessary to identify and improve a particular area of a project's functionality. This is impossible without source code.

In all of these situations, skills in the programming language can greatly reduce the amount of time required and the associated risks.

But knowledge of a programming language itself is really only the beginning. Open source software, and commercial software as well, is not constructed out of the programming language, but rather, out of all the reusable libraries of utilities and other special-purpose code. The real understanding of a language for open source purposes must include knowledge of these libraries, or at least skill in quickly understanding them. The Perl language has one of the most comprehensive collections of libraries at CPAN.org. As noted earlier, CPAN stands for the Comprehensive Perl Archive Network.

The most popular languages for open source development are:

C

> The C programming language is a low-level, standardized programming language developed in the early 1970s by Ken Thompson and Dennis Ritchie, for use on the Unix operating system.

C++

> Bjarne Stroustrup began C++ in 1978 as a "simulator for described computer systems." He wrote it for his Ph.D., at the Computing Laboratory at Cambridge University in England.

Perl

> Perl is a practical language for extracting information from text files and generating reports from that information. It was released by Larry Wall in 1987.

Python

> Python is a high-level scripting language invented by Guido van Rossum in 1989 to be powerful and easy to understand.

Java

> The Java language was created at Sun Microsystems in a project initiated by Patrick Naughton, Mike Sheridan, and James Gosling in 1991.

Ruby

> Ruby was created in 1993 by Yukihiro Matsumoto to be an object-oriented scripting language.

PHP

> PHP is a simple scripting language for personal use, created by Rasmus Lerdorf in 1995.

In Chapter 5, we analyze the issue of choosing a preference among these languages. The important issue for this chapter is determining what sort of skills are required at the different levels.

Use of source code by beginner and intermediate-level users is confined mostly to use of templates or small snippets of source code for configuration. At the advanced and expert levels, source code is read to understand the larger structure of the program for debugging or extending the program.

Open Source Community Skills

The storehouse of knowledge in open source projects is other people. To make the community work for you, you must know the community's rules, ethics, and style. Remember, open source projects are not staffed by people who are paid to help you. No amount of yelling or abuse can get the community's attention. If you come to the community with a last-minute request, it is not likely that anyone will drop everything to help you, unless implementing that request is somehow interesting to them. Losing "one throat to choke"—a vendor that is on the hook to help—is one of the greatest fears of those who are suspicious of open source.

This warning aside, open source communities generally are extremely friendly and are populated by people who are more than willing to help others who are making a sincere effort and are not asking lazy questions.

Evaluating the maturity of open source

As we discovered when writing this book, evaluating open source is an art, not a science. One of the key skills for anyone who seeks to use open source is the ability to evaluate an open source project and determine what it will take to use and support it. Beginner/intermediate-level users are mostly interested in what it does out of the box, while advanced/expert-level users will perform a deeper evaluation.

The key is to develop your own efficient style of evaluation. In Chapter 2, we presented one style based on the evaluation of hundreds of open source projects we had researched for this book. Your style will depend on your skills and the skills you want to develop. Most of the time, a beginner/intermediate-level evaluation tries to determine what the project claims to do, how well it does what it claims, what new skills will be required, and how it can be supported. The advanced/expert analysis dives more deeply into the project's architecture, the size and nature of the community surrounding the project, the quality and management style of the project's leadership, and the project's long-term prospects.

Networking with open source developers

Open source users at all skill levels must be able to unlock the value of the community. The forums and resources at open source project web sites are just the beginning of the trail to tracking down information. The people who post and answer questions are potentially valuable resources who can be tapped to help out, accelerate learning, and provide consulting services. The key skill is engaging such people in a respectful way. The approach can mean everything. "Hello, I have a problem.

Please do my work for me," is seldom a winning line of inquiry. Rather, if you have done research and you show the person that she might learn from you, it is much more likely that you will be able to engage her in a productive conversation.

Key social skills are not sales oriented, but rather, depend on polite directness, respect for the time of others, and a demonstrated willingness to work to research problems and share the results. In the article "How to ask questions the smart way," Eric Raymond distills the conventional wisdom: do your homework first (i.e., search the web or forum archives before asking), ask politely (i.e., provide all the relevant details and only the relevant details), and follow up when you find the solution.

How Maturity Affects Required Skills and Resources

One policy that is reasonable, especially for beginners, in the early stages of skill building is to just forget about all but the most mature open source projects. This means that many powerful programs are available—Linux, Apache, Mozilla, MySQL—but it perhaps misses the point of pursuing an open source strategy.

In fact, the most mature rank of open source is only the tip of the iceberg. A huge number of open source projects are less mature but still extremely valuable. Some of the biggest wins in open source can come from using a well-built but obscure program created to solve just the problem an IT department has. The key to success in using such software is to evaluate and experiment to really understand what you are getting into.

For example, different gaps in maturity require different skills:

- A beginner can overcome a lack of documentation, but evidence of bugs that require expertise to fix are showstoppers.

- As a beginner, all the needed features must be included. But an advanced- or expert-level team can add them.

- If the community is small, plan on time for reading code, experimenting, and figuring things out for yourself.

The odds are against most projects—even the ones that deserve to be more popular. So, it is wise to plan for how the product will be supported if development slows to a crawl.

The good news is that flying blind is not required. The only things standing in the way of evaluating a project are skill and time.

Skills and Risks

One useful exercise when considering open source is to define your organizational personality with regard to risk. The more risk an IT department assumes, the greater the immaturity of the projects it can use. Supporting mission-critical applications with open source requires maintaining a larger pool of institutional skills.

The decision to use open source should be made carefully in the context of how critical a system is to business operations. The more important the system, the more skills are required to support an open source project.

The key question is how the demands for skill change as the risk goes up. Here are some categories of importance for systems:

Experimental
If an experimental application breaks, it generally is not a big problem. Nobody expected it to work in the first place. When a system is installed for evaluation or on a trial basis to support one project, for example, a failure might not be a disaster.

Low priority
A low-priority system can be down for a day without bothering anyone. This provides time to resolve problems, and life goes on without major interruptions in the case of an outage. A Wiki used for documentation or project management, or a weblog used for internal use, can fall into this category.

Operational
Operational systems must run well and not be down for more than an hour or two. This is where the required understanding of an open source program and the skill level start to creep out of the intermediate level and toward the advanced level. An address book or calendaring system, or any actively used database, might fall into this category. People can find a way of living without the system for an hour or so, but they need it to be working soon.

Mission critical
These systems must work to keep the business running. Downtime is not acceptable. Such systems generally should have a failover plan so that in the event of a problem, service is maintained. For beginners, these requirements make only the most mature open source acceptable, unless some help is available. Intermediates can probably support templates in a mission-critical environment. Using less mature software for this context is probably prudent only in the case of advanced or expert-level teams. A web server and applications for e-commerce, or really any system connected directly to producing revenue, is an example of a mission-critical system.

Open Source Skill Building

Using technology to solve problems in business is rarely easy. Many traps and obstacles lie waiting. Open source projects are not immune to any of the common failures of requirements gathering, project management, or technical glitches that knock projects off track. IT departments must learn to be on the lookout for such problems and understand how to prevent them.

The point of this chapter was to show that open source is a seductively powerful tool. You can quickly make it do amazing things. This can lead an IT department to rush ahead and take advantage of the power of open source without asking the right questions about how it will be supported.

The most common nightmare is that one person understands open source and creates infrastructure or applications using it that nobody else in the IT department understands. When that person leaves, the department is left with an unmaintainable mess. Of course, the same thing happens with custom code or ancient applications. The remedy is a systematic identification of skills needed to support open source and a program for maintaining them inside a department. Compared to the thrill of getting a new open source project working, this is a relatively mundane activity, but one that is required to avoid a nightmare.

Skill building is a gradual process. Don't expect to get everything right the first time you try anything with open source. Adapting even the most mature open source projects to a normal IT environment will usually involve learning something new or figuring something out. If you hate the thought of this, and you would rather spend time on the phone to a support center than wading through a puzzle of different interlocking open source software programs, open source won't be a fun or profitable experience for you.

From a management point of view, this means that open source has a different problem resolution process than commercial software. Instead of talking on the phone to a technical support person, the next steps for resolving a problem involve running a diagnostic process inside the department. With open source, all the information and access required are available. It is the IT department's job to make sure the skills are available as well.

Open source, like most technology, can be thought of as a puzzle. If the idea of facing that puzzle, conquering it, and getting the reward from using the software is exciting to you, open source will probably be exciting to you as well. This book is in many ways about helping IT departments understand the size of the puzzles they choose to face, the skills and amount of time it will take to solve them, and whether there is much to gain by solving these puzzles in the first place.

CHAPTER 4

Making the ROI Case

One of the first things that is asked of any new project in a modern IT department is that a cost benefit analysis be created to determine if the investment of time and resources makes sense. This takes many forms, but at many companies the idea of return on investment, or ROI, is king.

Management's goal in asking for an ROI analysis is simple: explain why an open source project (or any other project) is going to help the organization succeed by increasing revenue or saving money. Technologists frequently are annoyed by the request to analyze ROI, for several reasons:

- It is hard to create a defensible approach. The results of almost any ROI analysis can be changed massively, by adjusting assumptions.

- Intangible benefits, such as flexibility or creating a simpler architecture, are frequently undervalued or are not included.

- Besides reducing technical costs, technologists have difficulty making reasonable estimates about how the new technology will increase revenue.

Despite these difficulties, ROI is here to stay, and almost every IT department that intends to use open source must figure out a way to determine the ROI of open source. Reasonable managers will not give open source a pass on faith. This chapter will provide an informal guide to analyzing the ROI of using open source.

ROI Fashions

The need for ROI comes and goes. In boom times, when IT is being asked to support more business activity as quickly as possible, ROI is no longer king. It gets deposed and becomes a proletariat. However, when the return is out there for the taking, if you can execute a business strategy quickly, the investment in IT to speed execution is not scrutinized nearly as closely. During times such as these the CEO or VP of sales might be most influential in promoting IT investment. But when times are sour, the CFO emerges as the most important gatekeeper—and CFOs love ROI analysis.

Most managers know that ROI is difficult to create. When something makes sense but is hard or impossible to quantify, managers are inventive when it comes to finding ways to justify investments without ROI. One common approach is to call something a *strategic* investment, meaning the investment makes sense and will improve the company's position despite the fact that a hard dollar analysis is nebulous. Billions of dollars are spent on strategic projects.

Technology vendors are very hip to the value of an authoritative ROI study. Most software vendor web sites contain and prominently feature ROI studies for specific uses of the software or for specific industries. Microsoft, for example, has commissioned several ROI studies about Linux. They all show—surprise, surprise—that Linux is more expensive, using assumptions that match few real-world situations. Some of the commercial companies promoting the ROI of Linux have also created studies showing that Linux costs less than the alternatives, but they use assumptions that apply to only a few companies.

For most uses of open source, there is no vendor preparing an ROI study. Even a specious ROI study can be adjusted with assumptions that match more closely the conditions at your company. Getting ROI correct is always a "do it yourself" proposition. With that in mind, let's discuss how you can determine the ROI of an open source project.

What Is ROI for Open Source?

At a high level, calculating ROI for open source is pretty much the same as for commercial software. The equation looks something like this:

$$\frac{\text{Return: (Increased Revenue + Savings)}}{\text{Investment: (Evaluation costs + License and Maintenance costs + Installation and Configuration costs + Integration and Customization costs + Operations and Support costs)}} = \text{ROI}$$

Of course, for such an equation to make sense we must understand many things:

- What is the time horizon for the analysis? How long will we get to count revenue or savings against this investment? One year? Two years?

- Is it possible to compare alternatives? Should we choose the fastest time to payback or the largest savings over the long term?

- What are the interest rate assumptions? What is the *hurdle rate*—that is, the minimum return—for any investment for the company?

- What costs will be included and what will be assumed to be born as infrastructure costs? ROI analyses frequently don't include the extra costs of electric power or bandwidth. Sometimes ROI analysis includes hosting, and other times it doesn't.

- Should reduced costs in the future, or costs than can be avoided, be included? How can such costs be reasonably estimated?

- Are the same costs between the alternatives being compared? Has the analysis for one product assumed away costs, or underestimated them? What costs are vendors concealing or disregarding?

The answers to these questions can vary widely, and they illustrate why ROI calculation is much more an art than a science. The vendor ROI studies sponsored by Microsoft carefully tune the assumptions against Linux by comparing mainframe-like machines from IBM running Linux with large PCs running Windows. Microsoft is not unique in its manipulation of assumptions. Almost all vendors do this to some extent. No defensible set of assumptions applies to all situations.

Other questions are of great significance to how an ROI analysis is constructed. Is there a minimum payback period for all IT investments? How much will it cost the company, and how much can it earn from alternative investments? If interest rates are high or a company has profitable businesses that need money to grow, the bar for investing in IT can become high indeed.

The last point in the list about using equivalent costs is the one that makes comparing commercial and open source software most difficult. The costs of open source have a different shape than the costs of commercial software.

How Open Source Costs Differ from Commercial Software Costs

On the return side of the equation there is not much difference between open source and commercial software. Revenue is revenue, and if a computer system helps support it, that's great. It is possible for two different alternatives to meet the goals of creating revenue in different ways, but we can draw no generality about open source always being better to support the creation of revenue. For savings the situation is much the same. Once the estimated savings are determined for each alternative, there is not much to do but compare.

Calculating savings is another black art. It is easiest to do when known costs are eliminated or are replaced with a new set of lower costs. But an honest analysis of savings would have to quantify savings due to differences in reliability, downtime, maintenance procedures, and so on. Many of these issues are hard to quantify in a defensible manner.

The nature of the costs of open source and commercial software is truly different, however.

Evaluation Costs

The costs of evaluating open source can be considered part of the ROI analysis, so it might not be included in the ROI equation, but it does take time, more time generally than for commercial software. At some level it should be included in management's thinking about the costs and benefits of using open source.

During the sales process for commercial software, vendors are eager to educate potential buyers about why their software is valuable. To buy software, an IT department must be convinced that:

- Their organization has a need for some software in a certain space.
- The vendor's offering is the best choice.
- Right now is the time to buy the product.

Vendors spend a lot of money on whitepapers, marketing materials, conferences, and other content to communicate all three of these points. Many IT executives use vendor materials heavily to "get smart" about a space.

For open source, few such materials exist. Open source projects rarely come with whitepapers explaining why you need the software. Open source communities just assume that you need it; that's why you are visiting the site. The product description of open source materials often happens at a relatively detailed level. ("This is a content management system. Here is the API documentation. See the code samples for further clarification.") And open source projects really don't care if you have a need now, or sometime in the future.

So, to really understand what an open source project can do, an IT department must install it and play with it, and this takes time and different sorts of resources. A typical commercial software evaluation might take place with the sales staff or with IT managers who screen the products, bringing in the architects or developers later only if the product looks promising. For an open source evaluation, the developers and architects should probably take the lead. An architect or developer's time might be worth more in some organizations than a manager's time. This must be planned for. The amount of time it takes to install a product is based on the IT organization's skills. Expert and advanced users can install and get most open source software operating in two or three hours. A user at a strong, intermediate skill level should be able to have most open source software running within a day.

In addition to the cost of creating a trial installation, the IT staff must learn enough about the software to play around with it and understand its functionality to determine if it can meet the company's requirements. While this is another activity that consumes technical resources, it also removes a significant amount of risk from the process. By using an open source product to create prototypes, the IT staff can compare the actual functionality with the requirements, and can validate the requirements by having users interact with the prototypes.

Arranging a similar installation of commercial software might require any or all of the following:

- Negotiation of a trial license that might have a time limit
- Payment of service fees to support the trial installation
- Training
- Trial licenses for additional related software

Vendors might or might not be open to a trial installation. After all, the investment in all the educational and marketing materials is supposed to make the value and functionality of the software clear.

In the end, the evaluation of open source can involve more technical resources than an IT department is accustomed to, but can also result in a deeper understanding of both the software and the requirements. With commercial software, management might take the leading role, and with open source the technologist might be the primary analyst. In either case, care must be taken to ensure that one side doesn't dominate the evaluation and create a disconnect between the business and technology requirements.

License and Maintenance Costs

An extremely naïve view of open source, one frequently promoted by technologists who are eager to use open source, focuses solely on the fact that there are no license or maintenance fees to pay. License and maintenance fees for commercial products can range from as low as a few percentage points to as much as 20 points or more of the total solution. But the savings in license fees is no guarantee that open source is the right choice.

First of all—and this might come as a shock—some open source does come with what amounts to licensing fees. Companies are frequently happy to pay subscription fees for Linux distributions from Red Hat or SuSE to get a coherent collection of software, packaged consistently, with a nice installation program and a steady stream of updates. Other projects such as JBoss charge licensing fees for documentation, and

Resin actually requires licensing fees for commercial use, even though it seems like open source. Open source is no guarantee of zero licensing costs.

While there is no maintenance fee for open source—upgrades are free—you often have to spend more time with an open source project to figure out what is in the upgrade. Perhaps the best news is that upgrades are never forced on you, the way they so often are with commercial software. An IT department can move from one version to the next whenever the time is right for the company, not when the vendor can no longer afford to support maintenance of older versions.

Increasingly, however, it is possible to find traditional support and maintenance for open source software. Several start-ups offer support for various open source projects and useful combinations of projects. One of the reasons companies like using commercial software is that it means an organization exists that can be held accountable for the software. The new wave of start-ups is responding to this need and is providing "one throat to choke" in exchange for a fee.

Installation and Configuration Costs

Installation and configuration of open source can be time consuming, especially for beginner or intermediate organizations that are not deeply skilled in the use of open source tools. To install an open source program and then get it running can require a fair bit of fiddling, especially with more immature products that have not been used much outside their native environment. Commercial software generally comes with some sort of install wizard that guides the user through installation and basic configuration. While more and more open source projects are showing this degree of professionalism, the use of such wizards is still not widespread.

Configuring the software, the process of changing all the settings so that the software behaves as desired, can also take longer for open source, as the mechanisms of configuration are discovered more through trial and error or reading code rather than through some comprehensive documentation. At a fine-grained level, especially for large programs, configuring a commercial software program can be a black art as well. Undocumented settings are routine in the commercial world and frequently are discovered by IT departments only after lengthy support calls or expensive engagements for services.

The real factor in determining whether installation and configuration will require a significant time commitment is an organization's skill level in using open source development tools, system administration, and operations. In general, beginners and those at the intermediate skill level will spend more time on installation and configuration than will more highly skilled IT departments.

Integration and Customization Costs

Careful assessment of integration and customization costs in many ways is the key to avoiding an open source nightmare. Unlike commercial products, open source projects are not usually created with the modern IT infrastructure environment in mind. Integration with single sign-on or support for monitoring protocols such as SNMP might not exist. Support for databases might be narrow and limited to a few choices or to one database. Support for standards might be lacking.

Most of the time, the same problems exist in emerging commercial software that is early in its life cycle. But as the commercial program is installed in more and more IT environments, smart vendors seek to productize the most common integrations so that the same work is not required again with each new client.

Some companies have unique integration problems that will always have to be solved through custom coding, regardless of whether open source or commercial software is used. The question is how easy that integration will be to create. And that can be determined only on a case-by-case basis. It is possible to argue that open source integration can be less expensive, because access to source code means you can always do the work yourself.

The need for customization arises when the open source project must be extended to meet the requirements at hand. Here, open source becomes a gray area between a buy versus build decision. Open source represents the decision not to buy, but to build as little as possible. And don't forget: the skills to customize an open source product must be created inside an organization or be obtained through consulting services.

With an open source program it is far more likely that an IT department will have to solve an integration or customization problem on its own. Then the question once again boils down to having the needed skills or renting them. If a web content management system, for example, doesn't support a single sign-on mechanism, someone will have to write the code to add that support.

Once such code is written, it can be either donated to the community and maintained as part of the project's source code, or kept as a proprietary modification that must be maintained and updated with each new release. In general, beginner and intermediate-level users require some sort of consulting help in creating such integrations, and advanced and expert users can do it on their own if they choose.

It's hard to generalize about whether this is a strength or a weakness of open source. It is clearly a weakness to the extent that more integration work is probably needed for the average open source project than for the average commercial project, which might have productized some of the integration. On the other hand, the answer is never "no" when it comes to integrating open source. Almost everyone who has used commercial software to support a business has come across a need that requires changing the software in a special way to optimize support. Perhaps a company has a custom-built operational monitoring system or a clever use of a data warehouse or the desire to integrate tightly with a desktop application. Commercial vendors frequently won't make such modifications for an IT department, and they won't provide the source so that an IT department can do it for themselves. Anything can be done with open source, so the barrier to creating the optimal system for supporting a business process is often lower. The higher the skill level, the lower the bar will be.

Operations and Support Costs

On the surface, operations and support costs do not look that different between open source and commercial software. Once software is installed, configured, and integrated, it is just software, whether it is open source or not. Skill levels play a large role in determining the time required to support both commercial and open source software. But when it comes to configuring a professional environment, open source leaps way ahead.

Commercial software vendors might require licensing fees for any of the following situations:

- Creating a development environment on each developer's workstation
- Creating a test environment or a staging environment
- Adding servers for scalability
- Adding servers for disaster recovery or for a hot backup site

For a vendor, all of this makes perfect sense. The more an IT department uses a product, the more value it gets from that product and the more it should pay for the product. But as a practical matter these ancillary licensing fees increase the cost and get in the way of optimizing the performance and stability of an environment. It can be a nasty surprise to find out that an expensive license stands in the way of scaling an application or creating the right disaster recovery site.

The Cost of Narrowness

Looking back on the difference between the costs of open source and commercial software, a theme emerges. In open source, the burden is on the IT department to develop or find the skills to evaluate, install, configure, operate, and support the software. If this burden is accepted, anything is possible.

For commercial software, these burdens can take less time and cost more money, but the range of possibilities is narrower and is confined to the common needs of the marketplace the vendor should support. The cost of this narrowness is the defining issue. How can you measure the cost of commercial software's narrowness and rigidity? If you never run into a barrier, the cost is zero. If you have a great need for a certain feature, it can be huge.

The same question must be asked of the functionality of the open source project. If there is a large gap between the needs of an IT department and the use cases that are the focus of the open source project, that gap might need to be filled. Doing so might require a significant time investment and a certain level of skill.

If you have a clear understanding of how a piece of software is going to be used, and you are confident that it is stable and unlikely to change or need optimization, perhaps the bias should be in favor of commercial software. On the other hand, if you need software that is optimized and tuned to meet perfectly the needs of a crucial business process, perhaps open source is the right choice. We will return to this analysis in detail in Chapter 5.

Making Your Own ROI Model

The bottom line is that you must do ROI analysis for yourself, whether using commercial or open source solutions. And while the true costs are rarely quantifiable or authoritative, doing the analysis for an open source project is vital, because it can expose the true costs and risks, and help an IT department prepare for them.

Now that all of the ideas about costs are swirling before you, let's take a close look at how you can create an ROI model to express all of these factors. There are, of course, many ways to go about creating such a model. This section will walk through a flexible approach that should apply to most situations faced by IT departments.

Creating the ROI Analysis Spreadsheet

A reasonable way to start an ROI analysis is to start with a spreadsheet that represents the equation mentioned at the beginning of this chapter. Let's assume a three-year analysis. The first page of the spreadsheet will have one row each for revenue and expenses, and one row for category of cost. At the bottom is a row that totals up the column according to the ROI formula (see Figure 4-1).

Each column represents a time period; let's assume one quarter.

After the first page of the worksheet is one worksheet page dedicated to each of the revenue and expense categories. The columns of these worksheets are the quarterly periods, just like on the summary sheet. The rows are the specified line items that make up the cost estimates. All the costs are estimated in dollars. If hourly time estimates must be created, they can be done on the rows of the worksheets or on other worksheets. The rest of this chapter will provide suggestions for what might make up the rows of each worksheet.

Creating the Estimates

Consistency in approach is perhaps more important than accuracy in such an analysis, for two reasons. First, accuracy is hard to come by. For some data, it will be possible to get numbers to back up estimates. For example, if an application can be retired and replaced with open source, maintenance no longer needs to be paid and

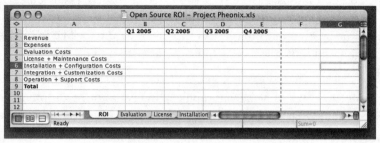

Figure 4-1. *ROI analysis spreadsheet*

the resulting savings will be clear. But how much time will be spent installing, evaluating, integrating, maintaining, and supporting the open source solution? These numbers will be hard to come by, especially if an IT department does not have a lot of experience with open source.

Second, if some sort of consistent approach is used, the analysis can be adjusted at the detail or summary level, with some hope that the model will not break down. In this way, it becomes clear to everyone reading the model that certain estimates are based on guesses, all of which are constructed in the same manner. The analysis should explicitly state how the guesses were constructed and why they are justified. For example, an IT department assumes that there will be four production servers and that configuring the first one will take 20 hours. The department can then replicate that configuration to three identical servers in two hours each. It will be possible to track this configuration time and then plug the real data into the model to see how it has changed. Another example: if it turns out that the configuration was underestimated by about 30% in the first 2 of 10 configurations, a new model can be created by reducing the 8 configuration estimates by 30%, if all of them were constructed in the same way.

So, in general, the more granular and measurable the analysis is, the better a planning tool it will be. As an IT department becomes more experienced with open source, its ability to estimate specific costs will improve.

Elements of Evaluation Costs

As we noted earlier in this chapter, evaluation costs for open source are generally higher and require different resources than for commercial software. An engineer, for example, will spend a significant amount of time researching and implementing an open source program. The following is a list of jobs an engineer will spend time performing while evaluating an open source project (these could also be included as line items in a cost estimate):

- Searching for open source

- Creating a test environment

- Installing and configuring software

- Writing test programs

- Researching questions and problems

- Researching integration techniques and costs

- Networking with open source community members and looking for answers to questions

Elements of Installation and Configuration Costs

Installation and configuration costs are the costs of figuring out how to install the software in your test and production environment, and make it work the way you want it to work, by using the settings and parameters that are intended for that purpose. Elements of installation and configuration costs include:

- Engineer time spent learning how to install the software in a development environment

- Engineer time spent learning how to install the software in a test environment

- Engineer time spent learning how to install the software in a production environment

- Engineer time spent doing basic performance testing

- Engineer time spent developing backup scripts

- Engineer time spent learning how to operate the software

- Engineer time spent learning how to monitor the software

- Engineer time spent integrating the software into production monitoring and alerting systems

- Training time for developers

- Training time for top operations staff

Elements of Integration and Customization Costs

Integration and customization costs include the planning, design, and development required to integrate the software into an IT department, and to extend the software's functionality to meet the needs at hand. Elements of integration and customization costs include:

- Engineer time spent gathering requirements for integration and customization

- Engineer time spent reading source code, documentation, and bulletin boards to understand the workings of the software

- Engineer time spent designing the integration and customization

- Engineer time spent coding the integration and customization

- Engineer time spent testing the integration and customization
- Fees for any consultants brought in to help the process

Elements of Operations and Support Costs

Operations and support costs are the costs incurred to run the open source project in production. Many of these costs are similar to those incurred for commercial software. Elements of operations and support costs include:

- Hardware costs
- Rack space
- Electric power
- Network bandwidth
- Operational monitoring
- Backups

Skills Versus Money

If this list seems long, remember that most of the elements represent time spent by an engineer to learn how best to use the software. In other words, the investment in open source is also an investment in increasing an IT department's skill level.

The commercial analog to most of these costs represents renting expertise that does not leave an IT department smarter. Sometimes money is more important than the time it takes to solve a problem. But in general, it is hard to argue that creating a more skilled organization is anything but a net positive for an IT department.

As an IT department's skills grow, more open source will become usable. The question then becomes which open source projects will provide the most benefit. In the next chapter, we turn to the issue of how to focus efforts according to a coherent strategy.

CHAPTER 5

Designing an Open Source Strategy

Figuring out how to make IT work for a company is no easy task. Any comprehensive strategy must take into account not only the company's technology concerns, but also its short- and long-term business plan, financial condition, competitive situation, existing applications and infrastructure, and consulting partners, as well as the skills and talents of its IT department. Creating such a strategy is hard work. The right strategy is rarely clear and usually involves making difficult and, at times, unpleasant tradeoffs.

Advice about strategy is rarely effective. Commonly rendered advice includes reducing the number of platforms, vendors, and skills; outsourcing noncritical tasks; and waiting six months before installing any new release. All these recommendations have merit. So does telling a stock market investor to "buy low, sell high." The question is how to execute such advice.

To become useful, general advice must be adapted to specific situations. The goal of this chapter is to synthesize the analysis we provided in the preceding chapters into a plan for adopting open source that will avoid major difficulties. Then the real teacher, experience, can direct users toward getting the most out of open source. IT departments can then follow a path of gradually building skills and expanding the adoption of open source to the point where benefits are discovered.

The first strategic question analyzed concerns how to get started with open source. This chapter will take you through the different stages of using open source that we described in Chapter 3, starting from scratch at a beginner level and moving all the way to the advanced and expert levels. We also will analyze the responsibilities and risk facing an IT department at each level.

The second strategic question concerns where to apply open source. You need to consider the IT needs of your business and your IT organization's skill level when answering this question.

The third category of strategic questions analyzed in this chapter concerns managing and living with the problems and challenges of using open source in a corporate environment. How can you control the use of open source? Are there differences between using open source as a platform for integration as opposed to an application? Is it possible to become a top-to-bottom open source enterprise?

This chapter will help IT departments proceed with open source development in an informed manner so that they avoid common mistakes.

Crafting a Strategy for Open Source Adoption

Before considering any serious use of open source, an IT department should check that it is willing to adopt two fundamental assumptions: a belief in skill building, and the slightest inclination to increase responsibility and control over its IT infrastructure. Even the simplest uses of open source require that some skills be brought into the organization, and unless an IT department wants to have a key-person problem, it must try to capture those skills. The second aspect is an ambition to take charge of more of the IT infrastructure. Open source provides greater control and comes with greater responsibility. If this is not of value to an IT department, open source will seem like a lot of work.

Many smart people and successful companies have neither of these attributes. General Motors, for example, has a policy of outsourcing all its IT to EDS. GM is not interested in control and responsibility. At GM, paying someone else to deliver is the fastest, most certain way to get value from IT. Will your business benefit from having a more skilled IT department? For many companies, where IT costs are not large and the use of IT is not a differentiator, perhaps the answer is no. Increasingly it is also possible to use open source by paying a consulting firm to install and maintain a program. This is not really using open source as much as it is using a service based on open source. While it might be a good idea for a company, it is not what we mean when we talk about open source adoption.

So, if an IT department is willing to adopt these two fundamental assumptions, the next question is, does it have the skills? In Chapter 3, we described several different layers of skills. If an IT department has these skills already, using open source will be less time consuming than if it is starting from scratch. Different skills are required to run open source as a computing platform as opposed to running open source applications. If an

IT department uses Unix systems heavily, it is likely to have most of the skills required to run Linux, the foundation of the open source computing platform. If a department is able to run only Microsoft .NET or Windows, running Linux requires a greater leap. It might make sense to run only open source applications that function well on Microsoft operating systems. It is a mistake to think that using Microsoft-friendly open source applications reduces the scope of the opportunity significantly. A huge amount of open source runs perfectly well on the Microsoft platform.

The next question is, which open source projects offer an IT department the most value? Answering this question requires developing the skill of evaluating open source that we described in Chapter 2, and just networking and looking for open source projects that might be useful. We hope an important part of this process for many people will be reading Appendices A through F, which provide a survey of the most promising open source projects for various areas of concern for IT departments.

Of course, the decision to go with open source always involves risk, but performing the sort of ROI analysis we described in Chapter 4 can give an IT department—as well as company management—a reasonable degree of certainty concerning how much it stands to gain by implementing open source.

Now, our analysis will turn to the subject of finding the right path to open source adoption.

Steps to Low-Risk Open Source Adoption

The approach we recommend is a sober one. You will gain nothing by waving the open source flag and applying it everywhere possible, without forethought and planning. This is impractical and rarely makes sense. Even the most highly skilled companies that are enthusiastic users of open source also use plenty of commercial products. Our method for addressing the right approach to using open source consists of the following:

- Understand your IT department's skills.

- Experiment in a safe environment, with open source of the appropriate maturity applied to well-understood requirements.

- Gradually build the skills needed to find open source and evaluate it, and then learn to install, configure, and operate open source in a production environment.

- Institutionalize those skills.

- Increase adoption of open source as opportunities arise.

By following these steps, you will discover whether open source is a natural fit for your IT department. If the initial burst of enthusiasm is followed by a sense of dread at doing the work involved, perhaps open source is the right choice in only a small number of situations where open source projects are as productized and mature as commercial software. However, if the spark of excitement at doing it yourself with open source becomes a morale-boosting project that restores enthusiasm and creativity to a department, expanding the use of open source probably makes sense.

The following narrative describes how skills might develop at an IT department that is starting from scratch and does not have existing skills in Unix or Linux system administration.

Starting from Scratch

The extreme case of starting from scratch occurs when an IT department that knows very little about open source is interested in finding out if open source can help it achieve its goals.

When an IT department starts from scratch, it should begin by asking all the questions we outlined in the previous chapters. Is there any open source that can help? How mature is it? Do we have the skills to handle it? What are the fully loaded costs? Frankly, answering these questions through analysis alone will not produce high-quality results. To answer these key questions, an IT department has to install some open source and start using it in an experimental fashion.

Fortunately, highly productized open source products that are aimed at end users and can be used right away are available. The OpenOffice.org products provide a full suite of desktop productivity applications, including spreadsheets and word processors. The Mozilla.org products provide a first-rate email client. Other, more challenging products include SpamBayes, an extension to MS Outlook for filtering spam.

Depending on the environment, just using this category of open source can provide many major benefits. If classes of users use PCs for minimal word processing, web browsing, and email, the savings in licensing fees could be substantial. However, this makes sense only if a department is ready to learn how to provide support or create a relationship with a consultant or service provider to do so. In performing experiments using such software, an IT department can gain a much better understanding of whether the risks and responsibilities of open source feel right.

Such use of open source represents only a small fraction of the potential value open source can offer most IT departments. Rather, most IT departments will benefit by finding open source projects that either replace existing systems or extend the infrastructure in beneficial ways. In Appendices A through F, we suggest many open source projects that do both.

Assuming the IT department starting from scratch is Microsoft oriented, the next step is to look for mature open source applications that are Microsoft friendly. Such users will likely benefit more from open source projects focused on applications or useful tools such as Wikis, content management systems, or applications for specific job functions or tasks.

Getting these sorts of programs running, and supporting them for experimental use, is not difficult. However, just gaining the ability to solve the problems in getting mature open source to work is a significant step forward. In addition, unlike with open source projects for end users, this involves skill in understanding how the components that lurk underneath open source programs work together. Most of the types of programs we have mentioned use a database, a web server, and, sometimes, other utilities. If an IT department can easily make standard open source components work together, a huge world of open source applications opens up.

When you are starting from scratch with open source software, you should stop at the experimental stage until you are confident your organization has the skills we described in Chapter 3 to support the use of open source in production.

At this level, it is important to be skeptical of self-assessments of skills from the IT department. Instead, skills can be gauged by keeping track of how much time is being spent on open source projects to determine the actual costs incurred.

One cautionary note: an IT department starting from scratch might find that the experimental systems quickly become operational if the functionality provided becomes popular. This frequently happens with programs such as Wikis, which gain favor with end users and project managers, because they are easy to use and enable free-form communication. If an IT department is not careful, a support burden that it is ill prepared to handle or uninterested in assuming can be thrust on it by popular demand.

In summary, starting from scratch involves:

- Using productized open source aimed at the end user, possibly in production if support can be arranged

- On an experimental basis, using mature open source applications that can run on any platform to determine whether supporting applications built from many open source components is within the skill set of an IT department

- Avoiding the use of Linux as a platform at the outset

Becoming a Beginner

At the end of the starting-from-scratch period, an IT department has begun to understand the components of a mature open source application. Getting the parts working together experimentally is not difficult, but it is hard to determine in advance what sort of problems will be encountered. The real challenge at the beginner level is to figure out when you have mastered the components of an application to an extent that you can support them as part of your IT infrastructure.

For example, with a content management system such as Drupal, which is based on PHP, an IT department must be able to provide the same support that any professionally managed system requires. This includes scripts for start-up, shut-down, back-up, and operational monitoring of the open source software, as well as a playbook for diagnosing what is going on with the database, application, web server, and any other components. When something goes wrong, the solution should be to run a process, not to find a person.

If an IT department has established operational procedures, supporting open source means finding out how to run those processes against open source applications. IT departments get nervous as they approach the launch of an open source application, because if something goes wrong, there is no support hotline to call.

The only remedy for such nervousness is experience. Open source projects should be run experimentally with a lower service level until an IT department can develop and institutionalize the skills needed to support it. Then when a problem occurs, an IT department will feel more comfortable and be better able to resolve it.

The first applications IT departments should focus on at the beginner level are those that are mature and provide a specific function, without requiring a lot of configuration. Open source applications for bug tracking, Wikis, source code management, or weblogs fall into this category. The goal is to introduce complexity gradually. The productized end-user applications mentioned as a first step are the simplest and most familiar to use and support. The next step is to deploy the mature applications that do not require lots of configuration and customization. Then the challenge is to learn how to support these applications in a reliable and professional manner. This level of expertise, which is not hard to attain or institutionalize, opens up a vast world of applications to an IT department. Supporting open source at the beginner level also builds confidence for taking the next steps.

Additional challenges at the beginner level include carefully containing the rate of open source expansion. Enthusiasm from users and from within an IT department can easily result in products being pushed into production before proper support procedures have been designed and implemented.

At the later stages of the beginner level, an IT department should start two sorts of experiments. The first is to use more complicated open source applications that require more configuration, but only at an experimental level. Content management systems, application servers or development environments, and open source versions of large-scale enterprise applications for ERP or CRM fall into this category.

Gaining experience with more complicated open source will force most IT departments to decide how far along the open source path they intend to travel. Just as with commercial software, it is important to reduce the number of different skills that you need to learn and to leverage the skills that you already have. Maintaining an institutional skill level in any one open source language or component is not easy. The more components you choose to support, the greater the costs will be. Working with more complicated open source usually means understanding how to write code, or understanding the complicated workings of templating mechanisms or other complicated abstractions for controlling software behavior. At this point, an IT department becomes a Perl, Python, PHP, or Java shop, out of necessity.

The second sort of experiment at the beginner level is to install and use Linux. We consider starting with Linux a mistake, especially if an IT department does not already have Unix skills. The trip from no Unix skills to minimal Unix skills is much longer than the trip from one flavor of Unix to another. Learning Unix-style system administration is much less beneficial than simply using the sorts of open source applications that can be run on Microsoft operating systems. While this does put some open source out of reach, almost all of the more mature and most of the valuable open source runs well on Microsoft, including MySQL, Apache, Perl, Python, PHP, and many other major projects that are based on these technologies. The more mission critical the system is, the higher the level of Linux skills that will be required. Developing these new skills as an institution can take time. Support services of the sort we mention in Chapter 6 can help, but to use any platform in production, you must have a significant skill base, regardless of how much support is provided.

Despite the learning curve for supporting Linux, it is worth pursuing, because it provides a stable platform that allows the widest possible scope of open source to be used. Companies such as Amazon and Yahoo! have used Linux and other open source operating systems to build high-performance systems using the cheapest possible hardware.

To summarize, the beginner level involves:

- Using the simplest, most mature, and easiest-to-configure open source applications
- Developing support procedures for those applications and institutionalizing any new skills required
- Experimenting with more complicated open source applications that require more configuration
- Starting to think about which open source language and components will become a focus for skill building
- Experimenting with Linux or other open source applications as a platform

Moving to the Intermediate Level

The intermediate level of open source expertise is all most IT departments require to get the full benefit from open source. At the intermediate level, an IT department understands how to find, evaluate, install, configure, and support open source applications. These applications can be running on Linux or Windows.

The difference between the beginner and intermediate level is how well the open source applications are understood. Beginners understand open source projects well enough to run them in a stable and reliable manner. For more mature open source software, beginners still understand the software as a relatively simplistic black box. For intermediate-level users, software configuration, customization, and integration are the key skills, and their ability to understand how the applications work is far more sophisticated.

Here is where configuration of templates, or the complicated abstractions that control an application, starts to cross the boundary into software development. The task of integrating applications with one another and with commercial software usually also requires development, as does extending applications by adding new features. At the intermediate level, a department becomes comfortable performing simple development projects, and then testing, installing, and supporting them. All of this requires a staff that has an increased skill level.

One benefit of the increased confidence that is gained at the intermediate level is that support of mission-critical applications becomes possible, because the department now has a much more complete understanding of the software it is using, as well as how to support that software. At the beginner level, departments understand applications only as relatively large black boxes, which is not sufficient for mission-critical support.

However, as the skill level rises, so does the amount of work required for institutionalization. It is impossible for even a large IT department to be skilled in even a small fraction of the open source available today. Intermediate-level users must make important decisions concerning which open source components, languages, and projects the department will focus on. Once the department has chosen a focus, perhaps by concentrating on PHP, it becomes confined, in a way, to that type of open source. It becomes easier to use projects that are based on the chosen technology, because the institutional skill level is higher. Of course, this is a long way from vendor lock-in, but it is lock-in nonetheless.

Another source of lock-in at the intermediate level is the integration between open source components and the investment in application configuration, both of which represent an outlay that is not easy to replace.

It is at the intermediate level that the few who are masters of IT really can show their mettle. The decisions made at the intermediate level are vitally important because they essentially lock an IT department into certain components and skills in the same way that product choice binds an IT department to a vendor. The business as a whole will succeed or suffer based on how well these long-term choices match the business's requirements. Making these decisions properly is an art form that requires a deep understanding of the technology, the business requirements, and the forces driving the evolution of both.

The decisions made at the intermediate level determine whether an IT department is a Perl, Python, PHP, or Java shop, whether it uses MySQL or Postgres, and what key infrastructure is used for development and integration. At the intermediate level, a Windows shop can determine that it makes sense to use Linux or other open source operating systems. With an understanding of the true costs of supporting open source, an IT department can determine if it is worth the effort to reduce costs by using Linux instead of Windows. The answer should be based more on money than on open source religion. At the intermediate level, enough data should be available through experimentation and experience to make an informed decision.

There is no need for most IT departments to move beyond the intermediate level. Rising to the advanced and expert levels means becoming a full-fledged software development shop, which is a wise choice for only a small number of IT departments because of the high level of skill that must be maintained.

In summary, the intermediate level involves:

- Mastering the software development skills involved to configure, integrate, and extend open source applications

- Acquiring a deeper understanding of applications and support skills so that open source can be applied to mission-critical applications

- Choosing to focus on skills in particular languages, components, and applications that can be leveraged to solve many problems for an organization

- Deciding whether Linux or other open source operating systems will be part of the institutional skill set

When the Advanced and Expert Levels Make Sense

Moving to the advanced and expert levels will be a reasonable step for only the small number of IT departments that genuinely need to develop their own solutions. The advanced and expert levels are about using open source as a platform, integrating and extending applications, and creating new ones to meet a company's specific needs.

Development at the intermediate level is about extending an application in ways that have been anticipated or for which the context has been set by others. Development at the advanced and expert levels means designing and building an entire application from the ground up. This is a much more difficult skill to obtain and institutionalize.

At the advanced and expert levels, an IT department can do anything. This means that even more of the focus we described in the previous section is required to avoid spreading resources too thin. At this level of skill, an IT department can create a high-performance application to meet a business's precise requirements. The challenge, then, as with any custom development, is to properly document the development and maintain the skills to support it. Without careful attention to these matters, the high-performance custom solution of today can easily become the legacy albatross of tomorrow.

The other opportunity that advanced- and expert-level skills afford is the ability to participate in or lead development of open source projects. It is not uncommon for IT departments to encourage participation in the development of open source that is highly relevant to their requirements.

The largest danger for IT departments is to follow the lead of a single person who is able to perform at the advanced and expert levels and forgo the skill building and institutional support required to keep a project going once that person leaves the organization.

To summarize, the advanced and expert levels involve:

- Mastering software development using the open source platform
- Focusing development activities to create the most value for the business
- Institutionalizing development skills and properly documenting development

Institutional Skill Building

One of the biggest dangers in using open source, which also can appear in many other areas of IT, is pooling knowledge in one person, thereby creating a significant vulnerability should that person leave the company. One of the reasons IT departments rely on vendors and consultants is to avoid this situation, and instead to document or otherwise preserve the skills of the organization rather than of a single individual. Transferring skills from one person to other members of the team, and documenting and systematically preserving those skills, is the essence of institutionalization. At many points in this book, we have emphasized the concept of institutionalizing skills to avoid the key-person problem. Now we will explain what the process of institutionalizing skills involves.

First, let's look at what happens in the typical key-person problem. A talented programmer takes the lead on a project and creates a brilliant solution to an urgent problem facing the company. The IT department's managers often recognize that should that talented programmer leave the company, the department will be in a vulnerable position. But in the crush of day-to-day priorities, this priority gets lost in the shuffle. Then, something happens that lures the talented programmer away. In her final two weeks on the job, the talented programmer attempts to pass along the knowledge and skill required to support her efforts. Unfortunately, this attempt is rarely successful and the department must scramble to figure out how to support the talented programmer's work in her absence.

The better course of action, and the one required for prudent use of open source, is to identify systematically the skills that are required to support the talented programmer's work. This is harder than it appears, because it is not easy to create an accurate list of the skills required to support an open source project, and it is even more difficult to then document and transmit these skills.

Most of an IT department's skills are never documented or transmitted systematically. Instead, job descriptions define the sort of person needed to perform a job and the skills she requires. While on the job, she learns what is required from colleagues or other sources and maintains that knowledge by doing the work repeatedly.

The key to institutionalization is not only to identify the skills to include in a job description, but also to have a group of people who perform the work regularly and to maintain an appropriate level of documentation for the organization's future needs. In building systems for the space shuttle or a commercial software product, much more must be documented than for most of the systems in your average commercially oriented IT department.

As open source has grown in popularity, it is increasingly possible to purchase support services from a new category of company that has been created to sell support services for open source. Chapter 6 describes the sort of services being offered by such consultants. Creating relationships with small consulting firms or individuals who are expert in open source also can help provide access to skills. However, to choose the right firm or manage these relationships, you must already have some level of skill in-house. With open source, there really is no way out of developing and maintaining certain skills.

At the end of the journey toward open source adoption, what will a company achieve? In one word: empowerment. As we describe at length in Chapter 10, using open source changes an IT department into a more powerful and self-sufficient organization.

To achieve this level of benefits, however, two other thorny issues must be addressed: applying open source to the right problems, and creating processes required to manage the introduction of open source into an organization.

Crafting a Strategy for Applying Open Source

Our approach in this book has been to provide tools for thinking about the important questions involved in open source adoption. So far, we have looked at approaches for evaluating the maturity of open source, determining the skills of an IT department, and understanding the fully loaded costs of using open source. One more such tool, a taxonomy of IT systems, is required to help discover the right areas in which to apply open source.

This taxonomy sorts the IT systems into three categories: stable, flexible, and dynamic.

Stable systems are those for which the business requirements are well understood and are unlikely to change in any unanticipated way. A payroll system is a good example of a mission-critical stable system. Every year or so there are new tax tables, but the system doesn't need to be rewritten to accommodate them. Legacy applications that have been doing the same job for 20 years are another example of a stable system. Simple weblog analysis is yet a third example of a stable system.

Flexible systems are those that are changed once every couple of years. Flexible systems are configured or customized to a small degree to solve a problem, and then they are left alone. A simple collaboration system such as a discussion forum, email list manager, or basic weblog system is a good example of a flexible system. It must be installed and then adapted to meet a need, and every so often it is reconfigured as needs change.

Dynamic systems are those that are designed to support the key value-creating processes of a business. Dynamic systems are heavily customized and optimized. Dynamic systems are usually mission-critical, highly complex systems that are used to run a business. As the business's needs change, and as markets and competitors change, a dynamic system has to keep up. Frequently, dynamic systems are integrated with many different systems inside and outside the business so that the right information can be collected and used to make decisions. A high-volume e-commerce web site such as Amazon.com is one example of a dynamic system. Nike's supply-chain management application, which monitors the flow of materials to manufacturing facilities spread across the world, is another.

The goal of this taxonomy is to provide an early warning system for an IT department. By thinking through potential applications of open source using this taxonomy, an IT department will be better able to avoid applying open source in areas that are beyond its skill level.

The other dimension that must be considered is the importance of the system to the company. In Chapter 3, we described four categories of importance: experimental, low priority, operational, and mission critical.

The nature of the benefit of using open source is indicated by the type of system to which it is applied. Using open source for stable systems will most likely be an exercise in cost reduction. A stable commercial product will be replaced with an open source version that is cheaper or easier to support.

Applying open source to flexible systems is usually about expanding automation and support for business processes. Flexible systems change slowly, along with the business. Collaborative systems or systems that automate low-volume, operational processes fall into this category. The goal of applying open source to dynamic systems is to create a high-performance machine for a competitive advantage. Applying open source to dynamic systems is about controlling your own destiny in a vital area, but doing so requires the highest level of skill.

Another way to evaluate open source is to look at three ways to apply it:

- *Using open source applications* will happen at all skill levels and is the broadest and most beneficial way to apply open source.

- *Using open source as a computing platform* means using infrastructure starting with Linux or other open source operating systems. Beginners and intermediates without Unix skills will find this difficult.

- *Using open source for integration and development,* to make applications work together and to create new ones, is generally too complex for beginners. Intermediates can achieve simple integration, and advanced users and experts will find the most value.

Learning how to use open source and where to apply it provides an IT department with significant benefits. To manage all the risks, however, IT departments must learn how to address open source at every level of the organization.

Crafting a Strategy for Managing Open Source

Many CIOs and IT departments have yet to come to terms with open source and define their relationship to it. On the one hand, the press reports everyday about all sorts of companies saving a bundle with open source. Large players such as IBM and Novell are promoting open source projects and bundles that fit into their product strategy. Frequently the engineering and development staff is already using it to some extent. In many ways, the problem resembles the way that company web sites popped up spontaneously all over the Internet in the mid- to late 1990s.

The question we will address next is how that opportunity can be managed. What rules should govern progress toward greater adoption of open source in an organization? Which sorts of governance models are being used in which types of organizations?

Unique Challenges of Controlling Open Source Adoption

The vast potential of open source comes with a variety of risks that are not present in commercial software. To avoid uncoordinated chaos, these risks must be managed with some sort of governance structure or policy that prevents unmonitored and unauthorized use of open source. This governance structure is generally different from policies that are used to control other technology, for the following reasons:

- Open source is free of charge. Anybody can download an open source program and install it without paying a fee—and often they do it without any checks and balances. This means the purchasing process cannot be used to control the acquisition of open source.

- Open source can be easy to install and get running. This makes it alluring for frustrated users or IT departments that want to do things for themselves. Striking out on your own without adequate operational skills, however, frequently leads to disaster.

- Open source is available for almost every need. This adds to the allure for those who want to go it alone, yet lack the proper skill level.

- Open source comes with source code. With the required skills, anyone can modify and customize open source software. Although commercial software also can be customized, the customizations that can be applied to open source software are limitless. This provides an unrestricted potential for creating key-person risk.

- Open source licensing has important and subtle implications. The most dangerous situation is to use open source as part of a commercial product, without thinking things through carefully. Many open source projects can be safely included in commercial projects through licenses designed for this purpose, such as the Lesser General Public License (LGPL), a version of the GPL that makes including open source libraries less restrictive. However, if developers are not careful, using open source in sloppy ways can result in an obligation to make an entire product open source. While this can be remedied by removing the open source, few companies want to have any such ugly surprises. The other issue with licensing involves careful handling of intellectual property issues when releasing software as open source. Only open source to which a company has clear title should be released.

- Employees can contribute to open source projects. Sometimes encouraged by the company, sometimes on their own, employees can lead or contribute to open source projects. When this happens on company time and using company resources, questions of intellectual property ownership, such as who owns what and whether permission has been properly granted, must be handled carefully.

Different Companies, Different Responses

The right response to these issues changes dramatically based on an organization's size and the way it uses open source. For most IT departments, the issue concerns controlling the introduction of open source to avoid such problems as expanding the required skill set without careful deliberation, or making sure projects are properly supported and within the department's skills to support.

At a small company, the task of open source governance can be assigned to an individual who approves the use of open source. The approval can be based on formal or informal standards according to the company's style. The next problem is to make sure everyone knows that this person must approve any use of open source. This is about all that is needed for your average IT department that is not developing any software products and does not intend to release anything as open source or participate in development.

In a large company, the governance procedures must be far more formal. One person is no longer a reliable stopgap, and instead, the job is performed by one or several committees. Informal methods will no longer suffice, and the company must create a policy for all the issues involved, including the following:

- When is it appropriate to use open source? For what purposes and in what contexts should open source be used?

- What must be demonstrated and documented to gain approval?

- Which open source licenses are acceptable?

- When and how should open source be used in product development?

- When can internally developed software be released as open source, if at all?

- How will the company support open source development?

- How many employees should participate in open source development?

The goal of policies designed to cover these issues is to prevent the negative side effects of using open source too liberally. The specific policies that are right for a particular company depend on many factors, including the type of business the company is in, its tolerance for risk, and so on.

Hewlett-Packard is one of the most advanced corporations in terms of its approach to open source. At *http://opensource.hp.com/*, you can see all the projects in which HP is participating. HP's Open Source Program Office uses an Open Source Policy Document and an Open Source Review Process to ensure compliance with corporate standards.

Enthusiastic adoption by large enterprises such as IBM, HP, and Amazon.com—companies that are wary of undo risk exposure—indicates that it is possible to manage the risks of open source, as long as a proactive and rigorous approach is taken.

CHAPTER 6

Support Models for Open Source

At this point in the book, you might have the impression that open source is something you must learn to do yourself. Indeed, open source comes with many more responsibilities than most commercial software, but it also comes with many more opportunities—if you have the skills to take advantage of them.

Entrepreneurs and venture capitalists have noticed that the number of people who can benefit from open source is far larger than the number of people who have the skills to do so. While this book argues that the best way to take advantage of open source is to embark on a program of institutional skill building, startups, systems integrators, and software, vendors are coming to market with different offers of support. Moreover, a growing number of consulting services are designed to close the skills gap required to overcome the lack of productization and bring the value of open source to a wider audience.

From an IT department's perspective, perhaps the most attractive offer would be a fully integrated open source package that is configured to meet the department's precise needs. Do not hold your breath waiting for such an offer. To make a business viable, open source support providers, like all other service providers, will have to create one offer that can be delivered at an attractive price to the largest number of customers. This chapter will examine the offers that are available on the market, their advantages and disadvantages, and how they might appeal to IT departments along the continuum from beginner to expert.

Open Source Support Offers

The whole idea of open source support raises the following question: what does it mean to have support for any sort of software? For commercial vendors, support is stated as one thing, but IT departments purchase support for reasons other than those stated in the support agreements.

The Generic Commercial Software Support Offer

For the most part, commercial support agreements provide access to a team of support professionals who help ensure that the software you purchased works the way it is supposed to work. Another important aspect of support is access to a steady stream of software updates and bug fixes. Vendors often provide different levels of support, with more services or faster turnaround in exchange for a higher fee. Support can come in the form of a database of information about the product, or collections of technical notes about problems other customers have had and ways to solve them. However, support usually means an IT department can call a company, report a problem, and get help resolving it. IT departments that purchase commercial software usually pay from 15% to 25% of the total licensing fee per year for access to support services.

Software vendors that provide support are generally careful about defining what they will provide. Support is usually limited to software of a certain age, and it does not necessarily cover older versions. Part of the reason for this is to encourage upgrades to newer software. Another motivation, however, is the expense of keeping a team up-to-date on many different versions. Software companies also limit support to certain versions of operating systems and databases. You might be required to install specific patch levels to be eligible for support. It is not uncommon for a support call to begin with confirmation that the software you are running meets all the requirements for support services.

Then, of course, there is the issue of how the software should behave. Some software includes exhaustive documentation that specifies its behavior in all situations, but most does not. When software behavior is not clearly defined, software vendors and IT departments frequently argue about whether the behavior amounts to a bug that must be fixed or a feature that is just fine. If a bug is indeed found, it might be weeks or months before it is resolved.

As a practical matter, however, what IT departments are really buying when they pay for support are not the benefits mentioned so far, but rather, the peace of mind that comes with knowing someone is being paid money to be there to solve problems. Support is a form of insurance. For a commercial product, support means an IT department has one throat to choke.

Evaluating Open Source Support Providers

Supporting open source software is an IT department's responsibility. There is no one else to yell at or to blame. There is only the IT department and the source code. This can be a frightening prospect, especially for IT departments at the beginner or intermediate level. For all these reasons, as use of open source grows to areas that are increasingly mission critical, more IT departments will seek out support.

Commercial open source support providers cannot get around the basic economics of their business. They must answer the same questions as traditional support providers, and the way they answer these questions, and deliver and price their services, will ultimately determine whether they succeed. In addition, they have unique challenges, such as supporting software they did not write, which will be more or less difficult depending on the vagaries of each open source project. In the following analysis of different open source support models, we will examine how open source support providers answer these questions:

- What is being supported?
- What is the definition of proper software behavior?
- What operating system, database, and related software configurations are supported?
- How will support services such as upgrades, patches, and hot lines be provided?
- How much will support cost?

What Kind of Open Source Will Be Supported?

Given the vast range of quality in open source programs, it is clear that some are practically impossible to support, and others are fairly easy.

Emerging open source projects that are evolving rapidly will never be included in a generic open source support model. Companies will be able to find support for such software, if they require it, but the support likely will come in the form of a consulting relationship with people involved in the project.

At the other end of the spectrum are the most mature products that have become commodities. Linux, Apache, and MySQL are robust, stable products. For the most popular configurations, they work well, and most open source support provided today focuses on these products. The question for this sort of open source is not whether it can be supported, but how much that support is really needed. For the most common uses, this sort of open source software just works. But then again, most commercial software also works great for its intended purpose, yet companies still feel they need support. Support for stable software is clearly something organizations want and are willing to pay for, and companies offering commercial open source support planning meet that need as one of their first priorities.

What about the open source software in between the fast-moving early projects and the stable commodity products? This software is excellent for certain uses, but it might not be appropriate in lots of different configurations. The definition of what this software does is not as poor as that for emerging products and not as clear as that for commodity products. It is this category of software that represents a large amount of value and a large amount of risk for different sorts of commercial open source support companies described later.

Chet Kapoor, an executive at BEA Systems, Inc., has studied how corporations use open source and has analyzed how it is likely to be supported. In Kapoor's view, a large number of IT departments have been using open source for development and non-mission-critical applications for many years. Now, many more of them are starting to use open source for production, which is going to create a large opportunity for support services.

Kapoor's view is that open source projects, like other technologies, will proceed through the following stages:

New
　　When the project is just introduced

Adoption
　　When the project is starting to become popular

Standardized
　　When the project starts to work in a uniform way, with increasing productization

Commoditized
　　When the project is absorbed into the technology stack that supports computing

Kapoor thinks the big opportunity for support providers comes when an open source project has reached the standardized stage. This is when the software is generally applicable enough for a service provider to make money supporting it.

Now that you're armed with a clear understanding of the types of open source software that can be supported commercially, let's turn to the different types of support services being offered.

Subscriptions

The earliest support for open source came in the form of a subscription. Companies including Red Hat, Mandrake, and SuSE collected the public distribution of Linux and other related programs into a neat package that came with regular updates. For an added fee, users could upgrade these subscriptions to include support provided by technical experts over the phone, just like with commercial software. Red Hat has been especially aggressive in terms of increasing the breadth of the software offered through its subscription and supported by its technical support services.

Now, what sort of support do you get with these subscription products? Mostly, you get support for proper product installation and configuration, plus limited support for software operation. Interested in doing some kernel hacking? Subscription support is not likely to help. What if one of the APIs on your content management product is behaving strangely? Subscription support will probably do no more than point you to the web site for that content management product.

Subscription support provides a valuable service by collecting a useful bundle of stable software into one package, and making sure that all the integration or compatibility problems are resolved. Custom installation scripts and documentation make up for lack of productization, and can help an IT department overcome the skills gap. Subscription bundles usually employ stable software at or close to the operating-system level, which doesn't require a lot of support.

Subscription support has been around for several years. While the amount of support provided is low, the price is also low. This is not the focus of the companies that were just coming out of the gate at the beginning of 2005.

Certified bundles

New companies such as SourceLabs (*http://www.sourcelabs.com/*), SpikeSource (*http://www.spikesource.com/*), and Wild Open Source (*http://www.wildopensource.com/*) are reaching beyond the realm of commodity software and are providing bundles designed to meet the needs of narrower but still common use cases. SourceLabs, for example, is providing certified bundles of commonly used software that works together, such as Linux, Apache, PHP, and MySQL. SpikeSource is providing another sort of certified bundle, and Wild Open Source will customize a Linux distribution for use in an embedded system or high-performance context, and then support the customized distribution.

As with the subscription model, these companies package up a collection of software, resolve problems concerning interdependencies, and make up for some of the lack of productization by creating easy-to-use installation scripts and providing documentation. However, companies supporting certified bundles include a much wider variety of software and intend to support many different bundles aimed at different audiences. The bundles might be tested for reliability and be configured for high-performance operation.

For example, SpikeSource offers a certified bundle that contains 50 products, including Apache, JBoss, MySQL, Tomcat, Axis, Hibernate, and PHP, which are certified to run several different installations of Linux. Other companies such as SourceLabs offer other sorts of certified bundles.

The goal of the companies offering support for certified bundles is to become the trusted provider for a collection of software that becomes the foundation of custom development. Companies offering certified bundles will be seeking to help independent software companies who might want to deliver their commercial products on an open source platform. Certified-bundle companies might also choose to offer support for the infrastructure of custom open source projects created by systems integrators.

The obvious challenge for companies offering certified bundles is to define bundles that are attractive to the greatest number of potential customers. However, another difficult challenge is to narrow their offerings so that support can be provided. As we mentioned earlier, at every opportunity commercial software vendors choose to limit the scope of supported configurations as much as possible. How will certified bundles be limited? What versions of what software products will be supported? How will the fast-moving nature of some open source projects be reconciled with the need for a stable configuration to support? Most of all, certified-bundle companies must determine what price they can charge for support, and whether this price will support a service organization. These are not easy questions to answer. The right answers will vary from bundle to bundle, and they will be found only through trial and error.

As the support market matures, competition will increase. In addition, unlike with commercial software, in which only one company can provide support for a given product, multiple vendors will be selling support services for the same open source software. Not only will this drive down the cost of support, but also, because the vendors are competing on service it might result in a new standard for the quality of support offered. This raises the following question: will these bundles become products with a new form of vendor lock-in, or will an organization be able to switch from one open source support provider to another? The answer depends in part on the decisions your company makes moving forward.

Custom enhancements

A close relative of the sort of custom distributions we mentioned in the previous section are custom enhancements to open source projects. These are generally created and then supported by experts. Programmers from Sony Pictures Imageworks, Industrial Light & Magic, and Rhythm & Hues participated in the development of Film Gimp, an enhanced version of the open source Gimp image-manipulation program, to make the program more appropriate for certain manipulations used in movie production. Frequently, these enhancements are contributed to the original project. However, even if they are, companies might want to engage the experts who created them in an ongoing basis to support the enhancements.

Open Source—Based Products

A variety of independent software vendors have noticed the power of open source development, and a new breed of commercial software based entirely on open source is cropping up. Under this model, a software vendor creates a product based exclusively on new development, using open source projects as a foundation. The products are licensed in a variety of ways that do not conflict with open source licenses. These products frequently come with support for the entire configuration of open source used to create and run them.

Companies such as Gluecode (bought by IBM in May 2005) create application development platforms for IT using open source as a foundation. Other software companies such as Compiere and SugarCRM have open source versions, either as a marketing technique or as a vehicle around which to sell consulting services.

Consulting Services

When systems integrators create solutions based on open source, the service frequently includes continuing support for the open source configuration at the foundation of the solution.

When Is Commercial Open Source Support the Right Choice?

The models in the previous section provide different ways to bridge the skills gap between IT departments and open source software. This section examines the pros and cons of each support model for IT departments with different skill levels.

Using commercial open source support providers effectively requires many of the same skills IT departments use to evaluate any vendor. An IT department has to understand what kind of support it needs, whether the offered services meet those needs, and whether the company can provide the services when they are needed. However, open source support has different characteristics and provides new choices that IT departments are not used to making. Consider these differences:

- Support for most commercial products comes from one provider: the software vendor. With open source support, however, several vendors might be offering different types of support services.

- Pricing for support will be negotiated much more intensely with open source products than with commercial products. There is no benchmark based on licenses. Customers will be able to cut deals.

- Support offerings will have to be evaluated carefully to determine what services will be provided. Offers will range widely in terms of scope and quality. Some emerging companies might promise levels of support they cannot deliver.

- Support might be used for high-risk periods and dropped when a product is proven stable. After all, with commercial support, you have to pay for updates, but with open source, the stream of updates is always freely available.

- Support might be used as a protective measure while an IT department builds skills.

Companies offering commercial open source support are well aware of all these differences, and they will fashion their offers to provide significant levels of service to clients as well as to protect their position. In the end, these companies are betting that the additional service, convenience, and quality they provide will be of enduring value to their intended customers.

In the next section, we will take a look at some of the most common situations in which commercial open source support is attractive to IT departments.

When Use of Open Source Is Mission Critical

For an IT department, applications that are mission critical, or that have high-performance requirements, must have a high level of support. With open source, this means becoming an expert yourself, engaging a consultant to be available in some way, or using a commercial open source support provider. IT departments at all skill levels will use some combination of these choices. IT departments at the expert or advanced level might have the skills to support an open source product but might prefer to apply those employees to other projects. Expert companies might also want a 24/7 hotline available as part of their operational processes. As systems become less mission critical, the support needs drop and support becomes easier, because downtime is more acceptable.

The problem for mission-critical systems concerns matching the support services offered to the needs of the IT department. This is never easy, even with commercial software where support is offered up and down the stack.

When a Certified Bundle Solves an Important Problem

Certified bundles are collections of open source projects that are packaged by support providers and are tuned to operate optimally with each other for a certain purpose. The initial collections of these bundles are focused on core infrastructure, such as matched sets of complimentary software like the Linux operating system, the MySQL database, the JRun servlet engine, and the Apache Web Server. Where these bundles will go is not clear yet. It is possible that bundles could be created to help build portals, to provide email infrastructure, to support collaboration, and for other purposes. It is possible that these bundles could become the equivalent of supported products and be attractive to an IT department. The key question is whether the bundles will work to solve a problem. The initial bundles are focused on infrastructure and software development support. It remains to be seen at the time of this writing whether other sorts of bundles will emerge and succeed.

When a Consultant Creates a Custom Feature

IT departments often extend open source software to meet specific needs. Experts will do this themselves and will likely support the extensions themselves. IT departments at the beginner, intermediate, and advanced levels might engage consultants to extend open source and then retain relationships with them to support those extensions. This support might be needed even if the extension finds its way back into the main distribution of the original open source project.

Accelerating Implementation and Building Skills

Services from commercial open source support providers and consultants can be used to accelerate the creation of an open source infrastructure, and to build skills. Systems integrators and consultants offer advice and services to help create strategies and execute pilot projects. Working with such experts can help an IT department to acquire skills quickly.

Buy Carefully

One of the biggest advantages that open source provides to IT departments is choice. Open source allows companies to avoid vendor lock-in, which can lead to higher costs and restricted options. On the other hand, choice can be a burden, because options must be evaluated, which might be difficult to do in an emerging market.

The best thing IT departments can do is test the offers provided to them in every way possible. It is likely that certified bundles will be available for installation on a trial basis. IT departments can call hotlines to determine the support staff's expertise and availability.

Commercial open source support services are one way of closing the skills gap. However, they might not work for every situation. Sometimes the skills, not the software, require support. It is possible that commercial open source support services could evolve in this direction and offer education as well as support services. As more IT departments experiment with open source, they likely will find that they need support of some kind. After all, it is a lot easier to get open source working than it is to configure it, tune it, and solve its problems.

This year is shaping up to be a period of intense learning for IT departments as well as for commercial open source support providers. Eventually, if the services can be provided for a reasonable price to a large enough base of customers, a mature and stable open source support offering will be defined. Until then, IT departments will need to be careful when evaluating and choosing open source support vendors.

One unintended effect of the arrival of commercial open source service providers could be a slowdown of the innovation cycle. Once you purchase support, forget about recompiling what you have and adding your own customizations to the key components. If bundles become popular, commercial support providers might want to delay the rate at which changes are made to restrain the costs of supporting a wide variety of bundles. This could create tension between IT departments that want the benefit of rapid open source innovation and the support providers who want to maintain stability.

CHAPTER 7

Making Open Source Projects Easy to Adopt

In the preceding chapters, we outlined ways to build the necessary skills for using open source in the enterprise. But what happens when you are finished evaluating and implementing an open source project within an organization? In this chapter and the following two chapters, we will look at some of the emerging issues that are shaping the future of open source. At the same time, we will show how your company can manage the risks, and reap the rewards, of participating in the evolution of open source.

In Chapter 1, we proposed that the challenge to using open source was to overcome the lack of productization found in most open source projects. This chapter will examine what it means to be productized, the benefits that accrue to an open source project for doing a better job, and how IT departments can participate in productization to help build skills.

Productization tends to arrive late to open source products, if it comes at all. In many open source projects, the implied attitude toward productization is dismissive, as if the leaders of the project were declaring, "Look, you've got the source code; if you can't figure out what you need from there, perhaps you should not be using this software." This is a hard-line position: it insists that the only barrier to open source adoption is a skills gap. While few project leaders hold this view consciously, the lack of attention to productization says it all.

Who cares, really? Perhaps the lack of productization should just be seen as a fact of life for open source projects. The open source projects that take that view weaken their appeal for those of beginner and intermediate skill levels in IT departments and other groups. However, this chapter argues that for most open source projects a small investment in productization can yield tremendous benefits in terms of making the software available to a larger community.

Productization is not something that only serves the needs of beginners. When software is easy to use, has features that automate or assist common operations, and works easily with other programs in its intended environment, everybody is happier.

Productization can reduce the learning curve for potential project participants and make it easier for other projects to incorporate a project into their software. Some projects have turned their high-quality productization into a source of revenue by charging for documentation or by selling a fully productized commercial version. In addition, participating in improving productization provides a way for a larger part of the user community to contribute to an open source project. If you can't write code, but you are thrilled with how cool a project is, you can consider writing documentation to become part of the team.

This chapter also has a lot to say to IT departments in organizations considering the use of open source software. By making your needs known to open source development teams—and perhaps making contributions to productization—you can improve their software while expanding business opportunities for everyone in a project's ecosystem. IT departments using open source products are the biggest market for consulting and other services related to open source projects.

One Program for Productization

If you ask a CTO who has lived through creating a commercial software product when productization occurred, usually the answer is "At the last minute, only when we had to because we started to sell more software." At that point, productization becomes a huge priority, because the number of newly arrived customers at the beginner and intermediate levels starts to grow. They need to be educated and must be able to perform simple tasks for themselves. If productization is lacking, the company pays in terms of support costs or frustrated customers.

For open source projects, this "last minute" comes when the number of users participating in the project overwhelms the core development team, which frequently becomes annoyed that so many beginner-level questions are flooding mailing lists. The first response is usually to create a parallel support structure of user-only mailing lists and other community features, out of which the developers hope that users can create materials to help themselves.

Alert open source developers should try to stay ahead of their users and provide some support before becoming frantic. Here are some guidelines for providing this help for users at different skill levels:

- Provide basic information and community support for beginners and intermediates.
- Reduce the skills gap for getting started through installation scripts and administrative interfaces.
- Accelerate learning by providing architectural documentation and sample code for advanced- and expert-level users.
- Add features and functions to support integration with related systems.

These guidelines will help in terms of planning productization so that an open source project has a chance to perform productization before it becomes a problem for the user community and thwarts wider adoption.

Basic Information and Community Support

Beginner and intermediate users need education. First, they need to figure out what an open source project does, how mature it is, and whether they have the right skills to use it. Most frequently, these users look at the project's web site, download the software, and then try it out.

Beginner and intermediate users also need help with context. Many of the questions that flood mailing lists have nothing to do with how the open source project functions, but rather concern how it fits into the surrounding environment and what settings are needed to make databases, web servers, and network ports behave properly.

In the subsection that follow, we discuss the most important elements a project should include to help beginner and intermediate users.

Mission Statement

A mission statement or brief description of the project featured or linked to prominently on the home page of a web site is a great help to anyone trying to figure out what the project is all about. Here are some samples and excerpts:

OpenOffice.org
> "To create, as a community, the leading international office suite that will run on all major platforms and provide access to all functionality and data through open-component based APIs and an XML-based file format."

Drupal
> "A dynamic web site platform which allows an individual or community of users to publish, manage, and organize a variety of content, Drupal integrates many popular features of content management systems, weblogs, collaborative tools, and discussion-based community software into one easy-to-use package."

Babeldoc

> "Universal document processor. The open source tool for business-to-business and systems integrators and enterprises wishing to connect data and documents centers. Babeldoc is intended for systems integrators and EAI projects."

Examples and Working Sites

If the project's mission is clear, the next step many users take is to look at working examples. For some software, such as OpenOffice.org, this can mean showing screenshots. For others, such as Drupal, this can mean links to a huge number of other web sites built with the project. For an infrastructure, such as Babeldoc, this can mean a whitepaper on the site that mentions who is using it and for what purpose.

Question-and-Answer Archive

Short of a well-written book, perhaps the single most useful tool to help encourage use of an open source project is an active bulletin board system that the project team scans regularly and that is complemented by a well-maintained FAQ. It is here that beginner and intermediate users can find answers to simple questions about the context in which the software runs. Such a structure tends to allow people to support each other, with simple questions being answered by those with a little knowledge and the leaders of the project team weighing in on the most difficult problems. While an open source project cannot force the creation of a community to use tools such as bulletin boards and FAQs, it can provide them and answer questions on them to get the ball rolling.

Of course, bulletin boards and FAQs are no substitute for a well-written manual or book. But a well-written manual is hard to come by, and FAQs and bulletin boards are easier to maintain by a larger group, which usually makes them the first stop, even when a manual exists.

Documentation

Only the most mature projects have documentation worth the screen it was written on. Most projects have *README* files and a small amount of documentation aimed at saving those with a high skill level some time searching through the source code. However, frequently these are more like notes to the project's internal members than documentation designed to communicate to newcomers how the software works. For those at the beginner and intermediate levels, the most useful documentation comprises a step-by-step tutorial of how to get a project running so that users can play with it and figure it out through experimentation. We will discuss documentation for more advanced users a bit later in this chapter.

Most of the time, adequate documentation arrives in one of three ways:

- The community supporting a project grows large enough to attract people who feel moved to create documentation as a way to contribute to the project. This generally doesn't happen until projects are on their way to larger-scale adoption.

- Authors and publishers notice a project, prompting the project's leaders or other experts to write books.

- The project leaders make it a priority to write documentation, because they want to encourage adoption or they want to charge for it.

Given that documentation is so rare, it can be one of the easiest ways for a project to distinguish itself as being professional.

Reducing the Skills Gap for Getting Started

The next step in productization is to make an open source project easy to use. This means automating as much of it as possible so that beginners can avoid as many complexities as possible.

Installation Scripts

Most projects come with some scripts that help unpack the project from its compressed form. Then, a *README* file explains the steps required to compile and install the project. This is where people with beginner and intermediate skills start to get nervous. Most of the time, they don't know how to get the project from its unpacked state to a working state. Some projects don't offer an installation script that can actually anticipate all the different settings and configuration options that might be needed to get a project running. However, if an easy-to-use installation script is available, beginners and intermediates will appreciate the quick start and it won't get in the way of advanced and expert users.

Tools are available for making open source easier to install, such as RPM. However, the installers that come with open source software are rarely as easy to use as the ones on consumer PC systems. The easier that open source installers are to install, the easier it will be for users of all levels to use open source.

Configuration Tools

While installation is the process of fitting software into the environment in which it will run, *configuration* is the process of controlling the software's behavior. Most software has a variety of mechanisms controlling its behavior, from settings in property files and databases to small scripts that are executed at predefined points. The worst case is when these mechanisms are undocumented and can be understood only by reading the source code. Sometimes documentation in the form of comments is included in property files. The best programs have interactive environments for changing settings in a way that makes it easy and clear, and protects the user from common errors or combinations of settings that do not make sense.

Administrative Interfaces

Many programs include common configuration tasks that are performed repeatedly, such as adding users or changing permissions. The same sorts of interfaces that make configuration easy are also needed for administration.

Operational and Diagnostic Consoles

Most large-scale software has a log file that various parts of the program write messages to during normal operations. Software diagnosis frequently begins with an examination of these log files. One of the biggest favors that any software designer can do for future users is to build diagnostic functionality into the software that goes beyond log files to confirm the operation of various software components, thereby making it much easier to diagnose problems. Such diagnostic routines are generally found only in the highest-quality software.

For example, if an application relies on getting data from a service on the Internet, a simple diagnostic routine could confirm proper operation of that service. Alternatively, if an application is implemented by services that run on several different servers, a diagnostic console could confirm the proper operation of those services.

With these tools, beginner and intermediate users can extend their abilities, and expert and advanced users can save a significant amount of time.

Accelerating Learning

The productization described so far satisfies most beginner and intermediate users' needs. But as use of the software grows, more users of all types will arrive and intermediates will grow to the expert level. Other projects will also start using the software for purposes that were not originally anticipated. All of this happens late in a project's life cycle and much more slowly than the initial arrival of beginners. But open source projects can increase adoption further by providing productization designed to serve the needs of expert and advanced users.

Sample Code

Intermediate users require sample code for managing the sort of templating and simple scripting they engage in. Expert- and advanced-level users require sample code that shows how to use the APIs that allow other programs to invoke the functionality of another piece of software. Generally, the more sample code there is, the better. Once a project provides an area for sample code and support for community collaboration around it, users tend to provide more than enough samples.

API Documentation

While sample code is a good way to start supporting developers, open source projects should proceed to the next stage and perform actual documentation. A good first document is a catalog of all APIs available to programmers and a basic tutorial on how they can be used. Well-commented sample code is a great help, but just a few pages that describe the general idea of each API and the different subroutines or services that can be invoked can save a programmer hours of time.

Architecture Documentation

At the expert and advanced levels, the problems get harder. Instead of trying to configure or administer a program, developers are generally asking deeper questions about how they can extend an open source project to solve a new problem or integrate it into another program. Users at this level frequently are able to understand quickly what a project is all about by reading the code. A project can save them time and encourage participation and adoption by providing a high level of architectural documentation. Such documentation should cover the design principles used in the software and the structure of the program's components or modules. Frequently, such documentation lacks an overview and dives right into the details of APIs. Apache.org has a good example of architectural documentation under the documentation section of the Apache project (*http://httpd.apache.org/docs-2.1/*).

Guide to Embedded Components

Another useful sort of expert and advanced documentation is a guide to how an open source project uses other open source projects that are included as components. Many open source projects come with a list of other open source that must be installed. Documentation of what each embedded open source component does in an application can help to speed the learning process. The decisions that the core development team made in selecting a component can quickly help other expert and advanced users make sense of how an open source project is constructed.

Integration

The basic elements we just mentioned are important and go a long way to closing the skills gap and promoting wider adoption. The next step is to improve the integration of an open source project into the users' environment. This is a more advanced level of productization that can take place only after the core development team understands how a project is being used.

Better integration is the key to completing the goals of productization so that the installed software does everything the user wants it to do. For this discussion, *integration* means the software works with all the other parts of an IT infrastructure when it is installed. Basic productization involves making the process of understanding, installing, and configuring the software as easy as possible.

For example, Apache, MySQL, and PHP are used in thousands of applications all over the Internet, and most of the time they work together seamlessly. Sometimes, however, when one of the three is upgraded to a newer version, problems arise that are hard to track down. The more such problems are anticipated, planned for, and tested for, the better integrated a set of products will be.

Proper integration is not accomplished on a whiteboard. Generally, a fully productized, integrated product is the result of gathering feedback through a series of releases. Careful study of users' experiences with the software generates requirements that, if properly implemented, make using the software a pleasant experience.

TWiki: An Integration Case Study

One of the most successful, productized, and deeply integrated open source projects is TWiki™, an implementation of Ward Cunningham's Wiki concept for efficient collaboration. Peter Thoeny, founder of the TWiki project, deliberately focused on making TWiki friendly to the IT environment. Part of this is due to the fact that Peter introduced the idea of using Wikis to his employer, Wind River Systems. Peter used TWiki as the foundation of the company's systems for providing user support. Hundreds of contributors update and read content from a massive TWiki composed of 50,000 pages that are changed an average of 20,000 times each month.

Peter has consciously pursued a variety of productization elements and integration features intended to promote TWiki's use in engineering departments and corporations as an environment for intranets and knowledge bases. How his decisions worked to encourage adoption makes for an instructive story.

Choosing an Intranet Identity

The concept of a Wiki is so flexible that it is used by a huge variety of applications. In eXtreme Programming, Wiki is used to manage projects and to help record requirements. The Wikipedia uses Wiki as a publishing and knowledge management platform (in fact, we wrote this book using Wiki for project management and collaboration). When Peter Thoeny first encountered Wiki and was given the task of running a customer support department, he wanted to use Wiki for knowledge management.

True to form for open source protocol, Peter first grabbed an existing Wiki written in Java, called JOS Wiki, and used that for a while. Like most talented developers, his head quickly filled with ideas for improvements, and to scratch that itch, he created the TWiki project and wrote a Wiki based on the Perl language.

The early version of TWiki worked well enough within a small customer support department, but then the user community expanded and new requirements arose. Peter saw that TWiki needed to focus more on satisfying the needs of the IT department and not just those of content creators. Peter changed his vision of TWiki from a knowledge management tool to one that was also designed to operate as a corporate intranet.

Here are a few of the features he had to add to make this transition:

- The original TWiki, like many other Wiki implementations, had no access control; anybody could do anything to any page of information. Based on user feedback from many installations, Peter found that database and system administrators couldn't stomach the idea that TWiki had no access control. Peter added a simple mechanism that allowed access to portions of the TWiki that can be controlled by assigning permissions to users and groups of users.

- TWiki has its own user registration database along with the ability to use HTTP Auth to control access. While permissions must always be handled as part of administration, the original TWiki users found it annoying and difficult to have to maintain a parallel database of TWiki users when a perfectly good directory of users, usernames, emails, and other information was already part of the IT infrastructure. Peter added the ability to integrate with the namespace created by single sign-on mechanisms.

- The original Wiki implementations had no way to recover if a user deleted the contents of a Wiki page, whether by accident or on purpose. Peter added a version control mechanism to create an audit trail of how pages were created and to allow deleted information to be recovered.

- The original Wiki did not have a mechanism for attaching files to a page. Peter added this feature for use by his customer support department and it proved popular with users.

- Many pages created for Peter's customer support Wiki turned out to be lists of small items. Peter added the ability to create forms that allowed information on a page to be entered into fields. Adding such metadata turned pages into something similar to records in a database. This allowed new pages to be created that were lists of portions of other pages selected based on metadata. In this way, TWiki became similar to a database-driven content management system.

Peter communicated all of this to the world at large by declaring his commitment to the IT world in TWiki's mission statement: "TWiki is a leading-edge, web-based collaboration platform targeting the corporate intranet. TWiki fosters information flow within an organization; lets distributed teams work together seamlessly and productively; and eliminates the one webmaster syndrome of outdated intranet content."

TWiki's focus and its integration into the corporate IT environment have made it one of the most popular and widely adopted Wiki implementations. On *http://www.TWiki.org/*, success stories from Disney, Motorola, SAP, and Yahoo! explain different ways the software has been used in large environments.

One possible objection to this broader, advanced view of productization is that it really is inseparable from the task of just improving the product. There is no dividing line between making a product friendly to a new environment by adding a feature such as integration with single sign-on, which can be seen as an advanced form of productization, and adding a vital feature such as keeping an audit trail, which could be thought of as merely useful. The idea of advanced productization is to focus more on the audience and to anticipate their needs, which is what great products do.

Benefits of Increased Adoption

Productization is boring, for the most part. That's why it is so broadly ignored. The fact that many open source projects thrive for so long with such meager productization suggests that it is not vital to growth, at least in the early stages. Frankly, for some sorts of projects, productization really doesn't matter much.

For example, if you are creating a special extension to the Linux kernel that can be used only by those who compile their own Linux executable from the source code, productization is not that meaningful. The whole target audience is so sophisticated that a good *README* file will get everyone where they need to go.

However, open source is outgrowing its "by developers, for developers" ethos, where productization is a sideshow. At various points in this book, we noted how open source is bursting out of the basement of the infrastructure stack, where only developers and sophisticates pay attention, and increasingly is being used to create applications that the general population employs. Applications need productization to thrive.

When the purpose of an open source product is not just one developer scratching an itch, but rather, is to serve as a corporate marketing or collaboration device, or as the platform for a business, ease of use and productization matter mightily.

Achieving productization is primarily a function of leadership. Frankly, completing the productization is not a popular activity in commercial products. The cream of the development team rarely spends its time creating documentation, configuration and administration tools, installation scripts, and all the other aspects of productization we covered in this chapter. But better productization creates better software for all users. Somehow, someone has to be motivated to do the work. Junior people can be paired with senior people. The prestige of joining the development team can be held out as a carrot. Leaders of open source projects frequently break down and do the boring work themselves after realizing the project will not grow without it, or because they get sick of the bulletin boards being flooded with simple questions. Some projects turn productization into a line of business and charge for the best stuff.

The reason to execute on productization is to bring more people into the community of a project. For commercially oriented open source, where marketing or sales of services or hardware is the goal, increasing the community is clearly beneficial.

What about your normal itch-scratchers doing an application? What is in it for them to have a larger user community who benefits from productization? The answer depends on the project leaders' motivation. If the only goal is to create software for your own use, with help from other like-minded experts, expanding the community might be an annoyance rather than a benefit. If, however, the project leaders are interested in creating a product for the ages, a great work of software art, more people at all levels are required to hasten the pace at which features are vetted by usage and new requirements are suggested. Opening the door to more users means opening the door to more use, and that means better software.

Opportunities for Skill Building

So far, we directed this chapter at open source project leaders. But worry not; something is lurking in here for IT departments, the heroes of this book.

Productization provides an opportunity for beginners and intermediate players to do service to projects they find useful and want to see succeed. Just writing beginner-level documentation can be a great service and will earn the gratitude of project leaders, who will no doubt be inclined to be more friendly and helpful.

Beyond that, working on writing actual code for simple productization tasks such as creating code samples or administrative interfaces under the direction of more experienced people can be an excellent way to improve an IT department's skill level.

Contributing features to an open source project not only builds skills and increases understanding, but it also initiates contact with more experienced developers in a project, who might review and evaluate the code. Being a major contributor to an open source project can also enhance the technical reputation of an IT department. Ticketmaster, a heavy user of Perl, has provided significant support for Perl.org, which has had the effect of attracting talented developers to the company.

Nothing will make productization fun, but, like flossing your teeth, there are many important reasons why everyone should do it.

CHAPTER 8

A Comparison of Open Source Licenses

This chapter covers the legal underpinnings of open source software as embodied in the licenses created to protect and extend the aims of the software's creators. From the foundation provided by the GPL that Richard Stallman created for his GNU project, which governs the use and distribution of Linux today, to its predecessors developed by MIT and UC Berkeley, open source licenses have since evolved into more than 50 "flavors" administrated by universities, individuals, and increasingly, corporations including IBM, Apple, and Sun.

How much time an IT department must spend worrying about licenses depends on how open source will be used. For most CIOs and CTOs, who are interested in using open source software only to meet their day-to-day needs, there is little to be concerned about. This group will benefit from this chapter's explanations of licenses as they related to the SCO case, which is discussed in more detail in Chapter 9, as well as discussions of other software debates and policy issues.

For companies that are developing software that includes open source as components, it is critical to understand the aims and restrictions of these licenses. Even upper management should study the principles involved. One license might require sharing any new code created with the open source community, and another might mean handing over that code to a software giant's private developers. The current generation of licenses might also prove to be a model for the terms under which new or formerly proprietary software projects are released as an open source effort.

Many Flavors of Licenses

The casual use of the terms *open source* and *free software* among programmers and in the press has led to a popular, albeit hazy, impression that open source software exists in the public domain, or that the software's creators have otherwise volunteered not to exercise their copyrights (or to file for patents). This misconception is born from another misconception: that open source advocates are anti-capitalist, anti-intellectual property zealots out to destroy the commercial software business. (Actually, only a few of them are.)

The open source movement and community are governed by a broad spectrum of widely used licenses with distinct, strict provisions for the use, modification, and distribution of source code and the "derivative works" compiled from that source code. The OSI lists 54 approved licenses on its web site.

In this chapter, even the phrase *open source* is up for dispute, redefinition, and then hairsplitting by the advocates of competing licenses. Richard Stallman, who in 1984 created for his GNU project the first and still most popular open source license, the GPL, actually hates the term *open source* and demands the use of *free software* instead. This is not a marketing dispute; an avowed "pragmatic idealist," Stallman expressly designed the GPL so that any software that uses it as a license is open to modification, and so that any larger software project that incorporates code issued under the GPL is automatically bound by the GPL. Developers should think carefully before including GPL-protected code in the next version of their software, especially if there is any chance that one day it might become a product. However, if code is protected under a different license—such as BSD and the BSD license—developers can use that open source code as a foundation for proprietary products. (This is exactly what Apple did when it utilized parts of BSD in Mac OS X. It created layers, and kept open source in one layer and put the proprietary parts of the operating system in another. In addition, Sun used BSD Unix as the foundation for its Solaris operating system.)

Understanding the overlap and incompatibilities among different licenses is critical for any developer seeking to harness an open source project or mix-and-match open source code. (The GPL, for example, has a list of conditions that determine whether software bound by a different license is "compatible.") Conversely, the fine print on these licenses often offers a cut-and-paste foundation for a custom license governing the release of formerly proprietary software as an open source project.

The legal scope of the rights, privileges, and protections granted by these licenses has become an extremely contentious subject over the past few years. The first real test was in the lawsuit filed by the former Linux distributor, SCO, against IBM in 2003. SCO claims to have purchased the original rights to the Unix operating system, and that IBM programmers illegally incorporated pieces of copyrighted Unix code into Linux. In effect, SCO claims to own Linux, and is involved in litigation on a number of fronts to reinforce this claim. (We cover the details and future implications of these continuing suits in Chapter 9.)

The rest of this chapter will explore and compare the terms of the most popular open source licenses to date. We will start with the "classic" licenses invented by individuals and universities—the GPL, BSD, and MIT licenses—before moving on to the second and third waves of project-specific licenses (e.g., Perl's Artistic license) and corporate license (such as those of Apple, IBM, and Sun) to emerge in the last decade.

The Classic Licenses

The classic licenses cover a huge swath of open source software. Each has its own personality based on how and why it came into being.

In the Beginning: The GPL

Considered the progenitor of all open source licenses, and still the overwhelming favorite among programmers (85% of all projects, by some estimates), Richard Stallman's GPL underpins Linux and the constellation of software around it—everything from email clients to MySQL to more C++ compilers than you could ever possibly need.

The GPL stems from Stallman's ideological stance that creating "free," as opposed to closed and proprietary, software is the ethical responsibility of programmers and end users. Whether you subscribe to Stallman's belief in the "Free World" does not prevent you from using GPL-protected code or profiting from it, as MySQL and commercial distributors of Linux can attest. Nevertheless, understanding where Stallman is starting from is key to grasping the full implications of his central innovation: Copyleft.

Free, open, and Copylefted

All open source licenses share the principle that anyone should be able to use, copy, and distribute—perhaps with modifications and under the right circumstances—source code and the executable software compiled from it. As you will see in this chapter, proprietary software makers dabbling in open source projects tend to have the most restrictive licenses, and the GPL does the most to ensure that software stays open.

The GPL has one notable restriction, however, and that is the idea of Copyleft. While other licenses, such as BSD's, allow users to build proprietary software on top of open source foundations, Copylefted software does not grant that right. Under the GPL, any software developed from source code licensed under the GPL is also automatically bound by the GPL. The term *viral licensing*, which the Free Software Foundation rejects, was invented to describe the effects of the GPL—new code based on GPL-protected work is "infected" by the terms of the license, with no allowances for the size of the code involved or its relative importance to the derivative work. (When someone uses the words *viral* and *infect* to describe the GPL, it usually means they are hostile to open source.)

The intent was to guarantee that a commercial third party would never modify and productize Copylefted open source code down the road. Use is free, to modify is free, but if you distribute the code or any modifications, you must do so under GPL terms. In some ways, this makes it harder for a programmer to make money with open source, because the software can always be downloaded for free. But it guarantees to the entire user base that all subsequent improvements will be freely available, and it eliminates the possibility of forking due to commercialization.

Mixing Copylefted code with proprietary software or attempting to distribute a closed, proprietary work based on such code is a violation of the GPL that the lawyers of Stallman's Free Software Foundation will enforce. So far, they haven't taken anyone to court, although they do actively search for violations and have become involved in disputes. The abundant amount of community hostility toward those who violate these rules helps with enforcement. Because of the GPL's mindshare among programmers and its widespread use in open source projects, the question of whether a given piece of code is compatible with the GPL is often asked during open source projects. The upcoming discussions of other licenses will indicate whether a license is compatible with the GPL.

That said, end users can modify Copylefted code and can mix it with proprietary systems, provided they keep the resulting code in-house and under wraps. The key here is *distribution*—software developed internally on GPL code to drive business processes is allowed under the GPL. But any form of distribution—not just for sale but also passed along to a partner or shared with a third-party developer—triggers the GPL, forcing the company in question to make the source code available to anyone who asks. Nondisclosure agreements do not technically override the GPL, and those inclined to play fast and loose with the licensing agreement should consider that the discovery of a GPL violation that is also part of a critical piece of software could cripple a business.

For most end users, access to the source code is of theoretical value only because programs are used as they are, and are not modified. When they are modified, the modifications are rarely distributed. The most common form of distribution is to send bug fixes or extensions back to the core development team.

The "Lesser" GPL

A less restrictive version of the GPL also exists for use with code libraries that are used in precompiled binary form and do not require access to source code. When Stallman recognized the fact that programmers might prefer to link certain libraries to the GPL—statically, or using a shared library and proprietary applications simultaneously—he created the Lesser GPL to grant them this right. Applicable only to libraries, the majority of the primary GPL's conditions still stand—the source code of modified libraries must be made freely available, etc.—but the Lesser GPL allows open source applications to fit more snugly into a preexisting product development process.

Using the GPL in Your Own Work

Licensing code under the GPL is almost as simple as cutting and pasting. The Free Software Foundation's web site (*http://www.fsf.org/*) contains a full text version and multiple language translations of the GPL, along with step-by-step instructions for adding copyright notices and other pieces of necessary boilerplate language.

The Free Software Foundation does not recommend using the GPL itself as the template for a homegrown license, as the creation of a new, alternative Copyleft to the GPL's is almost certain to render it incompatible with the GPL itself and all software, including Linux, licensed through it.

The BSD Licenses: FreeBSD, OpenBSD, and NetBSD

First developed in the 1970s, BSD and its contemporary offspring all use variations of an open source license that is short, simple, and generally GPL compatible, yet still allows proprietary products to be built and sold from BSD code without requiring that the source code be given away.

Unlike the GPL, which arose from one person's set of beliefs about software, the motivation behind the original "Berkeley license" had to do with the fact that taxpayer money was used to fund the research at a public university. The Berkeley license was thus designed to make that original work available to all. The three main flavors of BSD today are still licensed under variations of the original license. All of these include:

- A copyright notice

- A disclaimer of warranty

- A brief set of conditions, stating that redistributions of the source code and/or compiled code must contain the following:
  - The copyright notice
  - The disclaimer
  - This list of conditions

And that, generally, is it.

BSD is considered a very permissive license, much more so than the GPL. Its terms allow for the unrestrained borrowing of source code for other software projects or commercialized versions of BSD itself, with no provision for the sharing of source code, modified or not. This has to do with the software's public university origins— because taxpayers had funded the project, it was believed that any U.S. citizen should be allowed to do what they wanted with it.

Apple proudly incorporated code from FreeBSD into Mac OS X via its Darwin open source project (we provide details on the Apple license later in this chapter). Some open source advocates worry that the BSD license is a recipe for the private appropriation of free code written by the volunteers of the various BSD projects. The BSD license is considered to be an historical one at this point, used only by the BSD projects themselves.

The MIT License

Similar to the BSD license, the MIT license, developed originally to cover software including the X Window System for Unix, grants users the right to "use, copy, modify, merge, publish, distribute, sublicense, and/or sell copies of the software," according to its license. As with BSD, a copyright notice, a disclaimer, and the instructions covering both must be reproduced in the code. The MIT license is GPL compatible.

Second-Generation/Single-Project Licenses

The popularization of the Internet and the Web in the mid-1990s was spurred by the creation and release of a number of open source tools and software, particularly the Apache Web Server and the Perl scripting language, that quickly became part of every web developer's arsenal. The project leaders of these programs invented licenses separate from, and not necessarily compatible with, the GPL. While these licenses are generally considered historical and relevant only to the software they were created for, companies interested in using Apache or Perl (or those already using at least one of the two) should note their restrictions and approach to open source licensing.

The Apache License 2.0

The Apache Web Server is one of the best-known and most flexible open source projects in existence. Having begun life as a series of patches to another early open source server, Apache is now widely considered to be superior to many similar commercial offerings. Its use is overseen by the not-for-profit Apache Software Foundation (ASF), which approved a 2.0 version of its license in January 2004.

The Apache license is rooted in the BSD/MIT models. The 2.0 release contains several contemporary additions, including a grant of both a copyright and a patent license to the user by each past "contributor" to Apache's source code. (The patent clause is partly designed to protect Apache from litigation by contributors who might later claim that their own patented code was added to Apache maliciously or by mistake. Including code without having clear rights to it is a key issue in the SCO lawsuit against IBM that we discuss in Chapter 9.)

Otherwise, the requirements are familiar: the inclusion of a copyright notice, a disclaimer, and the license in any object code or source code produced from Apache, with the added condition that any redistributions of modified Apache code must highlight the changes and refrain from using the Apache name. Creating and selling customized versions of Apache is allowed.

Whether the Apache 2.0 license is GPL compatible is currently up for debate. The ASF has asserted that it is, while the Free Software Foundation contests this because of a requirement that Apache documentation must provide an acknowledgment to the ASF, which the Free Software Foundation considers unreasonable. Discussions between the two groups are ongoing.

The Artistic License (Perl)

Developed for the Perl scripting language and used as a model for several open source licenses that followed, the Artistic license vaguely resembles Apache's but has several important differences.

The Artistic license allows for the identical copying and redistribution of source code, contingent on including all relevant copyrights, etc. Changes made to the source code are allowable, assuming the user meets one of the following conditions: he makes these changes public domain; or he uses only modified code within a company or organization or renames modified code so that it does not conflict with the standard version (which must be included in any redistribution).

Some open source advocates consider the Artistic license to be sloppy, and it certainly contains several loopholes that undermine its noncommercial aims. While the license expressly states that users cannot charge a fee for the software package covered, it almost immediately follows this with the caveat that the package can be bundled with other programs and sold as a larger package, with no restrictions on the size or complexity of software it's bundled with. Another loophole allows users (under the right conditions) to make modifications proprietary. Despite these criticisms, the Artistic license is GPL compatible.

Another odd license worth mentioning is Donald Knuth's license for the TEX and METAFONT programs, in which he grants freedom to use his software but not to change it without his permission. He has stated he will fix only serious bugs and that after his death the programs will remain in their most recent state.

Corporate Licenses

The embrace of open source software by such IT companies as IBM, Sun, Apple, Intel, and many others has led to a third generation of licenses issued by corporations rather than individuals or not-for-profit foundations. While the terms of each license vary and typically concern specific projects and source code bases, they have become the second most popular model, after the GPL, for the creation of new licenses, and hence are worthy of study by any organization considering a similar path.

The Netscape Public License (NPL) and Mozilla Public License (MPL)

In 1998, Netscape released the source code for its pioneering Navigator web browser under an open source license. By this time, Navigator had lost significant market share to Microsoft's Internet Explorer in the "Browser Wars," and the decision was widely seen as a last-ditch effort by Netscape to recruit the army of programmers needed to keep pace with Microsoft. Netscape kept the Navigator name for its own commercial browser and released the source code under the name Mozilla, which had until then been an internal reference to the browser. Today, the Mozilla effort is run as a not-for-profit foundation (publishing popular programs such as the Firefox web browser and the Thunderbird email client), and its license, which has undergone several iterations, has proven to be one of the most popular contemporary alternatives to the GPL.

When drafting the original Netscape Public License (NPL), Netscape's executives first considered the classic models—GPL, BSD, and MIT—but elected not to follow them due to concerns about protecting its intellectual property. The NPL granted programmers the right to use, modify, and redistribute source code freely, but it quickly came under fire by the open source community because of provisions that granted Netscape special rights. Netscape programmers would be allowed to borrow contributed code for use in commercial Netscape products, and to relicense this code under more restrictive terms—including the right not to reveal the source code. Netscape said at the time that such terms were necessary because of the company's responsibilities to prior commercial licensees. To placate open source developers, Netscape released the Mozilla Public License (MPL), which removed these special privileges and is still in use today.

The MPL resembles the GPL in that modifications to MPL-covered source code must be made freely available to the development community. However, the MPL differs in one very important way: larger pieces of software that incorporate Mozilla code are not required to have their source code made available. Unlike the viral GPL—which infects larger pieces of software with its license if GPL-covered code is used—the MPL allows developers to use Mozilla code for the creation and distribution of "larger work" (in MPL terminology) that can be sold commercially and without the source code. In a qualifying software framework, MPL-protected code would run separately from proprietary code, which would interact with the open source portions through a defined API. The user can then patent these larger works.

The main advantage of the MPL, then, is that it creates an incentive for corporate and third-party developers to improve the open source code base while protecting intellectual property. The possible drawback for end users is a scenario in which competitors make substantial functional upgrades proprietary, leading to competing versions and less overall development of the code base. The MPL is not GPL compatible on its own, although the Mozilla Foundation has started an effort to relicense all Mozilla code under a triple license with the GPL and LGPL, thus granting developers the option to incorporate pieces of Mozilla code separately into GPL-covered projects.

The Sun Industry Standards Source License (SISSL)

Similar to the MPL, the Sun Industry Standards Source License (SISSL) is one of several open source licenses Sun has developed for specific projects. (Sun developed one such Sun license, the Sun Community Source License, to cover Java, and due to several restrictions, it is not recognized as open source at all.)

As they can under the MPL, under SISSL developers can modify and distribute source code freely or integrate the source code into larger, commercial projects without divulging the modified code. To reduce the risk of proprietary forking inherent in the MPL, SISSL adds the stipulation that developers who choose to license their larger work in a proprietary manner must declare their deviation from the source code through a public description as well as through a public reference implementation of those deviations. SISSL is not GPL compatible.

The Apple Public Source License (APSL)

Also similar to the MPL, the Apple Public Source License (APSL), which Apple developed for its Darwin OS initiative and since has applied to its Rendezvous networking technology and other projects, protects source code modifications while allowing its use in larger, commercial works. Users can distribute unmodified code freely, but are required to include a notice, along with the usual copyrights and disclaimers, with modified code. As with the MPL, with the APSL users can incorporate source code into larger works and then distribute it under another license. The Apple license, however, does not grant patent rights that Apple retains. Although it grants rights to use the software, it is possible for Apple one day to require a license to one of its patents. The APSL is incompatible with the GPL.

The IBM/Eclipse Public License (EPL)

Advocates hailed as an open source victory IBM's decision to release the source code of its Eclipse development environment. IBM created the Eclipse Public License (EPL) to spur open source programmers to contribute to the project, while protecting IBM's private consulting relationships and intellectual property. The EPL provides for a strong Copylefting of source code and a grant of patent licenses for any patents covering the software, but contains an exception for the distribution of object code.

Developers who choose to distribute only modified object code can distribute it under any license they want, commercial or otherwise, although IBM's disclaimers must still appear and the end user must receive a copy of the source code, even if the larger community does not. The client can also be restricted from distributing the source code (a no-no under the GPL). The result is that developers can use the EPL to create custom software solutions for clients without surrendering the source code to the larger community (and thus competitors). Naturally, this license is incompatible with the GPL.

The Lucent Public License (Plan 9)

When Lucent Technologies released its Plan 9 operating system as an open source project several years ago, many open source developers pointed to the accompanying license as an example of an overly restrictive open source license. Among their complaints: the requirement that the original contributor, Lucent, reserved the right to ask any contributor for copies of any source code and object code modifications, effectively barring the private use of modified source code. The license also reserves the right for any contributor to relicense the modifications of any other contributor, a clause that raised eyebrows among open source developers. Plan 9 is not GPL compatible.

Other Corporate Licenses

As more corporations weigh the pros and cons of open source projects and tailor licensing agreements to reflect their interests, the number of corporations offering open source licenses continues to climb. The ones we outlined in this chapter are perhaps the most notable, but open source licenses are also offered from the likes of Intel, Nokia, RealNetworks, and Sybase. Many companies, such as Sun, are also developing different licenses tailored to each project. As of this printing, Sun has publicly vowed to make its very proprietary Solaris operating system open source, but has yet to choose or design a license to govern its use.

Why Pick Just One? The Dual Licensing Option

In an attempt to reconcile the competing interests of open source developers devoted to the freedoms of the GPL and putting corporate customers at ease, several sellers of open source software have adopted a dual licensing approach. Simply put, they offer their user base the option of choosing either a GPL option—for those who want to modify and support their own versions of the software—or a more conventional commercial license to allow its inclusion in a larger, proprietary software package.

So far, the open source database makers MySQL and Sleepycat, and the programming component maker Trolltech, have used this strategy successfully. In all three cases, each company controls all the copyrights to the work being distributed. Companies that are considering releasing proprietary software as an open source project should study this option, although it comes with the potential headache of having to manage licensees and potential conflicts with the GPL carefully.

CHAPTER 9

Open Source Under Attack

One of the clearest indications that open source is gaining traction and gathering allies in the IT marketplace is the steadily rising resistance being mounted by some commercial software vendors, and the vicious attacks being mounted by others. To offset the attraction of the open source model, its growing number of enemies is seeking to sow fear, uncertainty, and doubt (a.k.a. FUD) among its potential customers, a classic Silicon Valley strategy deployed whenever a company's market share begins to look shaky.

The question IT departments must ask themselves is whether they should believe any of this FUD. In this chapter, we will discuss the current wave of FUD against open source, created by the SCO Group's 2003 lawsuit against IBM and its aftermath, and we will try to anticipate what future attacks might look like. It appears that the current FUD has, by and large, failed to bully companies into avoiding open source—SCO's case isn't considered a particularly sound one, and it likely is not a threat to open source users or allies such as IBM. However, there is no doubt that since open source software can create billions of dollars in value and can change the competitive landscape of Silicon Valley FUD is here to stay.

SCO Versus IBM and the Legal Quandary of Open Source

We will start with the big picture of the SCO dispute, and in later sections, we will explore the details and implications. Until two years ago, CIOs and CTOs could be forgiven for never having heard of the SCO Group, an amalgam of two not particularly successful companies. SCO (rhymes with *snow*) was formed through a 2002 merger of the Santa Cruz Operation, a small company that had bought from Novell a number of the original patents to Unix, and the commercial Linux reseller, Caldera. SCO was thought of as an also-ran in the open source community, when it was thought of at all.

That changed in March 2003, when SCO dropped a bombshell. Thanks to the Santa Cruz Operation's copyrights and patents, SCO believed it now owned the patents and intellectual property rights to Unix. In addition, those rights were being infringed upon by IBM software engineers, who were deliberately adding chunks of that company's proprietary Unix flavor, AIX, to the open source code base of Linux. SCO promptly sued IBM for $1 billion. Two months later, SCO announced it had discovered more code inside Linux—independent of whatever it is IBM is alleged to have added—which also infringed on its rights. SCO sent a letter to every Fortune 1,000 company, serving notice that SCO was owed a licensing fee for every processor running Linux that was used or sold.

SCO and IBM's original dispute has descended into a morass of litigation and allegations. Evidence then came to light that Microsoft had brokered venture capital investment in SCO so that the company could pay its legal bills, now in the tens of millions of dollars. This prompted open source advocates to wonder aloud whether SCO is the software giant's puppet and whether Microsoft will try to litigate the open source movement to death. Others, such as Sun, are looking to profit from the confusion by playing both sides against each other and preying on corporate users' fears.

Against this backdrop of FUD, many corporations are wondering whether SCO's claims are real, and whether they should go forward with their open source implementations. For example, the city government of Munich—which had announced it would switch its 16,000 PCs from Windows to Linux in a big PR win for open source—has publicly gone back and forth about whether to continue because of patent fears. (Munich's mayor has vowed it will continue.)

While open source advocates are confident they will prevail and legal scholars are not convinced that SCO has a case, the current crisis has turned a spotlight on both the legal issues of open source software and the movement's enemies, who are studying, with varying degrees of openness, how best to exploit these issues. What, if anything, is the threat from SCO? What will future attacks on open source look like? Are any of these threats real, or are they just a nuisance? And if a Microsoft FUD campaign really is behind it all, does that mean open source has truly come of age?

FUD or no FUD, using any software, commercial or open source, involves risk. Copyrights and patents can be unknowingly violated and aggrieved parties can sue. There is no foolproof blanket indemnity that protects a company in all situations. The important task for IT departments it to identify and evaluate real risks and take appropriate steps to manage them. Knowing the details of the disputes that we provide in the rest of this chapter is a good starting point for forming your own opinion.

What You Need to Know About SCO

The story of this dispute begins at Novell, which initially turned its nose up at open source as a business model. This decision triggered a series of events that led to the current situation.

A Brief History of SCO

SCO's origins lie in a secret project developed at Novell in the early 1990s—one that could have been a pioneering commercialized form of Linux. However, Novell scrapped the project, and the core members left to start Caldera, which rode the Linux wave of the late '90s to an IPO and crashed, along with the rest of the sector, shortly thereafter.

Meanwhile, Novell bought the original Unix patents and all accompanying rights from AT&T in 1993. After a management shake-up, it decided to flip those assets to the Santa Cruz Operation, signing a contract in 1995 that handed some, and then allegedly all, of the patents to that company. Caldera bought them, along with the company's name, in 2001, and became the SCO Group a year later.

The renamed company had a management change of its own in 2002. Darl McBride, a Novell veteran and serial entrepreneur, took over as CEO and began revamping the business plan. According to press reports, McBride had developed and honed a business model at one of his prior companies that was built on constant patenting and licensing. Instead of making software products, his company focused on accumulating patents through research, which it then used to hit up companies with competing technologies for a licensing fee. In exchange for the fee, McBride and company promised not to make any legal trouble for the licensee. In Silicon Valley, such exchanges are written off as an occasional cost of doing business.

Whatever the idea's origins, McBride decided to take this path with SCO. In January 2003, he set up a new division, SCOsource, in charge of administering and enforcing licenses of SCO's Unix patents. The company hired David Boies (a lawyer who had successfully led the government's antitrust case against Microsoft) to be its brand-name enforcer. He did his job: in May 2003, SCO sued IBM, claiming patent infringement, for $1 billion.

2003: SCO Versus IBM

SCO claimed IBM engineers had willfully copied swaths of code from AIX (IBM's in-house Unix flavor) into Linux as part of the company's initiative to upgrade Linux for use in its various enterprise software projects. SCO claimed that IBM had violated the licensing agreement for AIX that it had originally signed with AT&T and that SCO now owned. SCO also refused to make the majority of the allegedly copycat code public, sparking a war of words with open source advocates already disinclined to believe SCO's claims. But Microsoft and Sun were quick to comply, signing licensing agreements and purchasing stock warrants in SCO for more than $25 million, causing many in that community to wonder if the two companies were willing to use SCO as a stalking horse against open source.

Two months later, SCO claimed to have found more Unix code floating inside of Linux, and sent a letter to every Fortune 1000 and Fortune Global 500 company, effectively stating that it owned Linux and asking for a $699 licensing fee for every processor in every product running Linux inside each company. Few companies complied: the SCO division reported just $11,000 in revenues during the second quarter of 2004, a clear sign that everyone other than Microsoft and Sun was willing to wait and see if SCO was bluffing.

At the end of May 2004, Novell spoke up, claiming that SCO had no legal foundation on which to sue IBM, as it still owned the copyrights and patents SCO needed to make its case. It had sold some patents to the Santa Cruz Operation in 1995, but perhaps not the relevant ones. SCO sued Novell while legal scholars pored over the original contract and pronounced it impenetrable, with no clear-cut terms about ownership. Before SCO versus IBM could be properly resolved, this point had to be litigated first.

Meanwhile, open source activists, such as the members of the OSI and its president, the evangelist Eric Raymond, tore into SCO's claims. A paper that Raymond and the OSI published in June 2003 (see *http://www.opensource.org/sco-vs-ibm.html*) neatly dissected many of SCO's claims, including the following:

SCO's assertion that Linux was not a scalable, robust operating system able to compete with Unix until IBM (allegedly) dumped AIX code into it
> Not true, Raymond said. None of the five core abilities Linux needs for enterprise-strength computing (symmetric multiprocessing, journaling filesystems, logical volume management, nonuniform memory access, and hot swapping) can be traced to historical Unix code through IBM.

SCO's protests that IBM had infringed on proprietary code
> SCO, in its previous life as the Linux vendor Caldera, Raymond claimed, had actually released large portions of the code in question under the GPL!

While many Linux contributors have volunteered to rip the supposedly infringing code from the Linux kernel and replace it with clean code, SCO has steadfastly refused to release the bulk of the source code in dispute.

In August 2003, SCO produced a very small sample of this code in court. It was quickly leaked to open source web sites, where Raymond, among many others, dissected SCO's arguments again.

In Raymond's analysis (*http://www.catb.org/~esr/writings/smoking-fizzle.html*), the majority of the code reproduced was released as open source by SCO in 2002; didn't come through IBM; is not present in 90% of all Linux distributions in use; and was actually removed from the Linux kernel in July 2003 as an example of inefficient code.

He did concede that SCO could plausibly claim that its code had been copied, and that the terms of the GPL had been violated by whoever had done it. But the actual risk to IBM, and especially the open source community at large, seemed minute.

The Microsoft Connection

SCO was not about to back down. With its licensing efforts failing to gain traction, SCO sued two Linux end users—DaimlerChrylser and AutoZone—in March 2004, thus serving notice that it could be coming for your business next. Its legal bills had continued to mount, however.

But SCO had no trouble raising a war chest. The company had more than $25 million from Microsoft and Sun in the bank, and its stock rose from $1.09 in mid-February 2003 to $20.50 by October, when the venture firm BayStar Capital invested $50 million in the company.

Six months later, evidence became known that Microsoft had played matchmaker, and a BayStar principal openly admitted as much. A SCO internal memo, which fell into open source advocates' hands (*http://www.opensource.org/halloween/halloween10.html*), suggested that Microsoft had helped line up between $66 million and $106 million in financing for the company. Not everyone Microsoft matched up with SCO was happy with the end result (BayStar has since demanded its money back), but there appeared to be clear evidence that Microsoft was ready and willing to keep the company's lawsuit—and its ability to sow FUD—aloft for the foreseeable future.

What It All Means: The Implications of the SCO Crisis

The SCO lawsuits will likely drag on for years, and might even be succeeded by similar suits (discussed shortly). It highlights the flaws in the open source development model, which is what opened the door to litigation (and FUD) in the first place.

The SCO suits have exposed the myth that open source software, and Linux in particular, is immune from questions of authorship and ownership. Haters of Microsoft and Windows have been able to point to the open source model as the one alternative the software giant can't defeat in the marketplace, or purchase once it has lost. In this line of thinking, open source software is ownerless, thanks to the GPL.

From a legal standpoint, the copyright precedents for Linux and most open source projects are not as clear as its advocates might like. From a copyright perspective, it is not entirely clear whether it is a work of "joint authorship," a "compilation," or an endless series of "derivative works" that expands again when someone new tweaks the code. When Richard Stallman drafted the GPL in 1984, he tried to be very careful in basing his Copyleft model on contemporary copyright law, and his successors have been even more scrupulous. However, the GPL and its descendents have not been tested in the courts, meaning there is little precedent for how the SCO suit might play out.

The legal counsel for Stallman's Free Software Foundation has a simple explanation for this—there is a lack of precedence because the GPL works. No one has seriously tried to challenge it. "The GPL has succeeded for the last decade, while I have been tending it, because it worked, not because it failed or was in doubt," Free Software Foundation counsel, Eben Moglen, said in a speech at Harvard University in February 2004 (*http://www.gnu.org/philosophy/moglen-harvard-speech-2004.html*).

SCO's original assertion was that IBM had not only violated the GPL (by contributing code to Linux for which it did not own the copyrights), but also had done so by violating the terms of its original licensing agreement with AT&T (an agreement now owned by SCO) to create the AIX flavor of Unix.

Anyone seriously spooked by SCO's claims should pay careful attention to that last sentence, and to this next point. SCO, as it turns out, is not asserting that IBM had added code to Linux which SCO happened to own. SCO claims that IBM engineers added code they had written themselves for AIX, an alleged move that violated SCO's rights. This is considered a very aggressive interpretation of its licensing deal with IBM. Furthermore, it means SCO cannot claim that IBM copied code verbatim from SCO, but merely borrowed the "structure, sequence, and/or organization" of Unix code for its contributions to Unix. The Linux code SCO is fighting over merely resembles the code it happens to own; it isn't a perfect copy. The last time the U.S. Supreme Court wrestled with a similar case, it ended in a 4–4 draw.

What's the upshot for open source users? Despite SCO's attempts to bully companies with its $699 licensing fee demand, its case against IBM is tenuous at the very best and isn't really relevant. (Of course, if SCO loses its dispute with Novell, it doesn't even have a case, but that's another story.) IBM's engineers assumed they were in the right, whether they recycled AIX code into Linux or not. Maybe they were, maybe they weren't. IBM will have to pay the costs of litigation, but Linux and the GPL themselves are hardly fatally flawed.

That said, the GPL is not and never has been a defense against the kind of intellectual property violations that SCO has alleged. Of course, no commercial license is, even ones that offer indemnification. But the weakness SCO has exposed will be sure to dog the open source movement for years to come, as lawsuits and their accompanying FUD will continue to focus on the idea, and difficulty in proving otherwise, that other people's copyrighted code is floating around inside of Linux.

Richard Stallman did anticipate this problem when he wrote the GPL, which is why his GNU project demanded that would-be contributors hand over proof that they were the copyright holders of their own submissions, and that they formally hand over the rights to the Free Software Foundation.

This approach created a legally sound foundation for the GNU project, but very likely inhibited its growth. When Linus Torvalds solicited contributions to his Linux kernel, he adopted the GPL but failed to put a similar copyright enforcement mechanism in place, leaving Linux open to exactly the kind of claims SCO has made. The flip side is that Linux might never have reached its tipping point among developers if it had made onerous demands similar to Stallman's.

However, Torvalds' unwillingness means that thousands of contributions to the Linux kernel (or any other open source application) are now a potential Trojan horse of litigation. The possibility that unethical developers dumped proprietary source code into Linux—code copyrighted by their employers, perhaps, or else pirated—leaves the door open to potentially hundreds of lawsuits by developers claiming that their proprietary code was added to Linux without permission by someone else. And then all Linux users would be served notice to pay a licensing fee. Commercial software has the same potential problem as well, or it did until legal precedent was established, thus curtailing future suits. Conceivably, a similar precedent will be applied to open source in the wake of the SCO lawsuit, or one of its successors.

Open source advocates have vowed repeatedly to rip out and rewrite from scratch the code allegedly stolen from SCO, provided SCO pointed to the code in question. Their vow, along with Raymond's assertion that at least one piece of offending code has already been flushed from the Linux kernel, speaks to one of open source's greatest strengths: the ability to easily locate, replace, and improve failed code. Whether that code suffered legal failure or runtime failure is almost beside the point.

The glimmer of a future campaign might have been revealed by Steve Ballmer, Microsoft's CEO, in a November 2004 speech at Microsoft's Asian Government Leaders Forum. In the speech, he claimed that, based on a report by the consultancy Open Source Risk Management, Linux infringes on 283 patents. The authors of the report said Ballmer "misconstrued" their research, which indicated that Linux might "potentially" infringe on 283 patents. The authors of the report also pointed out that there is no reason to think that commercial operating systems have any less risk of infringement than Linux, and that while many commercial software makers have been sued for infringement, not one open source or free software project has ever been sued for infringing a patent.

More FUD, Dead Ahead?

If, and when, SCO's claims against IBM and Linux in general are repelled by the courts, the question becomes who will step up and take SCO's place. Whether their chances in court would be better than SCO's is beside the point. What it does create is the specter of an endless series of lawsuits—some frivolous, perhaps, and some not—against open source leaders, consuming millions of dollars in legal fees and spooking potential customers for years to come. Or at least that's the fear component of this particular piece of FUD. The reality is that, so far, there has been little cost for those who have embraced open source. While the flag bearers of the movement battle SCO, only DaimlerChrylser and AutoZone have been targeted among all other end users. SCO's threatening letters to the Fortune 1000 otherwise came to nothing.

Still, who would like to see this happen? Certainly any proponent of old-fashioned proprietary software. So, how about Microsoft?

The company's shadowy relationship with SCO has raised the fear in the open source community that Microsoft is actively recruiting stalking horses to sue the open source movement into submission. The SCO consultant who claims to have brokered the relationship between the two companies has since said publicly that he believes Microsoft "may have 50 or more of these lawsuits in the queue" (*http://www.newsforge.com/trends/04/03/12/1731252.shtml*).

Microsoft knows better than any company how quickly a competitive landscape can shift while the legal system hums along slowly behind it. Netscape management might have been proven right when Microsoft was later found guilty of antitrust violations, but by that time, Netscape had been swallowed by AOL, and it wasn't given back its former market share.

Indemnification: Could Sun Be a Safe Harbor with Open Source Solaris?

Anticipating this possible future, Hewlett-Packard, Novell, and other open source-friendly organizations have begun offering "indemnification" to open source customers (although, as with commercial licenses, their legal protection goes only so far, and it often isn't far at all). Often, the warranty is voided if the user modifies the software—a move that limits the value of the indemnification for the small group who actually change Linux—and others are only SCO specific. A handful of start-ups hope to offer what amounts to insurance policies against being sued.

Even more curious is Sun's role in all of this. After paying more than $10 million to SCO for an all-encompassing license (and some warrants to purchase stock), Sun is fully indemnified against SCO's claims. Therefore, the company's announcement that it soon will make Solaris open source creates the possibility that Sun might be able to offer the only legally safe version of Linux on the market. To do that, Sun won't be able to offer customers code under the GPL—SCO has already indicated it will not allow this, and Sun has historically been conservative with its own open source projects. But an open source Solaris would offer a safe middle ground for corporations hoping to use open source without needing special counsel on call 24/7.

Is the tradeoff between security and freedom—the freedom to modify and share code, or reap the benefits of others' work—really worth all the fuss? The answer to that depends, of course, on the needs, objective, and risk tolerance of the end user asking the question. Having to endure the saber rattling of SCO's successors down the road might become part of the open source equation for a lower TCO.

Patents: A Growing Concern

An area of emerging concern for software of all sorts is the explosion of patents that have been issued in the last 10 years. Patents, which in the U.S. protect an idea for 20 years from the date of filing, represent a threat different from copyright infringement. It is possible to violate a patent without knowing you are doing so. This is possible with copyright infringement, but only if there is a chain of copying from the source to you. But with a patent, an idea or technique is protected regardless of how you came upon the idea.

Various investor groups have formed to buy patents and then use them to pursue licensing deals. There have been some notable successes by firms pursuing this model, who have been able to force license fees after patents were upheld in court.

An unscrupulous technique called the *submarine patent* is also sometimes pursued. In this technique, someone files a patent for a device and then delays filing the details, while watching the market develop. The goal is to patent techniques that become crucial to an emerging technology.

It is possible that patents could be a threat to open source, but if so, they would be no less a threat to commercial source. Patent protection could be selectively pursued against open source, but this would likely bring the same players to the battlefield as are currently waging war in the SCO suits.

In the European Union, the future of patent protection for software is still being worked out, which has led some players to wait on the sidelines.

Worst-Case Scenarios

The potential risks in open source lawsuits are not easy to calculate. For example, what if SCO writes you a letter asking for a license fee. You could pay the $699 for each Linux installation you have. That's one way of calculating the size of the risk of using Linux. Another approach is to ignore the letter and wait for a lawsuit. Yet another is to try to get help from IBM or Sun. An organization called Open Source Risk Management offers indemnification against the risk of open source lawsuits for those who want to limit liability before the fact.

Nobody can say that for certain the risks are always small, even though they appear that way. Just as commercial software comes with risk, so does developing your own software. Anytime almost anything is created, it might infringe on a patent. To use any software involves risks of many different kinds. The question is whether the risks are acceptable. For millions of people around the world, the answer seems to be yes, despite a considerable amount of bullying and dissemination of FUD intended to make them think otherwise.

CHAPTER 10

Open Source Empowerment

For those of us who toil in IT, the puzzle that open source represents really is just a new version of the choice to build or to buy. Open source offers a "middle" way, a way to acquire technology that is almost built, without having to buy.

However, choosing to use open source changes a company that takes up the challenge, which is perhaps its biggest reward. Building the skill to handle open source empowers a company to save money, attract more talented employees, gain more leverage when negotiating with vendors, and, most of all, better meet the needs of a business. This final chapter will take a look at important issues that will arise in choosing to use open source, and the way an IT department will be transformed once that choice is made.

One of the strongest objections voiced regarding the use of open source in the enterprise is the lack of "one throat to choke." This concept refers to the accountability that commercial vendors have for solving problems with their products. IT departments get a feeling of comfort from knowing that if anything goes wrong with a commercial product, they can always call up the vendor and get some sort of assistance, or at least have someone to yell at. Oh, and let's not forget, having someone to blame. Commercial open source support companies think they will be successful because they will become the "one throat to choke" for open source.

Examined closely, one throat to choke is a pathetic form of recourse for an IT executive. It is like a salesperson hiring a sales consultant to have someone to blame in case he does not make his quota. Nobody managing a sales staff would ever stand for this.

IT executives should know the products they rely on, what they do well, and what they do poorly. When problems arise, they should have contingency plans and failovers in place that provides adequate time for problem solving. Needing one throat to choke means an IT executive is not doing his job of understanding requirements, making appropriate choices, and designing robust systems. IT departments that use vendor software in the way that it is intended do not need one throat to choke.

To be the sort of IT executive that does not need one throat to choke you have to be confident that you understand the products you are choosing, and that you understand your needs. From such a perspective, open source is much less scary.

If an IT executive or anyone else claims that open source is not viable because they want one throat to choke, perhaps the response should be "Why are we planning on having any throats to choke?"

Two Poles of IT: Buy Versus Build

The argument against one throat to choke is not an argument against using commercial software. Rather, it is an argument against using commercial software as an improper crutch to avoid obtaining an adequate level of competence and a robust design for IT infrastructure.

The choice that the manager of every IT department must make, and the choice that presents itself repeatedly in different contexts, is how much to buy and how much to build. There is no right answer in general; everything depends on understanding the requirements, the technology being considered, the department's skills, and the availability of time and money.

In practice, what happens is that the executive in charge of making these choices has to consider for each system whether he prefers to be a manager of resources (a bias toward buying a commercial solution), or whether he prefers to construct a solution on his own (a bias toward building with open source).

In fact, this is usually a false tradeoff. Commercial software is not all buy, and open source is not all build. In any project, commercial software must be extended and customized, which amounts to building. And open source software has lots of functionality that provides a running start.

One frequent mistake when choosing to buy is thinking that the simple act of buying solves a problem. Almost every purchased solution comes with a requirements gap between what the software does out of the box and what it should do at a particular company. In most cases, for a system of any size or importance, a significant amount of work will be involved to configure or customize that solution to solve that company's problem.

Open source projects don't have to be bought, but they don't have to be built from scratch either. This book has stated clearly that certain skills are involved in using open source. However, depending on the problem being solved, if an open source project is sufficiently productized, it might not require any more work than a commercial product.

There is no easy way out, and the art of IT is making this decision properly in each new context. All the companies that are famous for innovative use of open source are heavy users of commercial products. (Linus Torvalds himself caused a stir when he chose a commercial source-code management system for the Linux project. Why? Because it solved a well-understood problem better than open source alternatives did.) It rarely makes sense to be all buy or all build, yet when some IT executives argue against open source, they are essentially arguing that buy is always the right choice.

Making this tradeoff is an art and is one of the most important services that IT managers provide to their companies. There are two parts to it: deciding when to consider building and understanding how much work is involved.

Where to Buy, Where to Build

The best IT departments have a clear philosophy about when to buy and when to build. Some companies, such as General Motors, are very buy-leaning, and they have decided to focus on creating an IT department that knows how to buy. All IT at General Motors is outsourced. Some companies, such as Ernie Ball, the guitar-string maker, have foresworn use of commercial software. This doesn't mean they have created all the software they used from scratch, but it does mean they have taken on more responsibility for themselves to build and maintain skills. In aggressively adopting open source, Ernie Ball has become more build-leaning.

In Chapter 5, which discussed how to create an open source strategy, we introduced the idea of stable, flexible, and dynamic systems. The suggestion is that stable systems change infrequently, flexible systems change every one or two years, and dynamic systems change all the time.

The question of where to be more buy-leaning or build-leaning depends most heavily on the role that IT plays in a business. Is IT's role to provide and support a collection of stable systems, or is IT charged with delivering systems that provide a competitive advantage? The more that IT's mission involves stable systems, the more buy-leaning it will be, although much open source is maturing rapidly enough to be a plausible alternative for buy-leaning departments that have beginner or intermediate skill levels.

When an IT department is delivering systems to provide a competitive advantage, it is generally far more build-leaning. This might not be true everywhere inside the organization as much as in the area that counts most to the company. Systems that provide some sort of edge in the marketplace are generally more customized and dynamic. The more inexpensively such an application can be maintained and the faster it can be evolved, the better for the company.

These assertions raise important questions about an IT department's identity. Competent and skilled departments are comfortable making decisions about being buy-leaning or build-leaning, because they know exactly who they are as a department and what they are doing for the company.

Closing the Requirements Gap

Closing the requirements gap—that is, the gap between the software's out-of-the-box features and your particular needs—is always a major challenge for IT departments. It does not matter if a company is using commercial products or open source projects, or if it is developing from the ground up. The gap still must be closed. The difference between the options resides in the nature of the software, how well it is designed for configuration and adaptation, how much skill is required, and how much help is available.

There are three parts to this equation: requirements, software, and skills. Commercial software succeeds for the most part when an IT department's requirements fall squarely within the scope of the problems the software solves. The ideal, one that mature commercial software reaches frequently, is that a small amount of configuration makes the software work exactly as desired. That is probably why Linus Torvalds was happy to choose the commercial source-code management system. He knew what he needed from it and he knew his needs were not likely to change, so he didn't care that the software was commercial, as long as it did the job.

The risk with commercial software comes when new requirements appear that might be outside the original scope. This doesn't happen much with stable systems, which can be thought of as commodities. But for flexible and dynamic systems, requirements change all the time. If configuration cannot make the software work in a fashion that meets the company's needs, customization might be required. Sometimes commercial software cannot be extended in the desired manner.

With open source, every degree of customization is theoretically possible. The risk with open source projects is that an IT department might lack the skills and the development capacity to tailor the project to meet the requirements and then support the customization going forward.

Neither path is easy, but taking the commercial path leaves you beholden to a vendor that is seeking to maximize revenue, and using open source means you are in control and are responsible for your own destiny.

Open Source Empowerment

Building an IT department with the power to envision solutions, evaluate options, and lead evolutionary implementation is the best investment a company can make if IT is a strategic factor. The more an IT department is supporting stable systems, the more buy-leaning it should be, and the more IT becomes a commodity. The more strategic value that IT brings, the more likely it is that flexible and dynamic systems must be supported, and the more build-leaning a department should be. The more build-leaning a company is, the more it must take responsibility for its own destiny and create and maintain skills for requirements gathering, architectural design, and development.

Open source transforms companies, because it prepares them to be more build-leaning. As use of open source increases, IT departments take more responsibility as architects and creators of the solutions their companies need. (Doc Searles has an approach called "Do It Yourself IT" in which he recommends becoming more build-leaning.) To become more build-leaning, an IT department must develop a central architectural brain for crafting initial requirements, selecting from all the options available for implementation, and then leading the evolution of a better solution.

Creating a well-oiled IT department is difficult, whether a department is buy-leaning or build-leaning. If an IT department is buy-leaning, it had better have a brilliant understanding of requirements so that it does not find itself locked into inflexible solutions that do not meet the company's needs. If an IT department is build-leaning, it had better have rock-solid education and documentation practices to protect the department from key-person risk. Most successful IT departments combine elements of these two paths.

The best IT organizations are confident technology evaluators and component integrators. They have the skills to experiment and bring in partners to perform focused tasks. They do not ask anyone to solve their problems for them. They do not need one throat to choke. They have the creativity and drive of open source and the operational discipline and focus on process of traditional IT.

The more skills that an organization develops, the more open source will be a viable part of the solution. As we pointed out earlier in the book, using open source exclusively is probably appropriate only in extreme cases. Vendors will always be part of the picture of a healthy IT infrastructure, but the IT department must call the shots.

This book recommends that IT departments should become more build-leaning through open source adoption. First, in the right circumstances open source can lead to significant cost savings immediately. However, the following reasons apply as well:

- Acquiring and maintaining beginner- and intermediate-level skills allows for the use of open source of all maturities.

- Having open source skills in-house opens the door to using the most mature and productized open source to support stable systems, perhaps replacing commercial alternatives and saving money.

- For flexible and dynamic systems, using open source as the foundation for these applications and investing in skill building creates a stronger department rather than a richer vendor that is ever more deeply locked in.

- Highly skilled IT departments attract better-quality staff members, because talented technical people like being in a creative environment, surrounded by people from whom they can learn.

- Expanding the use of open source reduces vendor lock-in and increases available choices to solve problems.

Now, let's examine the implications of becoming more build-leaning through open source adoption.

Creating a Learning Culture

A build-leaning IT department is a learning organization in many ways and must be set up so that learning by the staff is a fundamental value and learning from experience is an ongoing process.

Learning by the staff is vital to institutionalize skills and create a culture of creativity and empowerment. Keeping skills alive and spreading them around happens only when knowledge is shared and people put their skills to work. To institutionalize skills, an IT department should take most of the following steps:

- Encourage ongoing education
- Allow ideas to bubble up from the staff
- Encourage people to download and test software
- Encourage people to contribute to free software
- Maintain open communication channels with the community
- Encourage staff to think of themselves first as members of a professional community, not as members of the IT department

The more that these characteristics are embraced, the more an IT department will become a dynamic force in its company. Why? Because the minds of the IT staff will be fully turned on. They will be engaged emotionally and intellectually in their work.

Of course, this focus on learning has to be governed by the department's needs. IT departments are not pure research institutions. They are also not no-research institutions. It is up to the department's leadership to find the right balance.

Learning as a process in a buy-leaning IT department is focused on getting a clear understanding of business requirements.

Often, IT departments are far too confident that their requirements are correct, and they find out only after implementation that they were terribly wrong and that the system doesn't help its users. Even after an IT department realizes it won't get it right the first time, there might be no time or money left for an evolutionary process to create a complete solution.

Another common problem is that the business organization frequently is not prepared to play the required role in evolution and, instead, expects a perfect solution on day one. Sometimes technologists in the company oversell what the solution can do and underestimate the work involved. Vendors consciously or subconsciously go along with all of this.

Unfortunately, the past 40 years of software development have determined that predicting requirements is a losing proposition. The waterfall development methodology based on studying requirements beforehand and building a system to meet them has been thoroughly criticized. The message of Agile development methodologies such as the Rational Unified Process, eXtreme Programming, SCRUM, and others is that it is best to take a humble view of one's ability to predict requirements, and instead to develop the skills to build software and rapidly evolve it. Iterative development works, because nobody is asked to construct a long-term prediction of what requirements will be and then stick to it. Instead, a short-term prediction is made, and then modified based on experience using the software.

In a build-leaning IT department focused on open source, the process of creating a solution for the business is always an iterative one. A department focused on learning from experience cuts the scope and spends much less money on the first version of the solution, knowing that the most important task is to get the application in users' hands so that learning can begin. Build-leaning departments allocate much more of the budget to resources for evolution than traditional IT.

Engineering Practices

This model of doing more development for yourself falls apart completely if the open source being deployed is not matched with strong engineering practices so that future generations of engineers in the department can understand and maintain it. Business executives responsible for IT would no doubt be frightened by the prospect of technologists creating custom-built applications and integrations that might easily become unsupportable. When this happens, if the developer who understands it leaves, that's when the systems integrators and vendors have to ride to the rescue.

What are strong engineering practices? All the things departments know they ought to do, but don't:

- Use source code management rigorously
- Build scripts that start by checking source code out from the authoritative repository, and then build the executable
- Deploy scripts to move versions in and out of production
- Maintain documentation at appropriate levels
- Rotate staff so that many people gain experience and skill with all of a department's key applications
- Conduct rigorous testing and quality assurance
- Conduct bug and issue tracking for technical support, and ongoing requirements engineering
- Properly separate development and operation control of production systems

In facing these issues, an IT department becomes ready to support its role as a development organization. Consciously or subconsciously cutting corners on engineering practices is a surefire path to an open source quagmire.

Building a Better Staff

Open source is not all peaches and cream. In the place of vendor lock-in, IT departments depend on maintaining a broader set of skills and more development capacity than most IT departments are used to. Pretending this is easy is a huge mistake. Finding the right people requires focused effort. One of the reasons that keeping technical skills in-house has such a bad reputation is that IT departments so frequently fail, and then systems integrators and vendors have to bail them out.

Open source skills are only part of the successful build-leaning IT department, however. The goal is to build an IT staff that is capable of understanding business requirements from top to bottom, and also can understand the available solutions in great detail. The best IT department has a strong understanding of business management and of those jobs focused on gathering requirements. This business requirements braintrust works closely with the technologists who have a deep understanding of the software used at the company. The technologists have to be highly skilled and intelligent to understand the details of the products they are using. It is the rare technologist who obtains this understanding by reading. Technologists obtain it through experience, and for this to happen, they must be working on the software and doing development. Keeping the right skill levels requires a steady stream of work. This does not mean doing everything yourself; it means doing only some of it yourself.

Maintaining such a department means providing a steady stream of interesting work for the technologists. While this model could work perfectly with commercial software, it is harder to achieve. Open source technology is simply more exciting to technical talent than commercial technology is. Once a talented technical team forms, for whatever reason, to work together on challenging business problems, open source will likely find its way in.

What types of people will be attracted to an empowered department? Most frequently, it will be creative, talented people who want to put their skills to work and learn from their colleagues. Once the core of an IT department has formed, word gets around pretty quickly, and attracting a talented staff requires less effort and becomes more self-sustaining because talent is drawn to the department.

Increasing Choice, Reducing Vendor Lock-In

Every IT department hates its vendors, or at least is frustrated by them. Most frequently this is because the software does not do exactly what the IT department wants it to do, and every time you want to change it you must pay some sort of consulting or licensing fee. Most of the time, the problem started during the sales process, when any mismatches between the IT department's requirements were papered over to get the deal done. IT executives who are excited about a product's functionality are all too willing to participate in this process.

One of the big attractions of open source is that it helps avoid vendor lock-in, which is another name for being stuck with a product that does not meet your needs adequately. Once IT departments decide on a product, it must last for a long time.

Empowered IT executives are in control of vendor relationships and are not beholden to them. Why? Because a build-leaning department has more choices. The vast potential of open source provides excellent leverage in negotiations with vendors. If you don't like what the vendor is offering, usually an open source alternative (or enough help from open source components that you can build what you want) is available. The more skill a build-leaning department has and the better able it is to learn, the less it needs to depend on vendors for consulting services. Open source can also be used for prototyping so that requirements can be better understood before a decision about lock-in must be made.

Lock-in is not avoided completely, however. The replacement for vendor lock-in is a lock-in to the skills required to maintain the software being used. But investment in this lock-in means investment in a more powerful staff.

Most vendors feel that open source is great for lowering the cost of providing their solutions, and that it can be an excellent companion to their products. However, they will invariably add, it is a completely crazy, unreliable, horrible choice as a replacement for their products. Open source is the vendor's friend when it promotes sales, but it's the vendor's enemy when it threatens sales.

The Vision and Challenge of IT

The process for successful use of IT in business, or for any purpose, is one of understanding the business's needs, understanding the technology's capabilities, and then crafting a process that meets the needs with help from the technology.

Most IT disasters stem from misunderstanding the business's needs and the technology's capabilities. Open source will not change this dynamic. For many companies it will simply provide a new form of technology to misunderstand. It won't help companies understand their needs.

The question of whether to use open source really calls into focus how an IT department sees itself. Confident, highly skilled IT departments never ask whether they should use open source. The staff simply looks for the best tools and uses them, regardless of the source, and figures out how to make it work for the company. The managers of these departments know what they are getting into and make sure engineering practices are strong to protect the department from cowboy tendencies.

But most IT departments are not Google, Amazon.com, Yahoo!, or Ticketmaster. You have to ask yourself: should you seek to emulate those companies, if not entirely, then in a small area where it would make a difference? Can you find just one open source application that would save the company money, provide some significant value, and help build the department's skills? If this process starts and is properly managed, it will transform and empower an IT department. If you want to be empowered, using open source can start you on the way.

Reading a book is an excellent way to prepare to learn. However, experience is the real teacher. Don't believe us. Pick up some open source, try to use it, and notice how it changes you and your company. You will not be disappointed.

Open source is a vast world to explore, and many treasures await those who can develop the right skills and adapt their organizations to sustain them.

The Open Source Platform

Once an IT department has used open source software successfully on a small scale to fill a gap in a data center's infrastructure, to reduce the cost for commodity functionality, or to provide the organization with an application of value, the appetite for open source can grow dangerously fast. Using one open source application or infrastructure is frequently a simple task, with modest implications. However, as each new instance of open source is added, modest implications can multiply into major headaches.

For example, if a company introduces Linux to replace a proprietary Unix implementation, it has now taken responsibility for maintaining the skills needed to support Linux. If a content management system such as Drupal is added, skills to understand and maintain that application are required, along with the ability to code in PHP, the language Drupal is written in. Of course, Drupal requires a database—usually MySQL—and a variety of other PHP components, as well as knowledge of Apache.

Let's say TWiki, a flexible, IT-oriented Wiki implementation, is installed. Now someone must understand how to support the TWiki application and the Perl language that TWiki is written in. In short order, an IT department can rapidly expand the pool of skills it needs to acquire.

It is easy for this pattern—the uncontrolled introduction of open source software with its accompanying demands on skills—to occur because the control processes associated with commercial software (the need to spend money to acquire and implement software) do not apply in the open source world. Download it, install it, and you're off.

In Chapter 5, we discussed a few different approaches to solving organizational problems faced when managing open source adoption. This appendix will shift focus to the technology itself and will use the concept of the *platform* to provide some guidance as to how to assemble the right portfolio of open source software.

The central idea is that each IT department should seek to minimize the number of skills required to support the open source portfolio it assembles. At the same time, IT departments should seek to leverage those skills repeatedly so that the investment in acquiring and maintaining them produces maximum value.

What Is a Platform?

The idea of a platform has gained great currency in technology strategy in the past few years. Most of the time, the term applies to a foundation layer on which other technology can be constructed. Intel's chip set is a platform. Microsoft Windows is a platform. Java is a platform. Much has been written about the rules for constructing and marketing a platform to gain the most control and to squeeze the most profit from its use.

Our perspective on platforms is much more modest. We use the idea of a platform to refer to the collection of software used for development, infrastructure, or applications. The goal is to assemble the smallest, least expensive, easiest-to-maintain infrastructure that meets all your needs.

The challenge in assembling a platform based on open source is that for the most part, no one is designing open source to be a platform. Some open source projects are used together so often that they are treated as a platform: the combination of Linux, Apache, and MySQL with Perl, Python, or PHP is referred to as the LAMP platform. But that doesn't mean it's easy to get a particular version of PHP working well with Apache or with MySQL. In short, the evolution of open source platforms, like open source itself, has left significant holes in the platform that IT departments should be aware of as they decide which open source to adopt.

Three Open Source Platforms

It is possible to consider a platform from many different levels and many different scopes. Linux, for example, was created on the GNU platform for software development. Bricolage, a content management and publishing system, was created on the platform created by the Perl language and the huge set of libraries written in Perl. The Yahoo! web site was created on a platform assembled from all sorts of software, infrastructure, and applications, from both the commercial and open source realms.

Our analysis will focus on three types of platforms:

* Platforms for application development

- Platforms for infrastructure
- Platforms for applications

Platforms for Application Development

Of the three types of platforms, open source is probably strongest as an application development platform. Open source has always been best at serving the needs of the developers who create it. The challenge for an IT department in choosing open source as an application platform is narrowing the choices to the smallest number of languages. Open source development can occur in C, C++, Perl, Python, PHP, or Java using a variety of different compilers, application servers, and libraries. The problem for IT departments is choosing among these languages. All of them are viable, stable languages that have been used to create great software. The sorts of questions an IT department should ask when looking at using open source as a platform for development include:

- What libraries are most important to our short-, medium-, and long-term development needs?
- What related infrastructure—such as application servers, source code management systems, and debugging and testing environments—is available?
- What other applications or important software infrastructure are written in the language?

By asking these questions, an IT department has a better chance of choosing a platform for development that will be reusable and will meet its long-term needs.

Platforms for Infrastructure

For the operating systems, application servers, web servers, and data center management software used to run a computing environment, open source has a variety of interesting platforms. Linux, of course, is the most popular operating system, but it's not the only one. BSD has remained popular. Apache is the most popular web server, with no real competition for general use. MySQL and PostgreSQL are two of many choices available for databases.

When choosing open source as an infrastructure platform, it is important to ask the following questions:

- What infrastructure software makes the most of the IT department's existing skills?
- What infrastructure is used by applications of interest to the department?
- How widely used and supported is the infrastructure component under consideration?
- How well does any infrastructure component work with existing parts of the department's infrastructure?

Platforms for Applications

Applications are the most difficult of the three forms of open source to assemble into a coherent platform. As most IT veterans know, the largest struggle in most IT departments is to make applications work seamlessly together. Most open source applications were built on open source development environments and infrastructure, but were not constructed to work with any other open source applications.

Another problem for open source applications are the large gaps in terms of the business process coverage that most IT departments need to support. Although open source solutions exist for ERP and CRM, the functional footprint of these applications is smaller than that of their commercial counterparts. The integration with other programs is also far less mature. Furthermore, vast swaths of enterprise applications, such as for SCM, PLM, HR, and SRM, are virtually untouched by open source.

Applications probably represent the largest opportunity for open source, but IT departments should take care to ask the following questions when choosing a set of open source applications:

- How closely will an application need to work with other applications?
- How integration friendly is the application?
- Is the application based on development and infrastructure environments that are already supported or are easily supported?
- How mature is the application?
- What APIs or other hooks are provided so that IT departments can develop higher layers of applications?

By asking these sorts of questions, an IT department has the best chance of choosing wisely as it finds its way to the optimal collection of open source.

Assembling Your Open Source Platform

Finding the optimal platform for your IT department is an iterative process. It is vitally important to be aware, from the moment you start implementing even a small open source application, that your goal must be to consciously design a platform that meets the requirements set forth at the beginning of this appendix. This process can mean making tradeoffs. Perhaps it is better to use a less mature application that is based on infrastructure and languages your department already supports than it is to use a superior open source project that requires support for new languages and new infrastructure.

The right choices depend highly on an IT department's existing conditions and skill levels. But we believe most IT departments can find many opportunities for using open source among the projects mentioned in the appendices that follow.

End-User Computing on the Desktop

End-user computing on the desktop is perhaps the most eagerly examined part of the open source stack. Thousands of megabytes of Internet bandwidth have been spent discussing the relative merits of the various options available, along with when and if they will be ready to replace the domination of Microsoft Windows and its Office suite. The good news is that they are. The bad news is that, as with other solutions in the open source space, caveats apply.

A large body of software exists in this space. Here, we will focus on the major areas that are of immediate use to the enterprise. In some cases, multiple open source alternatives to proprietary desktop applications are available. We evaluate and recommend alternatives based on attributes of value to an enterprise: ease of use, consistency, a well-defined migration path from vendor alternatives, and continuing interoperability with popular Office document formats.

We also focus on five primary user segments:

Fixed function
> Users who run only one application on the desktop and use the desktop only for that application.

Technical workstation
> Users who run industry-specific desktop applications, and don't care about the operating system or windowing environment being used to run the application.

They might use the desktop for basic email and web browsing as well as for instant messaging.

Transactional worker

Users who run several structured or forms-based web applications as their primary interaction with the desktop. They also use email and a web browser. Once again, the choice of operating system and windowing environment is secondary to the user experience.

Basic office

Users who rely on the desktop to implement business processes and for productivity applications (primarily word processors, spreadsheets, and presentation software). These are not power users, but they do collaborate extensively with users in other departments of the organization and with other organizations that are using interoperable document formats (the Microsoft Office suite, for example).

General purpose

Users who depend on the desktop for various Windows applications and are tied strongly to Microsoft Office formats.

Solutions

Solutions for the desktop space work in layers, with solutions at each layer depending on functionality and services from the layer below and providing functionality to the layers above. The key layers of the desktop are shown in Figure B-1.

Figure B-1. *Layers of desktop functionality*

We see two main migration scenarios:

Migrating users at all three layers simultaneously

In this scenario, we see a Linux distribution and a desktop environment and the productivity applications being replaced simultaneously. This is best accomplished by first doing a pilot among a representative subset of the user base.

Migrating from the top layer down

This scenario involves replacing the browser and Office application suite first, and then migrating the users to a different desktop environment and operating system.

Linux Distribution

A variety of Linux distribution choices are available for enterprise-wide deployment. The more cutting-edge distributions provide a lower level of support. But several mainstream options also are available, including Red Hat, Mandriva, SuSE, Debian, and Gentoo. The first three are company-supported distributions that come with the option of purchasing support contracts. The last two are community supported, mostly through mailing lists, forums, and chat rooms. When choosing a distribution, you should apply the following criteria:

Package management

All Linux distributions provide a method of distributing upgrades and updates. Red Hat, for example, provides updates via RPM. This is the single most important criterion when choosing a distribution, as it directly affects how easy (or hard) it will be to maintain the deployment base.

Productization

Some distributions are more polished than others. Depending on the technical skill level of the user base, a more polished distribution might be desirable.

Support

Some Linux distributions are available with company-backed support, and others offer only community-backed support. The system administrator's skill set should determine the level of support needed.

Desktop Environment

Desktop environment refers to the graphical interface where the user does her work. Complete desktop environments consist of a large number of tightly integrated but separate pieces of software. By default, GNOME uses a window manager called Metacity, and KDE uses kwin. The window manager is, of course, the most important part of the desktop. It handles window placement, movement, appearance, and user interaction with all the windows on the desktop. The choice of window manager is probably the most important factor in the success of a Linux migration on desktops.

Several window managers are available that offer a wide spectrum of options in the tradeoff between resource use and functionality. Table B-1 illustrates the point. XFCE4 is a less resource-intensive desktop environment. It is also highly customizable.

Table B-1. *Window managers and resource usage*

Desktop	Required RAM	Required CPU
XFCE4	128 MB	100 MHz
GNOME 2.x	384 MB	800 MHz
KDE 3.x	512 MB	1 GHz

In examining and evaluating desktop environments, consider the following enterprise-user requirements as paramount:

- Ease and consistency of use. An intuitive, integrated, and consistent experience for the end user is key.

- Ease of migration from Microsoft Windows.

Productivity Software

In examining productivity software, we confine ourselves to word processing, spreadsheet software, and presentation software, since meaningful alternatives to Microsoft Office exist in these three categories. We consider the following as requirements for enterprise users:

- Ease and consistency of use (i.e., an easy and integrated experience; e.g., the ability to create compound document spreadsheets or images embedded in a document)

- Ease of migration from Microsoft Office

- Interoperability with Microsoft Office document formats

Note that open source productivity software such as Open Office is steadily gaining ground on major proprietary platforms such as Microsoft Windows and Mac OS X.

Desktop Database Management

Applications in this category are alternatives to Microsoft Access, Microsoft FoxPro, and Adobe FileMaker. While local applications using a desktop database are fast becoming a rarity in enterprises, we recognize the continuing need for an alternative to Microsoft Access. Most open source productivity suites provide alternatives to Access by providing a usable interface to existing open source database servers such as MySQL or PostgreSQL.

Web Browsers

Applications in this category are alternatives to Microsoft Explorer. The security problems and lack of regular functionality updates in Microsoft Explorer have created an opportunity in this area, and the Mozilla Project has capitalized on it. Mozilla Firefox is a modern, stable, and secure web browser available for all major desktop environments.

Messaging Client

Since messaging is a collaboration tool, we provide a detailed explanation of messaging clients in Appendix D.

Capabilities

Table B-2 shows a grid of the major desktop functions and the key capabilities that every desktop solution should provide.

Table B-2. *Desktop requirements*

Desktop function	Key capabilities
Graphical desktop environment	Consistent look and feel Standardized menu and toolbars, keybindings, and color schemes Integrated help system Internationalization support Plenty of useful applications
Word processing	Ability to generate simple office documents such as memorandums and business forms Option to generate complex office documents with embedded spreadsheets and charts and tables Sophisticated style sheet support Auto correction and spellchecking Template support
Spreadsheets	Ability to generate simple formulae, charts, and statistics Ability to include the options for conditional coloring of cells and data display customization using various fonts
Presentations	Ability to insert and edit rich text Support for complex layouts of media objects Functions for playing presentations with transitions and other effects Publishing tools for exporting presentations as HTML to a web site
Database management	Small database management tools Mail merge
Web browsing	Availability of a standards-compliant rendering engine (HTML 4.x, XHTML, CSS, JavaScript) Full support for safe and secure web browsing (HTTP 1.1, SSL) Ability to support rich multimedia (Flash, streaming media such as RealNetworks and Windows Media)

Open Source Desktop Environments: KDE

While several strong candidates are included in this category, we recommend K Desktop Environment (KDE) as the easiest desktop environment for transitioning from Microsoft Windows. Not only does it provide a look and feel similar to Windows, but also it offers a consistent menu and windowing scheme for all applications.

KDE is an easy-to-use, modern, mature, and stable desktop environment that works on Unix systems. KDE's modular framework approach has resulted in applications that are tightly integrated and work well together. It also centralizes services that applications require to provide functionality to the end user. These include:

- Network-transparent input/output via KIO, which seamlessly supports major network protocols including HTTP, FTP, POP, IMAP, NFS, SMB, LDAP, and local files.

- A multimedia architecture based on the Analog Realtime Synthesizer that supports multiple concurrent audio and video streams.

- DCOP, a messaging protocol that interoperates with XML-RPC.

- Kparts, a component object model that handles all aspects of embedding components in applications.

- XML GUI Builder, which uses XML to build and manage most aspects of a GUI. This makes it possible to configure applications in a simplified and uniform manner.

- KHTML, a rendering engine that is fully standards compliant and efficient; it's so efficient that Apple chose to build its web browser, Safari, using KHTML.

KDE also has advanced features including a kiosk framework that allows KDE to be run on desktops in restricted environments and desktop sharing via VNC that allows for richer support and collaboration options.

Desktop Productivity Suites

Given our choice of KDE as a desktop environment, we are recommending KOffice and Open Office as productivity suites. KOffice should provide a unified experience for end users on KDE, and Open Office includes an option to migrate users away from Microsoft Office before migrating them away from the Microsoft Windows operating system. Both productivity suites supply major Microsoft Office functionality and full interoperability with Microsoft Office document formats. Table B-3 lists the three major Office applications, along with the KOffice and Open Office equivalents.

Table B-3. *Microsoft Office applications and open source equivalents*

Microsoft Office	KOffice	Open Office
Word	KWord	Writer
Excel	KSpread	Calc
PowerPoint	KPresenter	Impress

Desktop Database Management: MySQL

We recommend using MySQL with the Windows desktop as a replacement for Microsoft Access. While MySQL is a fully featured relational database management system (RDBMS), it is fast and lightweight enough to be used on a desktop system. You can use MySQL on the desktop in several different ways:

- On a Windows desktop, you can use Access as a frontend to MySQL using the MyODBC driver. Alternatively, you can install MySQL natively, and use it via GUI tools such as MySQL Query Browser.

- On a Linux desktop, you can easily install, use, and manage MySQL via web-based interfaces such as phpMyAdmin, KDE applications such as Kexi, or other GUI tools such as MySQL Query Browser.

MySQL is a fast, robust, and easy-to-use database. It is supported by MySQL AB, the company that funds MySQL development. It also has a large and active end-user community. MySQL's main features are:

- Broad ANSI SQL syntax support

- Multiple storage engine options, including MyISAM for performance and InnoDB for full transaction support and row-level locking

- Query caching and full text indexing

- Numerous third-party tools to help manage data

Web Browsing: Firefox

Web browsing on the desktop is a business-critical activity, and you have many mature open source web browser alternatives to Internet Explorer to choose from. We recommend using Firefox.

Firefox is a fast, easy-to-use web browser that provides a consistent user interface across multiple platforms. Its main features are:

- Pop-up blocking through a sophisticated mechanism that blocks unwanted pop-ups while allowing you to see the ones from sites you trust.

- Tabbed browsing for viewing multiple web sites in tabs of the same window, and the ability to bookmark multiple web sites that can be opened as tabs with one click. It loads tabs in the background to reduce the time users spend waiting for a page to load.

- Built-in search capability that accesses major search engines (Google, Yahoo!, Amazon, etc.), and the ability to plug in new search engines easily.

- Live bookmarks that are integrated with RSS.

- A smart download manager that makes it easy to find downloaded items.

- The ability to customize it with hundreds of useful extensions.

- A safe and secure environment, with several built-in controls to help protect users against malicious attacks.

- Standards compliance with the latest Internet protocols.

Open Source and Email

The utility of email-based communications in an enterprise is beyond question. With innovative uses such as monitoring critical systems via email alerts, group communications via carbon copy, and mailing lists, email has been and will continue to be the main application for enterprise-wide collaboration. Here we cover open source email server solutions, mailing list managers, and software that facilitate collaboration.

A Brief History of Email for Enterprise Use

From the very first one sent on Arpanet in 1971 to the billions sent today, email forms the heart of modern electronic communications. The growth of email use follows closely the growth of Internet use in general. As a result, virtually all Internet users rely on email. Early email use was entirely text based, with HTML email gaining prominence in the 1990s.

Graphical email clients appeared in the early 1990s and were a huge success because they made email easier to use. Microsoft Outlook quickly gained a majority of the market share for enterprise use after its first release in 1997. It displaced Eudora and other email clients, because of its superior graphical user interface and its approach to combining email with personal information management activities such as calendaring. Open source graphical clients, such as Novell Evolution and Mozilla Thunderbird, have been steadily gaining ground on Outlook, and they are now ready for prime-time use.

On the email server front, Microsoft Exchange is the dominant player in the enterprise, especially since Exchange Version 2000, which improved greatly upon earlier versions. Outside of big enterprises, open source email servers such as Sendmail, Postfix, and Exim dominate the landscape. Open source email servers lost ground to Exchange, because Exchange offers a comprehensive solution that meets an enterprise's email needs. This reduced the overhead for manageability significantly and made Exchange an attractive option for enterprises. However, with the proliferation of viruses and spam in recent years, coupled with Exchange's inability to keep up with the challenges posed, open source email servers are once again a viable alternative. While no one open source project is a "drop-in" replacement for Exchange, it is certainly possible to assemble a solution from open source parts. Furthermore, various open source products can be used effectively in conjunction with Exchange.

In this appendix, we will look at the four major product categories of open source email projects: client, server, antispam and antivirus, and mailing list managers.

Opportunities for IT Use of Open Source Email Products

Given the history of email adoption in enterprises, most IT departments in midsize to large companies are running Microsoft Exchange on the server and Microsoft Outlook on the desktop. Remote users or users checking email from home are using Outlook Web Access or Outlook Express.

We can subdivide each of these into three scenarios:

- You are using almost all the capabilities of Exchange, and while this is fine in terms of basic email and collaboration, you are overwhelmed by virus outbreaks via email attachments or are drowning in spam. The primary challenges in this scenario are managing increasingly frequent virus outbreaks and managing the nightmare of spam. Integrating open source content scanners into this environment can provide immediate relief on both fronts. A few specific examples are:
  - Creating a secure mail gateway, or a mail firewall, that will shield Microsoft Exchange or Lotus Notes from direct contact. This mail gateway can perform content filtering, including removing viruses and Microsoft Outlook exploits, and identify spam. This can be implemented using Postfix, SpamAssassin, or Anomy Sanitizer. This allows enterprises to implement short-term relief from viruses and spam, and immediately cuts the number of person hours that IT staff and end users spend dealing with the problem.
  - The SpamBayes Outlook plug-in can be deployed to users' desktop machines as a second-layer protection against spam. This can help catch any spam that server-based solutions are not catching. For smaller organizations, this might be the only solution needed for spam control, as it allows email administrators to plan the implementation of a server-side solution instead of dealing with it as an emergency.

- You are using only the basic email capabilities of Exchange and feel it is not worth the cost. So, you are exploring a low-cost alternative. Here are your options:
  - If your enterprise needs a shared address book and shared folders in addition to email, a combination of open source projects (OpenLDAP for a shared address book, Courier-IMAP for a mail delivery agent, and Postfix for a mail transfer agent) can save you from needing a Microsoft Exchange license.
  - Users with Outlook Express can be moved over to Mozilla Thunderbird to provide equivalent functionality and significantly reduced exposure to viruses and spam.
- You want a drop-in replacement for Exchange, and you want to continue to keep your end users on Outlook. In this scenario your out-of-the-box options are limited to a few products, such as Novell Open Exchange, but they are not open source. These products are significantly less expensive than Microsoft Exchange is, and they might be worth analyzing. Also, a do-it-yourself option of combining a solution out of various open source projects is available. Read the rest of this appendix for ideas.

Open Source Email Server Solutions

Open source solutions in the email server space tend to comprise combinations of open source projects. This is because comprehensive solutions such as Microsoft Exchange and Novell GroupWise have set the expectation of a single email system that takes care of all the enterprise's email serving needs, or at least those of a department within an enterprise. The open source community's answer to this challenge is to combine several open source projects that work well together.

Open source email server software provides a low-overhead way to manage large volumes of mail. With appropriate staff expertise, open source–based email server solutions can also reduce an IT group's exposure to the perils of spam and viruses.

Open Source Email Server Capabilities

It is instructive to look at Microsoft Exchange's capabilities, because Microsoft Exchange offers a feature set that meets most of an enterprise's common email requirements. We purposefully underemphasize collaboration features here since we address collaboration as a separate topic in Appendix D. Here is Microsoft Exchange's feature set:

- Full support for major email protocols like SMTP, POP3, IMAP, and WebDAV
- Active Directory integration with full support for global address lists across the enterprise

- Outlook web access and a full-featured web mail client, with S/MIME support, desktop-application-style shortcuts, task lists, and an integrated spellchecker

- Deep integration with Outlook 2003

- Security features such as S/MIME and HTTPS support, attachments, and complex HTML blocks that prevent propagation of viruses and malware attacks

- Advanced collaboration features such as public folders and shared calendars

- Support of clustered implementation for larger deployments across multiple locations

- Integrated support for mobile devices via Outlook Mobile Access, with support for related industry standards such as WAP 2.x, i-Mode (XHTML), and Compressed HTML (cHTML)

In addition to these features, an enterprise-grade email server should also have the following capabilities:

Advanced relay support

Advanced email servers are expected to distinguish legitimate email that originated from one of its end users and relay only that email. With some newer protocols, such as "pop-before," an email server relays outgoing email only from users who are currently actively receiving email via its POP server. With "smtp-auth," the email reader provides a username and password when sending email.

Administration features

These include mailbox quota-control support, as well as Webmin support for web-based administration.

Sendmail compatibility

Because of Sendmail's past dominance, many supporting programs and scripts assume the presence of Sendmail. As a result, most email servers aiming to replace Sendmail provide mechanisms so that the replacement is transparent to these supporting programs and scripts. Sendmail compatibility remains a key criterion for an email server to be a serious candidate for consideration in the enterprise.

Mailbox format support

This includes support for mbox and maildir. mbox is the traditional Unix mailbox format in which all messages are stored in one file and indexes are built to locate messages efficiently. maildir, on the other hand, uses the Unix filesystem to store one message per file. The maildir format was designed to avoid locking and to address other performance issues encountered by the mbox format in high-volume email scenarios.

Support for RDBMS

Newer email servers are experimenting with using a database to store messages, thus leveraging database technology for higher concurrency and reliability needs.

Content scanner support

This is the ability to hand a message's contents off to a content scanner (such as SpamAssassin or Clam AntiVirus) for analysis and custom actions such as flagging the message as spam or quarantining it based on its analysis.

Security and encryption

This is the ability to accept encrypted connections from email readers and provide the end user with a fully secure email experience.

Back-end support

The ability to verify senders or recipients with external directories, including LDAP-based directories or Active Directory-based directories, is vital.

Virtual host support

This is the ability to receive and send email on behalf of more than one domain.

Open Source Email Server Projects

We define open source email servers as a combination of Mail Transfer Agents (MTAs) and Mail Delivery Agents (MDAs). An MTA is a program responsible for transferring a mail message. When an MTA receives mail from a Mail User Agent (MUA) or another MTA, it stores it locally on a temporary basis and analyzes its recipients. The MTA either delivers the message by handing it to an MDA or passes it on to another MTA. An MDA is a program that delivers the message by storing it in the recipient's mailbox. Open source email server projects have been greatly improved and are more commonly used in enterprises. Open source email server software provides a low-overhead way to manage large volumes of email. With appropriate staff expertise, open source–based email server solutions reduce the exposure of an IT group to the perils of spam and viruses.

The field of open source email servers has a long and rich history. Since email was the first mass application on the Internet and it continues to be the most popular one today, the email server field is rich with mature choices. Sendmail was the first major email server and, at one point, had 80% or more of the market share—or so goes the folklore. However, Sendmail was designed and built to requirements that are obsolete today. What's more, it wasn't designed to scale on management, security, or performance fronts. Most current open source email server projects support common mailbox formats and provide various levels of integration. The key to easy adoption and effective use of open source email server projects is to identify a collection of projects that work well together. For example, using Courier-IMAP, Postfix, Clam AntiVirus, and SpamAssassin will provide a full MTA with shared folders, virus protection, and defense from spam. Some modern Linux distributions include, or make it very easy to install, these projects during installation.

Recommended Email Server Projects

In this section, we present three mail servers and the OpenLDAP data store that can support the mail server in an environment with many users.

Postfix

Postfix is an email server that was designed with performance security and Sendmail compatibility in mind. Like Qmail, Postfix is a collection of modules that create a pipeline to handle various aspects of transferring and delivering email. Unlike Qmail, it stores its configuration file in one monolithic file.

Product strengths

- It is flexible with configuration options and it handles large volumes of email effectively.
- It works well with popular content scanners.
- It provides easy-to-use spam relay control features.

Product weakness

- It has a complex configuration file.

Qmail

Qmail is a secure email server designed to be a drop-in replacement for Sendmail. It is designed as a collection of modules that create a pipeline to handle various stages of transferring and delivering email. Each program has its own configuration. Qmail works on the Unix system philosophy of "do one thing, and do it well." It also addresses security concerns by not running as root and by carefully managing trust relationships and intermodule communications.

Product strengths

- It provides easy-to-use spam relay control features.
- It is designed with security and performance in mind.

Product weaknesses

- Some critical Qmail functionality is available as patches, and several popular patches are not regression tested against one another.
- Configuration management is cumbersome due to multiple configuration files.

Exim

Exim is a general-purpose email server that is very flexible and powerful. It is also designed to be a drop-in Sendmail replacement. It is a monolithic program, very much like Sendmail, but unlike Sendmail, it is very easy to configure.

Product strengths

- It provides deep integration with SpamAssassin and does not accept delivery of email that is considered spam. This provides cutting-edge spam control.
- It provides deep integration with GNU Mailman.

Product weakness

- It has no Webmin support.

OpenLDAP

OpenLDAP is the de facto solution for open source directories. It is a popular, mature, stable, and widely used product, and is well supported by an active user and developer base. OpenLDAP has broad support for the latest version of LDAP (LDAPv3) and interoperates well with other LDAP servers (Microsoft Active Directory, Novell eDirectory, Netscape Directory Server, IBM Tivoli Directory Server, etc.). OpenLDAP is the common choice for implementing a directory when replacing a Microsoft Exchange server.

Open Source Email Client Solutions

Solutions in the email client space tend to be single-purpose applications that help the user read, send, and manage email as well as manage their address books. Microsoft Outlook is the commercial market leader in this space, as it is used on more than 60% of corporate desktops. Historically, these applications tended to be islands unto themselves, but now most are moving toward supporting external mail-related standards as they mature. For instance, LDAP is supported for address books, and the PGP, GPG, SSL, and TLS standards are supported for security.

Open Source Email Client Capabilities

All decent email clients should support the ability to read, send, and manage email. Features to sort the collection of messages by time and sender are also expected. Email clients should also allow users to easily manage their address books, at a bare minimum.

The state-of-the-art email clients, meanwhile, are expected to handle HTML mail and to thread together group messages related to a single conversation. The current trend is to improve search features that can quickly search across a large mailbox, as well as to provide dynamic filtering criteria that are kept up-to-date as new messages arrive. Another option to look for is support for *virtual folders*. Virtual folders allow the user to view messages in one folder that are located in several other folders, based on a search criterion. Novell Evolution provides support for virtual folders. Email *views* are another advanced feature that can be used to manage email. Views are search filters that are applied dynamically. One of this book's authors uses a TODO label and the TODO view to effectively use Mozilla Thunderbird as a mini personal information manager. Some email readers, such as Microsoft Outlook and Novell Evolution, feature built-in calendaring, but most email applications do not.

The ability to manage multiple email identities in one email reader is of extreme value these days. This allows a user to respond to a personal message that was accidentally sent to a work address from a personal address and continue the conversation there. Related to this is the ability to control the reply-to header, which allows the user to redirect responses to the email at a separate address. The ability to search across multiple email accounts is another useful feature.

Here is a detailed categorized listing of the most useful features of an email client. Microsoft Outlook 2003 supports these features, although its quality of implementation varies.

- Effective layout that doesn't confuse the novice user and doesn't limit the power user, including:
  — Support for two- and three-pane layouts
  — The ability to display and group messages via a variety of criteria, including sender, date, conversations (or threads), and topic (or subject)
  — The ability to mark or flag messages for later action, and to create custom flags
- Search capability that should include the ability to:
  — Search headers for senders, recipients, or subjects within a specified date range
  — Search the body of email text
  — Search across all message attributes or across certain headers
- Integrated address book support with:
  — A built-in address book
  — Auto completion of email addresses while composing email
  — Support for corporate address books via LDAP and Active Directory
  — Automatic building of an address book via regular use of the email client
- Integrated spelling support with:
  — A built-in spellchecker or use of spellchecking services provided by the operating system
  — The ability to spell as you type

- Content scanner support including:
  - Integration with client-side content scanners such as ClamWin and Spam-Bayes
  - Support for server-side content scanners such as Clam AntiVirus and Spam-Assassin
- Security and encryption support with:
  - Support for transport layer security mechanisms such as SSL and TLS
  - Support for message content security with mechanisms such as S/MIME, PGP, and GPG

Open Source Email Client Projects

Open source email client projects are finally starting to target the Windows platform and provide fixes for Microsoft Outlook's security vulnerabilities.

Email applications in commercial projects, such as Microsoft Outlook, tend to be a collection of related groupware functions: shared address books and calendars, journals, and other personal information management functions. However, their open source counterparts—Novell Evolution and KMail being two primary examples—are closing the gap and building a strong business case for an enterprise to standardize on them. There is also the promise of Chandler. Chandler is the next-generation personal information manager, designed by Mitch Kapor of Lotus Agenda fame. Being developed from scratch, Chandler uses email as the central application for messaging and collaboration and provides usage scenarios that are very different from the current standard (which is based largely on Outlook). Chandler is currently in pre-alpha stage, with no definite release date for Version 1.0, but due to its extraordinary promise, it is worth keeping an eye on.

We recommend some open source email clients for the most common enterprise usage scenarios. Novell Evolution is the current best bet for replacing an enterprise-grade client such as Microsoft Outlook. Mozilla Thunderbird is the best of the low-end clients and is a very suitable replacement for Outlook Express. Mutt is a text console-based client that is perfect for extended messaging needs in datacenter environments where an IT person might need to use mail but feels hampered by the default Unix mail client.

Novell Evolution

Novell's Evolution is a truly enterprise-ready email client. It is also a functional personal information manager. It has all the basic email reader functions and several advanced email functions not found in the competition or not nearly as well implemented. It has good support for enterprise email platforms, including Microsoft Exchange and Novell GroupWise, with better support expected in the next major release. This email client should be on every IT manager's short list of open source email clients.

Product strengths

- Several advanced features are well implemented (virtual folders, powerful search, etc.).

- It features Exchange connectivity.

Product weaknesses

- Performance is lagging.

- The Exchange connector is not yet open source.

Mozilla Thunderbird

Mozilla Thunderbird is a powerful and speedy email client that is great for home use and is ready for enterprise use, depending on the email server deployed. It provides excellent support for POP, good support for IMAP, and partial support for Microsoft Exchange via IMAP and LDAP, but it still lacks the smooth integrated corporate email experience for the enterprise that Microsoft Outlook provides. Thunderbird 1.0 was recently released after a long and stable beta-testing period. It continues to mature and enhance at a rapid pace, with several useful extensions also in the process of being released. It is well worth keeping an eye on.

Product strengths

- It has robust support for basic email client features.

- Several advanced features (threads, labels, search folders) provide a very customizable email workflow experience.

- It is very extensible; several useful extensions are already available.

- It integrates well with Mozilla Firefox and Sunbird.

- It features integrated support for other content syndication formats such as RSS.

Product weakness

- Message template support is less than mature.

Content Scanners

Antispam and antivirus are the two popular solutions in the content scanner area. Most are available on the server side; a few antispam and antivirus solutions are available on the client side as well. ClamWin, for instance, is a free antivirus checker that is available as an Outlook plug-in, and SpamBayes is an Outlook plug-in for spam control.

Most email clients in the open source arena are being designed and developed with antispam solutions built in. For example, Thunderbird has a naïve Bayes classifier for identifying spam that works well.

Antispam and antivirus software can be used independently if an enterprise has an email server solution already in place.

Antispam software integrates with either email servers or email clients to provide an effective means to block spam. For enterprise use, antispam software that works on the server side is recommended, as it is easier to manage and deploy.

Most open source antispam software tends to be immature, since blocking spam became necessary only in the last few years. However, the open source community has risen to the challenge of spam and has begun to provide software that is more effective in rescuing a user's mailbox from the brink of disaster. Various methodologies of spam detection are currently being tested, including Bayesian filtering and collaborative filtering. The best antispam control software uses a combination of these features.

Antivirus Software

We define *antivirus software* as software that integrates with email servers to provide an effective means to block or quarantine incoming email compromised by viruses. Open source virus detectors and blockers tend to be uncommon because of the need to keep the virus signature database up-to-date, but recently the open source community developed technology that reports new viruses in the wild. Again, a variety of techniques is being pioneered in various projects. Clam AntiVirus follows the standard "detect by virus signature," and MIMEDefang has extensible mechanisms to detect suspect email. Some antivirus software can also function as antispam software.

Content Scanner Capabilities

Basic features of email content scanners include:

Header analysis
> The ability to detect inconsistencies and discrepancies in email headers that are usually indicative of spam.

Text analysis
> The ability to analyze the full text of an email to detect patterns that indicate that the email is spam.

Learning classifier
> The ability to improve header and text analysis over time, by learning what messages a user marks (or unmarks) as spam.

Blacklist and whitelist support

The ability to support and manage a list of senders whose messages should never be considered spam (whitelist) and a list of senders whose messages should always be considered spam (blacklist). These lists can be a combination of lists indicated by the user, or those downloaded from external authorities, such as real-time blackhole lists (RBLs).

Real-time scanning

The ability to scan a message in real time and to keep up with email volume without introducing delays in delivering email.

Frequently updated database

A message signature database for antivirus software, and the database of rules to identify spam for antispam software.

MTA/MDA integration

Well-supported and documented support for major email servers; for example, Sendmail support (via milter).

Clam AntiVirus

Clam AntiVirus is a powerful antivirus software program and toolkit that integrates with most popular email servers for scanning attachments.

Product strengths

- It features a virus database that is kept up-to-date and is easy to update automatically via the Internet.

- It features a toolkit that makes virus scanning capability available for software development.

Product weakness

- It is not tightly integrated with Microsoft Exchange.

ClamWin

ClamWin is the Clam AntiVirus product but with a graphical user interface. It runs on Microsoft Windows and provides basic virus scanning functionality for the email client that Clam AntiVirus provides for the email server.

Product strength

- It offers full integration with Clam AntiVirus's virus database.

Product weakness

- It does not include an on-access real-time scanner.

SpamAssassin

SpamAssassin is the de facto choice for spam detection and control in open source circles. It uses many sophisticated techniques to identify and label spam. Labeled spam can then be filtered and/or deleted by email readers. It has a learning classifier that gets more precise with detecting spam over time, and it is designed for integration with email servers that handle large volumes of email.

Product strengths

- It features a wide variety of local and network tests to identify spam signatures. There is no single test that spammers can identify and circumvent.

- It is easy to extend, since rules, weights, and user-configurable options are in text files.

- It integrates with all major message transport agents, including Microsoft Exchange.

- It integrates with many popular distributed hash databases that store spam signatures, such as Vipul's Razor, DCC, and Pyzor.

- SpamAssassin technology is built into many commercial antispam products.

Product weakness

- Users need to implement at least client server configuration for good performance.

SpamBayes

SpamBayes does for email readers what SpamAssassin does for email servers. It is a Bayesian classifier that provides a web-browser-based interface that allows an end user to instruct SpamBayes how to classify incoming email as spam—or not.

Product strengths

- It learns very quickly how to classify your email properly, and it improves over time.

- It works on Microsoft Windows and has an easy-to-use web interface for learning and classification.

- It provides a plug-in for Microsoft Outlook.

Product weakness

- It offers no initial spam training set.

Mailing List Managers

We define *mailing list management software* as software that manages various aspects of running an email list. Such aspects include managing user subscriptions and privacy, spam and virus blocking, and sending daily digests and message archiving.

Mailing list managers are crucial in the open source development world, since mailing list archives can become a knowledge base for an open source project and can help foster a community around the project. A healthy community is critical to the success of an open source project.

Mailing List Manager Solutions

Solutions in the mailing list manager space tend to be software programs that are tightly integrated with email servers, use filesystems for storing messages, and provide a web- and email-based interface. They provide easy access to mailing list archives; more mature solutions also provide searchable archives.

Mailing List Manager Capabilities

Here is a list of mailing list manager capabilities:

List administration

> The ability to subscribe and unsubscribe to mailing lists and options to manage subscription such as per-message delivery or digest delivery

> Support for multiple languages and support for privacy options such as message archive privacy and list-membership database privacy

Membership management

> The ability to put subscriptions on hold temporarily and the ability to support real names

Content management

> The ability to handle MIME attachments

Delivery capabilities

> Support for delivery options such as per-message and digest delivery, and the ability to handle bounced messages properly

Archiving capabilities

> Seamless, built-in archiving or support for external list archives like MHonArc and Gmane

Reporting capabilities

> The ability to generate reports for list usage and subscription activity

Mailing List Manager Projects

Open source projects in the mailing list management space tend to be collected around a few stable solutions, such as Mailman, Majordomo, and ListProc. With the advent of RSS and web-based forums and the overwhelming amount of spam in a typical user's inbox, collaboration via email lists is not an area of active development.

The open source developer community—and technical users elsewhere—still use mailing lists effectively. Any enterprise should look into mailing lists as a low-cost way of building a community and a knowledge base of product support and best practices.

Mailman

Mailman is one of the first mailing list managers that moved over to a web-based interface paradigm successfully in the late 1990s. Today it is the de facto mailing list manager in the open source world. It is the default mailing list manager available on SourceForge.net, and it is used widely elsewhere. It offers all of the basic and most of the advanced features one could hope for in a mailing list manager, and it integrates with most email servers and email archivers. It is also well documented and has an active, vibrant community that provides support.

Product strengths

- It supports the list moderator's role separate from the list administrator's role, allowing one person to administer the system-specific issues of many mailing lists and delegate list moderator roles to someone else, such as power users in the mailing list.

- It enjoys a large and active user community.

Product weaknesses

- Its web-based interface is less than pretty.

- It has no built-in ability to search on message archives.

Dada Mail

Dada Mail is a general-purpose mailing list manager targeted toward small to midsize enterprises and personal web sites. It started out in the classic open source fashion: one guy—a self-described noncomputer geek—built and released a good first version and then kept up with support issues and enhancements to grow it into community-supported software. A professional version, with advanced features, is also available.

Product strengths

- It features a powerful and easy-to-use web-based control panel.

- It offers support for sending small "batches" for large subscriber bases.

- A book is available about the product.

Product weakness

- True community mailing lists are hard to configure.

Groupware, Portals, and Collaboration

We define *groupware* as software that allows the people in an enterprise to participate in three broad classes of activity:

Communication

> Activities involving information and data sharing. Email, of course, is the pri-
> mary medium of communication. In some instances, sharing information in a
> more structured manner, such as via discussion threads and by keeping archives
> and making them searchable, adds value to the information. Discussion forums
> (also called bulletin boards) are a popular and effective medium for this type of
> activity. Weblogs and Wiki Webs are emerging media that also address needs in
> distributed, non-real-time communications. Perhaps weblogs and Wikis are pop-
> ular because they are lightweight, are easy to use, and have few access control
> restrictions. For more immediate and real-time communications, instant messag-
> ing solutions are appropriate. Use of instant messaging in the enterprise is a
> recent phenomenon, and best practices in this area are still unclear. Because of
> the disruptive nature of real-time communication, options such as instant mes-
> saging should be used sparingly.

Collaboration

> A process that seeks to build and develop a shared understanding that the col-
> laborating parties did not have at the beginning of the process. Document shar-
> ing, Wikis, and discussion forums are popular ways of collaborating.

Coordination

Coordination introduces order to collaboration activities. Workflows, task delegation, and notifications during shared document authoring are examples of coordination activities. Discussion forums, Wikis, and blogs offer notification features, by email or RSS, for example, that facilitate workflow building and other coordination efforts.

Groupware and collaboration technologies can be categorized along two primary dimensions, as shown in Figure D-1.

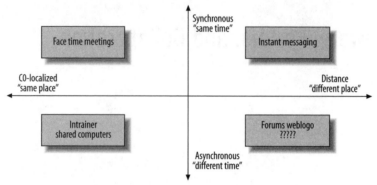

Figure D-1. *The dimensions of groupware and collaboration technologies*

It turns out that asynchronous distance collaboration methods, when aided by effective collaboration tools, also work well for groups that are collocated or are capable of synchronous collaboration but don't have the time for it. While it remains undisputed that face-to-face communication is the most effective means of collaboration and communication, it does come at a high cost.

The groupware field has a large number of open source projects because of the distributed nature of the open source development process. Most open source projects use more than one form of asynchronous, distance-based collaboration tool. Some projects also use real-time, distance-based collaboration tools, such as Internet Relay Chat (IRC), to conduct "meetings" among developers and to provide support.

Groupware

Solutions in the groupware space come in many different varieties. When designing collaboration processes, keep the following in mind:

- Collaboration can be highly disruptive. People take time to adapt to new collaboration processes.

- The collaboration process should be lightweight. Elaborate workflows and hierarchical access control rules tend to inhibit adoption.

- Cultural factors affect the outcome of the collaboration process. The primary reason Wikis are rejected is because they pose too much cultural change.

Therefore, you should implement new collaboration paradigms in phases and with great regard to the sensibilities of the users being affected.

Intranet Solutions

Intranet solutions range from basic document sharing solutions using a web server that is restricted to a LAN, to elaborate systems that provide everything from document management to project management and forums. A typical enterprise looking to set up or improve an intranet is trying to meet the high-level objectives of increased employee communication, collaboration, and knowledge management. More specifically, intranets are deployed to provide four common solutions: project management, software development process management, document management and distribution, and forums.

Project management

Managing projects, especially for distributed teams, is an effective use of intranets. Managing project schedules and documents is a common task that intranets support. Collaborating on and coordinating project documentation incrementally is another common solution facilitated by intranets.

Software development process management

Managing software development and maintenance is another common scenario where intranets can add value, particularly in regard to nightly software releases, bug-fix coordination, and other tasks related to software development. Intranet solutions also fit well in software documentation processes. A living document, such as a page on an intranet, is often more valuable than a static document that lives in a filesystem.

Document management and distribution

Managing documents is another common function that intranets provide. These activities range from collaboratively creating a document, to managing its various revisions and coordinating feedback during the review process. Distributing large documents across the enterprise via email is cumbersome, and intranets are a viable alternative. Several case studies show that large companies save significantly by distributing documents via an intranet rather than email.

Forums

Forums or message boards can be used as an effective, if informal, method of fostering collaboration inside an enterprise. An employee can build a knowledge base just by answering her fellow employees' questions.

Business Application Support

The collaboration tools we list in this appendix can provide a low-cost and effective mechanism for supporting a business application or service to external or internal users.

Forums

In scenarios where an enterprise application has users spread out in various locations, providing discussion forums for low-priority support requests (a defect tracking system should be used for high-priority requests), for community building, and for allowing users to support each other can be very effective.

Application/team weblog

Other mechanisms for providing product support are product weblogs and developer weblogs, where significant events in a product's development cycle can be posted. This gives interested users early information about an upcoming release. Similar information, when released via email, tends to affect the entire user base, when only a few users are interested in it. Weblogs also serve as an archive for this information.

Open Source Groupware Capabilities

In this section, we look at the features provided by open source projects.

Forums

Forums, or bulletin board software, are a popular and easy way to build, foster, and nurture a community. Basic web-based forums are easy to implement. Perhaps this why a lot of them are implemented in PHP. However, mature forum systems are hard to come by. What differentiates great forum software from the rest of the pack is its ability to allow a community to sustain itself and grow organically. It does this by providing granular access control in different levels of moderation, and by providing different features, such as the ability to let power users find unread posts, while not overwhelming novice users by providing sticky threads and a flexible search.

In the context of an enterprise, forums can be used to provide a variety of solutions, including community-managed product support.

Basic features

- Posting, replying, and editing topics and messages.
- Limited HTML tags for message styling.
- Automatic lost-password retrieval.
- Forum moderation.
- A moderation queue. In moderated forums, the moderator can view all unapproved messages and approve or delete them on the spot.

Content management and collaboration features

- Sticky/announcement messages that stay on top of the forum until they reach an expiry date

- Thread locking by forum administrators and moderators

- File extension control, allowing/disallowing uploading of certain files based on their extensions

- Fully customizable headers and footers, which can support PHP code

- Language filters that allow the administrator to replace certain offensive words

- Unread post tracking that automatically lets a user see which posts have not yet been read

- Extensive message filtering, by date, read/unread, forum, thread, and reply status

- Message reporting, which allows visitors to report inappropriate messages to the administrator

User management features

- Email confirmation of registered users

- Hidden, private, moderated, and password-protected forums

- Banning of users by their username and/or IP address or IP mask, email address filter, or login name filter to disallow users with privileged-sounding usernames or usernames from known problem email domains

- Cookie-based tracking system backed by sessions if the user cannot use cookies

- Polls (if allowed, users can create one or more polls on their messages)

Advanced usability features

- Post notification system, which can send notifications via email and RSS

- Forum and thread subscription system with an easy-to-use control panel that allows users to subscribe and unsubscribe from forums and threads

Recommended Open Source Groupware Projects

Many options are available in the open source forum software space. The most popular forum software is available on the LAMP platform and is written in PHP. We recommend phpBB because of its feature set, stability, and large installed user base, although vBulletin and Ultimate Bulletin Board are also viable choices. In the J2EE space, we recommend mvnForum, but we also consider JForum to be a solid choice.

phpBB

phpBB is a database-driven bulletin board package written in PHP. It works with major database servers, including MySQL, Access (via ODBC), MS-SQL, and PostgreSQL. It is user and administrator friendly, highly customizable, and very scalable.

Product strengths

- It supports all basic features.
- It features an integrated search facility.
- It includes versatile user groups and forum permissions.
- It offers powerful and friendly administration features.

mvnForum

mvnForum is an easy-to-use and easy-to-administer bulletin board software program written in Java using JSPs and servlets. It works with any servlet container that supports JSP 1.2 and Servlet 2.3 standards.

Product strengths

- It supports all basic features.
- It offers an integrated search facility using Lucene.
- It provides up-to-date spam prevention methods.
- It includes friendly administration features.

Product weakness

- Better user documentation is needed.

Portals

Two industry analysts at Merrill Lynch coined the term *Enterprise Information Portal* in November 1998 as "an amalgamation of software applications that consolidate, manage, analyze, and distribute information across and outside of an enterprise (including business intelligence, content management, data warehouse, and data management applications)."

We define *portals* more generally as web sites that collect, organize, and display large amounts of dynamic information in an organized manner. Portals are so named because they are considered gateways to the wide Internet, or to internal systems and applications, or both. In the late 1990s, for a brief time portals were considered the "next big thing" and were the subject of much hype and investment. Today portals such as Yahoo! News and MSN are quietly serving millions of users and easing their daily consumption of news and other information. Portal functionality is implemented as a collection of portal components (also known as *portlets*). From a user interface perspective, portals are designed with two- or three-column layouts where a user can pick portlets to display and the column to display them in. In this way, portals help the user build a personalized home page.

In the enterprise context, portals are used to streamline communication between management and employees, foster collaboration among employees, and give employees personalized access to the information and applications they need to do their work. Portals are cost effective, because they allow the possibility of consolidating servers and applications. Human resources information and news feeds are typical examples of the type of information that portals integrate well.

Portal Capabilities

It is important to note that portals share several features with content management systems, and many good content management systems provide an effective way to implement portals. This is why the open source projects we recommend in this appendix are content management systems that happen to be good at implementing portals.

Basic feature

- Two- or three-column layout

User management features

- User profile and personalization, such as my page, my preferences, etc.
- Integration with external authentication mechanisms such as LDAP

Content management features

- Integration with utility portlets, including address book and calendar
- Integration with information feeds, news feeds, weather feeds, and stock prices
- Integration with collaboration portlets such as instant messaging, forums, and surveys/polls

Recommended Open Source Portal Projects

In the following sections, we cover the open source portal projects we recommend.

Tikiwiki

Tikiwiki is a popular web publishing system written in PHP. It supports major databases (MySQL, PostgreSQL, Oracle, Sybase, and MS-SQL) and works with any web server that supports PHP, including Apache and IIS. Tikiwiki makes excellent use of external open source projects and boasts superior support for RSS. Tikiwiki supports Wiki markup and has a basic Wiki module, but you shouldn't confuse it with a Wiki.

Product strengths

- It supports all portal capabilities listed earlier.
- It includes an integrated keyword-based search facility.
- It supports numerous portal components out of the box.
- It boasts a large developer community with rapid releases.

Product weakness

- Performance of early releases was an issue.

Metadot

Metadot is a portal server written in Perl. It runs everywhere that Perl runs (all major flavors of Unix, as well as on Windows and Mac OS X systems). It also supports MySQL and Oracle databases.

Product strengths

- It supports all basic features.
- It features an integrated keyword-based search facility.
- It comes with portal components such as news and file management, a discussion forum, survey and calendar components, and many others.
- It is easy to use and is well documented.

Wikis

A Wiki (or a WikiWikiWeb) is a web site where all the pages are editable via the browser. *WikiWiki* means *quick* in Hawaiian, which is what Wiki webs are—quick to put together and quick to modify. More formally, Wiki webs are content management systems with very few hierarchies and controls. Wikis are well suited to building collaboration systems, since they have very flexible access controls and are easy to use. Wikis have simple text formatting rules that allow users to use rich markup tags without having to know any HTML. Wikis are implemented on a variety of platforms, with the LAMP platform leading the pack. Wikis use the filesystem or a small database as a content store and sometimes have a built-in caching layer.

In the enterprise context, Wikis can be used to provide a variety of solutions, including free-form collaboration sites, knowledge bases, and document management systems.

Wiki Capabilities

As you can see from the following subsections, Wikis have a variety of important capabilities in terms of content management and collaboration, as well as user management.

Basic features

- The ability to edit any page from a web browser
- Simple text formatting, the ability to create bold and italic words, and the ability to include hyperlinks to other Wiki pages and external web pages
- The ability to search across all Wiki pages

Content management and collaboration features

- The ability to attach files and build a simple document management process
- Revision control, which allows users to track changes to all files and attachments
- Templates and skins for changing the look and feel, headers, and footers of a collection of pages without affecting the content
- The ability to manage individual pages, and to delete and rename pages easily
- Topic locking, which keeps a page from being edited for a short time to prevent problems related to simultaneous page editing

User management features

- Access control, whereby users can control who gets access to different areas of the Wiki
- Web-based registration, with lost-password recovery
- Integration with existing authentication systems (e.g., Windows domain authentication or Active Directory)

Advanced usability feature

- Change notification of page updates through email or RSS

Recommended Open Source Wiki Projects

The Wiki software field is young, but at least one project is worth considering for every technology platform. Because Wikis get adopted in IT departments first, and because most installations undergo enhancements and customizations, the choice of platform is important. One particular flavor of Wiki stands out, in our opinion, especially in terms of features that make it a good fit for enterprises: TWiki (*http://www.twiki.org/*). Other projects to consider include MoinMoin, Media Wiki, and JSPWiki.

TWiki

TWiki is a flexible, powerful, and easy-to-use enterprise collaboration platform. It is a structured Wiki, typically used to run a project development space, a document management system, a knowledge base, or any other groupware tool, on an intranet or on the Internet. Web content can be created collaboratively by using just a browser. Developers can create new web applications based on a plug-in API.

Product strengths

- It is fully useable from the browser.

- It is extensible via plug-ins. Many plug-ins are available.

Product weakness

- Its installation process is complicated.

Messaging Systems

Messaging systems, such as instant messaging and IRC, provide real-time collaboration options analogous to asynchronous collaboration via forums and Wikis. Due to the distributed nature of open source development, messaging systems have long been used by developers to "meet" in real time to discuss, collaborate, and provide support to each other and to their users. When combined with logs of conversations, messaging systems can augment a knowledge base and add a much-needed real-time component to collaboration.

Instant messaging and chat-based messaging systems are on the leading edge of collaboration in the enterprise, even though the technology is popular in terms of general Internet use. This is probably because this form of collaboration first gained widespread use for social conversations. Enterprises can also have security concerns regarding network messaging traffic going through public servers such as AOL or Yahoo!, and being susceptible to eavesdroppers. Such concerns can be mitigated by running a private messaging server based on Jabber, or by using serverless instant messaging using Rendezvous. This ensures that all messaging traffic remains on local trusted networks.

The choice of an instant messaging client has a personal component for the user, since "conversations" via this medium are considered a form of personal expression, more than they are with other media such as email and forums. Mature clients address this by providing themes and other customizations to the user interface. Furthermore, large user communities exist in AIM, Yahoo!, MSN, ICQ, and IRC networks, and these networks use messaging protocols that are sometimes incompatible with each other. To address this issue, major clients provide support for simultaneous use of all major protocols. While the user will have to create an account on each network, the day-to-day experience of messaging with users on different networks is unified and seamless.

Messaging Capabilities

Messaging systems offer a variety of basic, collaboration, user management, usability, and security and privacy features.

Basic features

- One-on-one chat
- Presence management, customizable "away" messages
- Tabbed interface, for the ability to manage multiple chats in one window

Collaboration features

- Group chat
- Audio and video chat
- Ability to use multiple instant messaging networks simultaneously
- Ability to maintain multiple identities per instant messaging network
- Ability to send SMS messages

User management features

- Ability to categorize contact lists in groups
- Ability to store buddy lists on the server

Usability features

- Integrated spellchecker
- Notification of buddy logon
- Keyboard shortcuts
- Themes

Security and privacy features

- Secure instant messaging
- Serverless instant messaging via Rendezvous

Recommended Open Source Messaging Projects

The field of open source instant messaging clients is rich, with mature and stable clients available on every major platform. All of our recommendations meet most of the aforementioned features. We include Trillian in this list even though it is not an open source client. The basic client is available free of charge for noncommercial use. Here are our recommendations:

- Windows: Trillian and Gaim
- Mac OS X: AdiumX and Fire
- Linux: Gaim
- Jabber

Gaim

Gaim is a multiprotocol instant messaging client for Linux, BSD, Mac OS X, and Windows. It is compatible with AIM and ICQ (Oscar protocol), MSN, Yahoo! Messenger, IRC, Jabber, and other protocols. Gaim users can log into multiple accounts on multiple instant messaging networks simultaneously.

Product strengths

- It supports all basic features.
- It offers an integrated spellchecker.
- It is extensible via a plug-in API.
- It provides tabbed window support.

Product weakness

- It has no serverless (Rendezvous) support.

Trillian

Trillian is a full-featured, standalone, skinnable chat client that supports AIM, ICQ, MSN, Yahoo! Messenger, and IRC. It provides capabilities not available with original network clients, while supporting standard features such as audio chat, file transfers, group chat, chat rooms, buddy icons, multiple simultaneous connections to the same network, server-side contact importing, typing notification, direct connection (AIM), proxy support, encrypted messaging (AIM/ICQ), SMS support, and privacy settings.

Product strengths

- It supports all basic features.
- It includes an integrated spellchecker.
- It provides tabbed window support.

Product weaknesses

- It's free, but it's not open source.
- It's available for Microsoft Windows only.
- Advanced features are available in the Pro version only.

AdiumX

AdiumX is a multiprotocol instant messaging client for Mac OS X. It utilizes libgaim (the core part of Gaim) to connect via multiple protocols, and is based on a new plug-in architecture. Partial address book integration, a tabbed interface, multiple protocols for instant messaging, and a compact contact list are some of the many features of the new AdiumX.

Product strengths

- It supports all basic features.
- It offers wide support for protocol-level features via libgaim.
- It provides support for compact contact lists for smaller displays (like laptops).

Product weaknesses

- It is available for Mac OS X only.
- No logging ability is available for group conferences.

Fire

Fire is a multiprotocol Internet instant messaging client based on freely available libraries for each service. It is released under the GNU GPL. All services are built off libraries under GPL, including FireTalk, libicq2000, libmsn, Jabber, and libyahoo2. Fire can handle simultaneous connections to AIM, ICQ, Yahoo!, IRC, MSN, and Jabber.

Product strengths

- It supports all basic features.
- It offers per-contact notification settings.

Product weakness

- It is available for Mac OS X only.

Jabber

Jabber is an open, secure, ad-free alternative to consumer instant messaging services such as AIM, ICQ, MSN, and Yahoo!. Under the hood, Jabber is a set of streaming XML protocols and technologies that enable any two entities on the Internet to exchange messages, presence, and other structured information in close to real time. Open source clients and servers exist today to use Jabber-based instant messaging solutions. Since the protocol specification is open, it is a good choice for real-time messaging solutions for an enterprise. Visit the Jabber web site (*http://www.jabber.org/*) for a detailed list of servers and clients, and for further technical details.

Product strengths

- It is an open protocol, and it's XML-based (XMPP).
- It integrates with other messaging systems (AIM, Yahoo!, MSN, and ICQ) transparently, so phased migration is possible.
- Better presence management is built in, and asynchronous messaging is possible.

Product weakness

- XMPP is a verbose protocol, so you must plan for the additional network traffic.

APPENDIX E

Web Publishing and Content Management

Software for web publishing and content management is probably the most active area of open source use and development. The simple concept of a web site has taken on so many forms. Portals, intranets, extranets, knowledge hubs, and brochureware are examples of the sort of sites that are built with software for web publishing and content management. This explosion of solutions based on distributing information through web sites means that software for web publishing and content management applies to a greater variety of situations than any other type of open source.

For the most part, web publishing and content management are no longer optional capabilities for most companies. Many of the solutions we mention in this appendix are must-have items. The brochureware used for marketing in 1996 meant that a company was on the cutting edge. Now it is just another cost of doing business. Supporting web site creation and maintenance as efficiently and inexpensively as possible is an important task in almost every organization, and is one of the largest opportunities for open source to create value. One of the most popular projects for which open source is frequently considered is consolidation of the heterogeneous mixture of web publishing and content management systems onto a common platform.

In this appendix, we will review the most promising open source projects and explain how mature they are and for what solutions they are best suited. Before we do that, though, let's review the basic capabilities of online publishing, extranet, and intranet solutions.

Complete Content Management Systems

A complete content management system offers all the features needed to create, manage, and publish content for a web site by a team of people of varied technical backgrounds. After installation and initial configuration, such a system should allow users to perform most tasks via a rich and consistent user interface. The interface should be powerful enough to accommodate advanced users, yet intuitive and easy enough for beginners to use.

Basic Online Publishing Solutions

The common thread found in most online publishing solutions is that a company is using a web site to present information to some group of people outside the company.

Brochureware

Brochureware is perhaps the most common sort of web site in existence. It can be as simple as a set of HTML pages that act as an online resume for a company or an individual, or as complex as an interactive collection of web sites, each telling the story of a different part of the company.

Marketing collateral

Sites for marketing collateral present collections of whitepapers and other information that tells the story of a company or product.

Product information

Sites for product information include brochures on products, lists of features, downloads of development kits and other demonstrations, and possibly technical documentation.

Online publications

Online publications are newsletters or other sites that present information in the form of a publication rather than as brochureware. Most major products and other heavily marketed items now come with some sort of product-related site sponsored by the manufacturer. Sometimes these sites contain community features to encourage interaction among the site's visitors.

Weblogs

Weblogs are becoming a more popular feature of company sites that allow direct communication from key executives to their customers. In one sense, weblogs are simply another way to publish ideas and present them to the community; part of basic online publishing. But they can also encourage interaction with readers, and at that point weblogs become part of the collaborative systems we detailed in Appendix D.

How web publishing and content management systems help create basic online publishing solutions

Frequently the sites in this category start out as collections of HTML pages that are managed by a graphic designer using a tool such as Macromedia Dreamweaver. Web publishing and content management solutions become essential once the graphic designer gets overwhelmed with requests for changes, and the site's quality starts to slip as the number of pages grows.

Web publishing and content management solutions are used to implement sites that allow different groups to control the site's content, without having to go through an intermediary. The use of forms and templates to create content can help guarantee the site's quality. Workflow features ensure that all content appearing on the site is approved. Most web publishing and content management systems offer a large number of features that make sites easy to manage.

Extranet Solutions

Extranet solutions are about collaborating with people outside of a company via a web site. Usually, the web publishing and content management system provide only a portion of the solution that is made up of web content. Other applications for file sharing, specialized databases, or other functions are frequently part of extranets. Unlike basic online publishing solutions, extranet solutions frequently require users to register with the site and create an account so that they can be identified and have their access to the site verified.

Technical support

Most products have a web site that helps users solve problems by providing answers to their most common questions. Technical support sites usually act as a first level of support to allow customers to solve problems on their own, without having to call the company and speak to a support specialist. Complicated products such as large software programs can allow users and customers to search a database of bug reports. Such sites frequently allow customers to download updates or patches to fix certain problems or download tools and utilities to supplement the functionality of the main application.

Customer self-service

Customer self-service sites exist to allow customers to solve their problems on their own instead of having to rely on support specialists at call centers. Customer self-service sites at companies such as Federal Express and UPS allow customers to track packages. Many other companies are adding the same visibility into the process of fulfilling a customer order.

Training and e-learning

Training and e-learning sites exist to teach people how to use or support products. Such sites are frequently used to train people who are seeking some sort of certification as a support specialist or some other role that requires special knowledge.

Business-to-business relationship support

Frequently, as a precursor to a more automated relationship between two companies, a special-purpose web site is created that allows one company to interact with another company's systems. A web publishing system can be used to provide a gateway to an internal system, including all the training material required to understand the business processes and user interfaces.

How web publishing and content management systems help create extranet solutions

Most of the time, extranet solutions require some sort of registration, supporting content, and integration with another application. For this reason, it is natural to think of extranet solutions as more appropriate for a portal which specializes in creating one identity for the user and then allowing access to many different applications. But even in situations where a portal can be the right solution, a sizeable amount of content must be managed. It is important to recognize the potential of web publishing and content management solutions to provide portal-like solutions that include registration and integration of other applications.

Intranet Solutions

Intranet solutions are aimed at presenting information or collaborating inside a company. Web publishing and content management systems can be used to create several different types of sites for an internal audience.

Knowledge management

Knowledge management sites are dedicated to capturing and improving a body of knowledge about some topic that is important to a company. Knowledge management systems can be implemented in a variety of ways, but one popular model is to capture the knowledge as a series of articles on different topics. The articles are commented on by the company's employees, and then at certain points they are revised and updated.

Document management

The ability to upload files is a common feature of many web publishing and content management systems. Providing a centralized repository of documents that has versioning and the ability to track comments about each document can be a godsend for managing the documents related to a complex project.

Digital asset management

Frequently, digital assets such as images or engineering drawings can be managed using a web publishing and content management system. This sort of solution uses the web publishing system as a repository, just as in the document management solution, except digital assets are stored instead.

How web publishing and content management systems help create intranet solutions

Of course, any of the other solutions mentioned in the first two categories can be implemented on an intranet. The solutions we mention here as intranet solutions are focused on using the web publishing and content management system as an intelligent repository. Extremely advanced systems are available for managing knowledge, documents, and digital assets. But the first step toward using such advanced systems is understanding requirements; using a web publishing and content management system as a prototype can be a great way to start.

Web Publishing and Content Management System Capabilities

You can implement the solutions we listed earlier in many different ways. One of the most challenging aspects of evaluating web publishing and content management systems for a particular purpose is that so many different systems can be used to provide solutions, each in its own way and with its own set of capabilities.

The purpose of this section is to describe at a high and relatively detailed level the sort of capabilities that web publishing and content management systems provide. It is from these capabilities that the solutions we described earlier are constructed.

The challenge when summarizing the capabilities provided by web publishing and content management systems is the breadth of the functionality these systems offer. Perhaps the easiest way to approach the subject is to examine the three primary steps of most web publishing and content management processes:

Create
> The content is created or acquired.

Manage
> The content is manipulated, reviewed, and improved.

Deliver
> The content is rendered into publishable format and is presented to the audience.

Most content management systems have some subset of the capabilities covered in the following subsections.

Content Creation and Persistence

The capabilities in this category are focused on creating and storing content:

Content repository

> The repository is the star of the show for most web content management systems. The content that is eventually stored in pages is stored in this repository. It can be as simple as a filesystem or as complex as a special-purpose, object-oriented database. Most often, the content repository is a relational database.

Structured content types (record formats for addresses and forms for input)

> Web content management systems frequently are used for what some people call *database publishing*, which means forming web pages out of fields stored in a record in a database. An important feature to look for in a web content management system is support for structured content types that allow an existing database to be accessed and used when creating content.

End-user content creation tools

> Many web content management systems offer only the simplest web forms as a way to enter content. Adding just a little bit of markup, such as the ability to incorporate boldface and italics, can go a long way. Sometimes, with the help of browser plug-ins, a full-featured text editor can be delivered through the Web. XML editors are also often used to create and edit web content in both online and offline mode.

Integration with desktop editors

> Most content is created in word processors that make the job of writing much easier than with other tools, such as online editors or XML editors. Being able to accept content from Microsoft Word documents into a web content management system can greatly expand the pool of potential contributors, but opens up many quality control problems that can occur during conversion. Providing one-way support is seldom sufficient, because when an author wants to make changes, she will want to use the word processor, not an online interface.

Metadata management

> Metadata is data about the content in a web content management system. Metadata fields can be used to assign categories to content, to contain titles and summaries of articles, and to contain other fields such as the author, date of publication, and source for the content. Web content management systems sometimes have ways of automatically creating or assigning metadata and special interfaces for those responsible for focusing only on the metadata.

Versioning and change logs

> Keeping track of what has changed on a web site can be extremely valuable and is a common regulatory or compliance requirement. It can also help determine who changed what when, the usefulness of which goes way beyond finger

pointing. Some systems show reports that indicate what changed from one version of a piece of content to the next.

Workflow Management

Workflow is all about keeping track of who is doing what in a web content management system. Perhaps a better way to say it is that workflow is about who should be doing what, and whether they are doing it. Workflow is specified in most web content management systems in two ways:

State-based workflow

One of the most useful and simple workflow mechanisms is the ability to assign a state to a piece of content that determines what can be done with it. Typical states include approved, copyedited, and submitted. In a state-based workflow, a piece of content might have a person assigned as well, and perhaps a series of notes that reflect what everyone did.

Process-based workflow

A process-based workflow keeps track of more complicated activities that involve many different content items. It can be used in conjunction with a state-based workflow. A publishing process for documents about a new product might have many different stages, each with its own process. The planning stage defines what documents were to be created, and then a resource allocation stage might be executed to determine who would create each piece of content. Publication might not be allowed until all content items are in an "approved" state.

Search

Search capabilities range from being able to choose to see a list of all content that is in a certain category of metadata, to a full, free text search in which documents with specific words, phrases, and combinations thereof can be located. It is not uncommon for web content management systems to have a simple, moderately powerful search capability. Most of the time, full-featured search can be added with an open source project for that particular purpose.

Site Administration

Site administration is all about managing the day-to-day operations of a web content management system. The following capabilities of web content management systems should be considered:

Installation packages

Open source programs vary widely in the way that installation packages are created. The best programs have wizardlike functionality that guides users through software installation and basic configuration. Many open source programs have basic instructions and require more user expertise.

Administrative interfaces

Administrative interfaces assist system administrators and users in configuring software behavior. Open source programs have everything from form-based interfaces to property files containing settings that control system behavior.

Archiving

Content can proceed through a life cycle in many web content management systems. At the end of that life cycle, the content is removed from the repository and placed into an archive. Some web content management systems come with this as a prebuilt function, and others have toolkits that enable users to construct such functionality.

Task scheduling

Web content management systems support a variety of processes to maintain and update content. Most systems have a way of scheduling when a content item might be published to a site. Others have task scheduling systems that allow arbitrary tasks to be scheduled and executed.

Multisite support

Frequently in corporate environments, one database of content items might be used to create several different sites. Some web content management systems allow several different sets of templates to be maintained, each able to access the same repository of underlying content. Several sites can be created and maintained from one repository in this manner.

Security

Security in web content management systems ranges from simple role-based security that allows different users to perform different functions based on their role, to incredibly fine-grained security models that control read/write permissions to individual content items.

Page and User Interface Design

Capabilities in this section involve dealing with the design of pages where content will be displayed, as well as the user interface that content creators and administrators will deal with on a day-to-day basis:

Page templates

Templating is a core function of web content management systems. Templates allow users to design a page's form and publish many different instances of the form by substituting different content in specified locations of the template. The templating architecture of web content management systems ranges from substitution of variables, to HTML-like display templates, to clever use of XML and XSLT transformations, to incredibly elaborate templating languages that allow complex logic that is executed as part of the templating process.

Content components

Templating systems frequently have a component architecture in which certain types of content components are defined. Such content components might contain the navigation of a page, or interfaces to commonly used content from third parties.

Navigation

Templating systems frequently have specialized support for creating common navigation among a group of pages.

Print-friendly versions

Templating systems have strategies or prebuilt templates for creating print-friendly versions of articles.

Multilanguage support

Multilanguage support generally comes in two flavors: support for different languages in the navigation or "chrome" of the page and support for different languages in the body of the page. Multilanguage support for navigation involves building the site's templates in such a fashion that all natural-language elements are stored in property files. When a user accesses the system, the preferred language is identified and then site navigation is presented using the property files of that desired language, if they exist. Multilanguage support for content within the page's frame means that the content items in the repository can be rendered in different languages, and the correct version of the content items must be selected based on the viewer's preference.

Content Delivery and Distribution

Capabilities in this section involve delivering the content for distribution once it is published. The speed with which content can be delivered to the final distribution environment is often an important consideration when choosing or building a web content management system.

Page rendering

Templates and content items can be rendered into pages in a variety of different ways. Pages can be dynamic (created when requested), or they can be created in advance so that they can be delivered as quickly as possible. All sorts of other strategies are possible, including rendering parts of the pages in advance or creating an entire site in static HTML files.

Web server support

Most open source web content management systems support Apache, but other web servers such as Microsoft IIS and Netscape are frequently supported. Some web content management systems are not linked to a specific web server.

Email support

Publishing content through email or sending alerts about various events or workflow tasks is the most common way that email is supported in web content management systems.

Load balancing

Web content management systems can support different scalability strategies, such as replicating versions of the content across many web servers or allowing many page template engines to be replicated on top of a single repository.

Integration with Web-based Distributed Authoring and Versioning (WebDAV)

Many web content management systems support the WebDAV protocol to allow easy access to the repository using commonly available tools.

Integration with FTP

Many web content management systems support the FTP protocol to accept or distribute content.

Replication and distribution

Replication and distribution of content using XML, the ICE protocol, RDIST, or many other mechanisms are supported by web content management systems for syndicating content, or for other purposes.

Recommended Open Source Content Management System Projects

The projects we focus on in this section include:

Plone

Plone is a content management system that can be used as a portal, a document management system, an intranet server, an extranet server, or a collaboration server.

Drupal

Drupal is a content management system for building dynamic web sites for a broad range of projects, from personal weblogs to community-driven sites.

OpenCms

OpenCms is a content management system that can be used to build complex intranet and extranet sites quickly and cost effectively.

Plone

Plone is a turnkey content management system that is built on the powerful and free Zope application server. It requires minimal effort to set up, is deeply flexible, and provides a system for managing web content that is ideal for project groups, communities, and intranets.

Plone is good at many things, including workflows, content classification, and asset management. Users trying to build web sites focusing on digital media assets, collaboration, and even a custom project management site will benefit from Plone's strengths (see Table E-1).

Product strengths

- It offers good management defaults out of the box.
- It is standards compliant with XHTML, Dublin Core, RSS, and others.

Product weaknesses

- Many useful features are available via add-ons instead of via the core application.
- It is a big, complex system with a steep learning curve.

Table E-1. *Plone basic facts*

License	GPL (dual licensing scheme under consideration by Plone Foundation)
Home page	http://www.plone.org/
Version evaluated	2.0.2 (released May 20, 2004)

Drupal

Drupal is an open source platform and content management system for building dynamic web sites offering a broad range of features and services, including user administration, publishing workflow, discussion capabilities, news aggregation, metadata functionalities using controlled vocabularies, and XML publishing for content sharing purposes. Equipped with a powerful blend of features and configurability, Drupal can support a diverse range of web projects, from personal weblogs to large, community-driven sites.

Drupal's key strength is its flexible content classification capability, available via its taxonomy module. It is possible to assign every content item multiple classification keywords and then to build complex views of content based on this classification. Users building dynamic web sites where multiple views of content are a primary feature or a requirement will benefit from Drupal's strengths (see Table E-2).

Product strengths

- It features a powerful taxonomy and content classification system where content items are nodes and they can belong to multiple categories.
- It offers a mature code base that is actively supported.
- It is well documented, and is easy to install and configure in a few hours.

Product weaknesses

- No standardized PHP templating system is in use (e.g., Smarty).
- It has a relatively steep initial learning curve.

Table E-2. *Drupal basic facts*

License	GPL
Home page	http://www.drupal.org/
Version evaluated	4.4.1 (released May 1, 2004)

OpenCms

OpenCms helps users create and manage complex web sites easily, without knowledge of HTML. An integrated WYSIWYG editor with a user interface similar to that of well-known Office applications helps users create the content, and a sophisticated template engine enforces a sitewide corporate layout.

OpenCms excels at building custom web-based content management solutions from scratch, especially if the system's functional requirements are atypical and the system doesn't fit into any one popular category, such as portal or intranet server. The administrative interface is window-centric and has a low learning curve. The main window resembles Windows Explorer, and OpenCms provides a functional WYSIWYG page editor (see Table E-3).

Product strengths

- It offers a mature, widely deployed code base.
- It is very portable (it is Java and XML based).
- It is easily extensible via a modules API.

Product weakness

- Templating should better leverage open standards (e.g., JSTL, Velocity).

Table E-3. *OpenCms basic facts*

License	GPL
Home page	http://www.opencms.org/
Version evaluated	5.0.1 (released January 9, 2004)

Weblog Publishing Systems

Weblog publishing systems focus on publishing content that is short, timely, and usually presented in reverse chronological order. These systems are most often used by one person to generate concise text commenting on one or more articles found elsewhere on the Web. Therefore, content creation involves citing and linking to other content. Advanced weblog systems also offer the ability to categorize content easily, as it is being created, as well as collaborative content generation. Drupal and Blosxom have powerful categorization features. Geeklog excels at access control and workflows. Another common use of these systems is to allow readers to comment on the content. Slashdot is a good example of a powerful web discussions forum that works at a very active site and allows community moderation. Weblog publishing systems are an emerging section of the content management system field. While they started out as vanity online diaries, new and effective ways to use them in the enterprise are emerging, such as for project weblogs.

Geeklog

Geeklog is a small content management system for dynamic web sites that have simple workflows in the publish process. Geeklog also works well in situations where users should see different content details based on their access level. It is written in PHP and can be deployed on the LAMP platform.

Product strengths

- It offers flexible access control and workflow features.
- It is easily extensible via a modules API.

Product weakness

- It has difficult to modify user interface elements in Version 1.x.

Blosxom

Blosxom is a very small but powerful weblogging system. It has a simple and elegant design and packs a lot of functionality in a small code base. Since it is written in Perl, it can be deployed on Windows, Mac OS X, and Linux with equal ease.

Product strengths

- It is fast and flexible.
- It is easily extensible via a modules API, and it boasts a large collection of modules.

Product weakness

- Content is stored in flat files.

Content Management System Toolkits and Components

Often an enterprise wants to offer a content management system to a collection of internal users or customers, and none of the solutions available is a good fit for the requirements. In this scenario, it makes sense to go with a content management system that comes with a toolkit to extend and modify its functionality. By definition, all open source content management systems are toolkits, but some are designed better than others when it comes to being extensible. When evaluating candidates in this area, one should focus on code base quality (a well-defined API and good documentation), and the availability of the components in all major areas of a content management system (content creation, publishing, versioning, and workflows). All the projects we have recommended are good candidates for use as toolkits.

Content management system toolkits can be used to build custom content management systems that fit requirements developed internally. They help accelerate the progress of development by providing preexisting components and a functional API that allows developers to work on high-level concepts, such as workflow and site design, instead of inventing templating from scratch.

Apache AxKit

Apache AxKit is a content management system and XML application server that builds dynamic web sites. AxKit is built on top of mod_Perl and it uses XML and XSLT very effectively.

Product strengths

- It has a flexible pipeline of components, and it is easy to replace any component with a custom one.

- It offers full separation of content and presentation.

Product weakness

- It has a steep learning curve.

Application Development

Application servers are software systems that act as containers for deploying applications. They are typically implemented as virtual machines (VMs), which make it easier to manage running applications, and they coordinate an application's interactions with other server systems such as databases and web servers. An application server is a software framework that consists of APIs to coordinate and facilitate integration with other servers. They are typically deployed between a web server and a database server in a two- or three-system configuration.

The history of application servers and Internet technology is short but full of rapid innovations. During the early days, the Internet was full of static HTML documents and only web servers were required. With the growth of dynamic content, the Common Gateway Interface (CGI) protocol was invented and it quickly saw widespread use. This protocol was supposed to provide a standard way for web servers to interface with other servers. Nevertheless, it proved to be inadequate for supporting various complex interactions. To support the explosive growth of e-commerce and content-based web sites, three-tiered architecture approaches were quickly adopted as a best implementation practice.

Enterprise-class application servers are available for all major technology stacks—J2EE, .NET, LAMP, etc.—and have kept up with the technology trends by providing facilities to implement Service Oriented Architectures (SOAs) to address complex middleware integration challenges. The application server market is now heading toward commoditization, with mature open source application servers providing viable alternatives to proprietary options offered by vendors. This is especially true in the J2EE space, where professional open source companies such as JBoss have more than one-third of the market share (ahead of offerings from IBM and BEA).

This appendix covers the major open source application servers available today. When choosing an open source application server for use in enterprise applications, you should keep the following criteria in mind:

- Application server stability and performance should be of primary importance. Business-critical applications should not be deployed on unstable or immature platforms.

- Application servers provide a framework and integrate deeply with software written at an enterprise. Finding an application server that is a good fit with the developers' existing skill set is key. See Chapter 3 for more information about assessing your skill level.

- Often the functionality of a full application server is obtained by combining several open source projects.

Capabilities

Application servers provide facilities to support the creation of applications quickly and reliably using industry-standard best practices. They also provide facilities to operate and manage these applications in a reliable manner.

Presentation Management Facilities

Presentation management facilities include the following:

Template support
    Allows the creation of templates for various presentation views.

Model-View-Controller (MVC) support
    Allows the separation of development related to presentation from that related to business logic in an application. Application servers support this standard application design pattern to manage complexity and allow division of labor during application development.

Session Management Facilities

Session management facilities include the following:

Session persistence and failover support
    Allows support of many current users in an application, as well as graceful recovery if the application crashes

Administration, Configuration, and Diagnostic Facilities

Administration, configuration, and diagnostic facilities include the following:

Load balancing and clustering support
> Allows deployment of applications across multiple servers, and the ability to support a larger user base without changing the application code.

Debugging and logging framework support
> Provides facilities to debug and log application use and error conditions, and helps with bug fixes and other application improvements.

Subsystem monitoring and management
> Allows individual components within applications to restart, without having to restart the entire application server. This helps with releasing new versions of applications without incurring an outage.

External Systems Integration Support

External systems integration support includes the following:

Database server integration
> Allows database connection pools and object-to-relational-mapping tools.

Integration with external systems
> Allows for industry-standard integration technologies such as messaging systems and web services.

Open Source Application Servers

Since open source application development servers are used primarily to build and deploy applications, we present these servers here, grouped by technology rather than solution. The following subsections describe application servers in four technology groupings: Java, Perl, PHP, and Other (those deemed worthy of inclusion, but which do not fit into the other three categories).

Java Application Servers

A fully standards-compliant Java application server includes technologies to serve web pages using Java Server Pages (JSP) and servlets (typically called servlet containers), along with technologies to manage transactions with external systems, such as databases called Enterprise JavaBean™ (EJB) containers. As is common in other areas of the open source stack, a complete Java application server is a collection of open source projects. Apache Tomcat and Jetty are popular choices for a servlet container, and JBoss and JOnAS are popular EJB containers. For major platforms (Microsoft Windows, Linux, Solaris) bundled distributions of these two technologies are available for easy download and installation. The architecture of this solution is shown in Figure F-1.

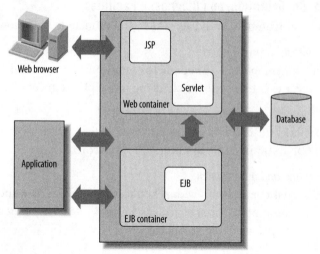

Figure F-1. *Typical J2EE application server*

A Java application server using Apache Tomcat as the servlet container and JBoss as the EJB container is a popular choice and is our recommendation. Other combinations using Jetty or JOnAS are also worth exploring.

Apache Tomcat

Apache Tomcat is an open source servlet container and the official reference implementation for Java servlet and JSP technologies. It is the most popular open source servlet container and is widely deployed. It features full Servlet 2.4 API support, and JSP 2.0 support for Tomcat Version 5.5.x and Servlet API 2.3 as well as JSP 1.2 support for Version 4.1.x. Tomcat has a very large user base and a very active developer community.

JBoss

JBoss is the only standards-compliant J2EE application server that is certified to the J2EE 1.4 specification. It has been deployed widely, has active community support, and is backed by a professional company that can provide enterprise-grade support. JBoss has a reputation for above-average performance.

Perl Application Servers

Most of the popular Perl application servers are based on mod_perl, which is a module for Apache Web Server that allows users to embed a Perl interpreter in the web server. This has the advantages of avoiding start-up overhead when running Perl applications, and allowing flexible web request processing made possible by close coupling of the Apache Web Server and the Perl interpreter. Several application frameworks built on top of mod_perl are worthy of consideration if you are in the market for a Perl application server.

HTML::Mason

HTML::Mason is a templating and presentation framework built on mod_perl. It provides facilities for building, serving, and managing large web sites. Mason excels in dealing with dynamic content and is a good fit for e-commerce sites.

Apache::AxKit

AxKit is an XML application server built on top of mod_perl. It provides a simple way to deliver content to multiple channels and devices in different formats. AxKit uses XSLT extensively.

PHP Application Servers

PHP-based application servers are typically architected as modules for web servers (mod_php for Apache and an ISAPI module for IIS). Additionally, PHP can be deployed via the CGI protocol. While no enterprise-grade, open source PHP application servers are available, several frameworks are available that you can combine to get the job done. Since this is an area of rapid innovation, we present an incomplete list of popular and mature frameworks, without a complete evaluation of their strengths and weaknesses.

PEAR

PEAR (*http://pear.php.net/*) is short for PHP Extension and Application Repository. PEAR's purpose is to provide a structured library of open source code for PHP users, and a system for code distribution and package maintenance. PEAR code is partitioned in *packages*. Each package is a separate project with its own development team, version number, release cycle, and documentation, and a defined relation to the other packages (including dependencies).

Mojavi

Mojavi (*http://www.mojavi.org/*) is an open source MVC framework for PHP, and is licensed under the LGPL. Developing with Mojavi enables you to easily divide your web application into tiers, allowing for independent development. It features a modular design, a logging system, built-in authentication and authorization, and a vibrant, active community.

Smarty

Smarty (*http://smarty.php.net/*) is a template/presentation framework. It provides the programmer and template designer with a wealth of tools for automating tasks commonly dealt with in an application's presentation layer. It features caching, easy maintainability via simple template syntax, and debugging support.

Other Application Servers

Lastly, we present some application servers and frameworks that don't fit our classification scheme but are still worth mentioning.

OpenACS

The Open Architecture Community System (OpenACS) is a framework for building scalable, community-oriented web applications. It runs on AOL's web server, an application server, TCL for scripting and templates, and PostgreSQL or Oracle as its relational database. OpenACS has been around since 1995 and has been used for some large deployments. It features a mature code base, significant out-of-the-box functionality, and an active and helpful community.

Zope

Zope is an open source web application server written primarily in the Python programming language. It features a transactional object database which can store not only content, but also custom data. Zope includes a content management framework that is used by an excellent content management system called Plone. Plone is featured in Appendix E.

 Index

A

AdiumX, 186
administration facilities, 205
administration interfaces, reducing skills gap
        with, 110
administrative interfaces, 196
Adobe FileMaker, alternatives to, 154
adopting open source
        becoming build-leaning by, 142
        benefits of, 114
        controlling it, 91
        crafting strategies for, 80–89
        productization and, 105–107
advanced skill level, 53–55
        accelerating learning of open
                source, 110
        moving to, 87
        productization and, 107
"Agile" development methodologies, 11, 143
Analog Realtime Synthesizer, 156
antispam software, 169
antivirus software, 169

Apache, 6
        example of formal community, 14
        helpful knowledge to have about, 61
        open source platforms for, 149
Apache AxKit application server, 202, 207
Apache License 2.0, 122
Apache Software Foundation (ASF), 122
Apache Tomcat application server, 35, 206
a-patch-y server, 12
API documentation, accelerating learning
                with, 110
Apple Public Source License (APSL), 125
application development platforms, 149
application servers, 203–208
        capabilities of, 204
        Java, 205
        Perl, 206
        PHP-based, 207
applications platforms, 150
applying open source, crafting strategies
                for, 89–91
APSL (Apple Public Source License), 125
architecture documentation, accelerating
                learning with, 111

architecture of program as evaluation
        factor, 38
archiving web content, 196
Artistic license (Perl), 123
ASF (Apache Software Foundation), 122
attacks against open source, 127–136
automating projects to reduce skills
        gap, 109

B

Ballmer, Steve, 133
BBS (bulletin board system) for
        projects, 108
beginner skill level, 51
    becoming a beginner, 83–85
    getting started with open source, 109
    productization and, 106
Bellendorf, Brian, 57
Berkeley license, 121
blacklist/whitelist support, 170
Blosxom, 201
Boies, David, 129
Bricolage, 19
brochureware, 190
browsing the web, 154
    with Firefox, 157
BSD licenses, 121
bundles of software, certified, 99
    reasons for choosing, 102
business-to-business relationship
        support, 192
buying versus building software, 138–140

C

C ++ programming language, 62
C programming language, 62
Caldera, 128–130
The Cathedral and the Bazaar, 10
certified bundles of software, 99
    reasons for choosing, 102
Chandler, 167
chat-based messaging systems, 184–187
Clam AntiVirus, 170
ClamWin, 170
code quality as evaluation factor, 37
collaboration technologies, 175–185
commercial conflicts as evaluation factor, 40

commercial open source support
        choosing the right one, 101–103
    evaluating providers for, 97
    "one throat to choke" approach, 137
    using care when buying, 103
commercial software, 19–22
    generic support offered by, 96
    life cycle of, 19–22
    open source-based products offered
        by, 101
    risks of, versus open source software,
        24–28
    ROI for, versus open source, 69–75
committers, 14
communities, building/nurturing with
        forums, 178
community skills for using open source, 63
community vitality as evaluation factor, 34
Compiere, 101
configuration costs for open source/
        commercial software, 72
    elements of, 77
configuration facilities, 205
configuration tools, reducing skills gap
        with, 109
consulting services, 101
    creating custom features using, 103
content management systems, 190–193
    capabilities of, 193–198
    for dynamic web sites, 201
    for groupware, 179
    for portal projects, 181
    for Wikis, 183
    recommended projects, 198–200
    toolkits/components, 202
content repository, 194
content scanners, 163, 168–171
Copyleft license, 9, 119–121, 132
copyright issues for open source
        projects, 131–133
corporate commitment as evaluation
        factor, 40
corporate licenses, 123–126
Courier-IMAP, 161
CPAN (Comprehensive Perl Archive
        Network), 58
Crossing the Chasm, 46, 48–50

culture as evaluation factor, 33
Cunningham, Ward, 112
custom enhancements to open source
        projects, 100
customer self-service sites, 191
customization costs for open source/
        commercial software, 73
    elements of, 77

D
Dada Mail, 173
database management system for desktop
        (MySQL), 156
database publishing, 194
definition of open source, 7–12
delivering web content for distribution, 197
dependencies as evaluation factor, 39
design quality as evaluation factor, 37
desktop database management, 154
desktop environments, 153
    KDE, 155
desktop functions and key capabilities, 155
desktop productivity suites, 156
desktop, end-user computing on, 151–157
developers, networking with, 63
development tools, creating using open
        source, 57
diagnostic facilities, 205
diagnostic routines, reducing skills gap
        with, 110
digital asset management, 193
distributing web content, 197
"Do It Yourself IT" approach, 141
documentation
    as evaluation factor, 35
    for projects, 108
    managing, using intranets, 177, 192
Drupal, 198, 201
dual licensing approach, 126
dynamic IT systems, applying open source
        to, 90, 139

E
early adopters (advanced skill level), 49
Eclipse project (IBM), 11
Eclipse Public License (EPL), 125
ecological balance of programs, 39
e-learning/training sites, 192
email and open source, 159–173

email client capabilities (open source), 165–
        167
email client projects (open source), 167
email content scanners, 168–171
email server capabilities (open source), 161–
        163
email server projects (open source), 163–
        165
embedded components guide, accelerating
        learning with, 111
empowering companies using open
        source, 137–146
end-of-life for commercial software, 22
end-user computing on desktop, 151–157
end-user content creation tools, 194
end-user support as evaluation factor, 34
engineering practices and open source
        projects, 143
enhancements (custom) to open source
        projects, 100
Enterprise Information Portal, 180
EPL (Eclipse Public License), 125
estimates for ROI model, creating, 75
evaluating open source, 6
evaluation costs for open source/commercial
        software, 70
    elements of, 76
Evolution (Novell), 166, 167
examples of projects, 108
Exchange (Microsoft), 160–161
Exim, 165
experimental applications and risks, 65
expert skill level, 55–57
    accelerating learning of open
        source, 110
    moving to, 87
    productization and, 107
external systems integration support, 205
extranet solutions, 191
eXtreme Programming, 11, 112, 143

F
failure risks, commercial software versus
        open source, 27
FAQs (frequently asked questions) for
        projects, 108
fear, uncertainty, and doubt (FUD), the
        sowing of, 127, 134
Ferguson, Scott, 33

Fire, 187
Firefox web browser, 157
flexibility of products, commercial software
        versus open source, 26
flexible IT systems, applying open source
        to, 90, 139
forking the project, 16
forums
        as evaluation factor, 35
        fostering collaboration using, 177–179
Four Freedoms, 9
Free Rider Problem, 9
free software, 9, 118
Free Software Foundation, 9, 121, 132
FreeBSD license, 121
freeware, 8
FUD (fear, uncertainty, and doubt), the
        sowing of, 127, 134

G
Gaim, 186
Geeklog, 201
Gluecode, 101
GNOME 2.x window manager, 153
GNU configure and build system, 58
GNU General Public License (GPL), 9, 118,
        119–121
Gosling, James, 62
governance models for open source, 91–93
GPL (GNU General Public License), 9, 118,
        119–121
groupware, 176–180
        features provided by open source
                projects, 178
        recommended projects, 179

H
history of email for the enterprise, 159
hosting environment and open source, 58
HTML::Mason application server, 207
hurdle rates, 69

I
IBM versus SCO Group, 127–136
indemnification offered to open source
        customers, 134
infrastructure components of open
        source, 60
infrastructure platforms, 149

innovators (experts), 49
installation costs for open source/
        commercial software, 72
        elements of, 77
installation packaging as evaluation
        factor, 36
installation scripts, reducing skills gap
        with, 109
instant messaging, 184–187
institutional skill building, 88
integration costs for open source/
        commercial software, 73
        elements of, 77
integration criteria, assessing maturity
        using, 42
integration of projects, improving, 111
interdependencies as evaluation factor, 39
intermediate skill level, 52–53
        getting started with open source, 109
        moving to, 85–87
        productization and, 106
intranet solutions, 192
        for groupware, 177
investing in productization, 106
IRC (Internet Relay Chat), 176, 184–187
IT departments, choosing to use open
        source, 137–146
IT systems, categories of, 89

J
Jabber, 187
Java application servers, 205
Java programming language, 62
Java-centric systems, 58
JBoss application server, 206
JForum, 179
JOS Wiki, 112
JSPWiki, 183

K
Kapoor, Chet, 98
Kapor, Mitch, 167
Katz, Phil, 8
KDE (K Desktop Environment), 155
KDE 3.x window manager, 153
key-person problem, 47, 55
        institutional skill building and, 88
King, Gavin, 33
knowledge management sites, 192

Knuth, Donald, 123
KOffice productivity suite, 156

L

LAMP platform, 148, 179, 201
LDAPv3, 165
leadership as evaluation factor, 32
learning culture, creating, 142
legal issues affecting open source, 127–136
Lerdorf, Rasmus, 62
LGPL (Lesser General Public License), 92
licenses, open source, 9
    comparison of, 117–126
    costs of, 71
    types of, as evaluation factor, 40
life cycle
    of commercial software, 19–22
    of open source, 16
Linux, 1
    distribution choices, 153
    helpful knowledge to have about, 60
ListProc, 172
lock-in by vendors, reducing, 145
low-priority systems and risks, 65
Lucent public license, 126

M

Mail Delivery Agents (MDAs), 163
Mail Transfer Agents (MTAs), 163
mailing list management software, 171–173
Mailman, 173
maintaining commercial software, 22
maintenance costs for open source/
    commercial software, 71
Majordomo, 172
managing open source, crafting strategies
    for, 91–93
marketing collateral, 190
marketing/selling open source, 8
Matsumoto, Yukihiro, 62
maturity of open source
    affect on skills and resources, 64
    elements of, 31–41
    evaluating, 63
    measuring, 29–44
McBride, Darl, 129
MDAs (Mail Delivery Agents), 163
Media Wiki, 183

message boards, fostering collaboration
    using, 177–179
messaging clients, 154
messaging systems, 184–187
metadata management on web sites, 194
Metadot, 182
METAFONT program, license for, 123
Microsoft Access/Microsoft FoxPro,
    alternatives to, 154
Microsoft and SCO lawsuit, 128, 131, 133
Microsoft Exchange, 160–161
Microsoft Office, 156
Microsoft Outlook, 159–162
migration scenarios, 152
MIMEDefang, 169
mission statements of projects, 107
mission-critical systems
    commercial open source support
      for, 102
    risks and, 65
MIT license, 122
mod_perl, 206
models for evaluating open source, 5
Moglen, Eben, 132
MoinMoin, 183
Mojavi application server, 207
momentum as evaluation factor, 37
money versus skills, 78
Moore, Geoffrey, 46, 48–50
Mozilla Public License (MPL), 124
Mozilla Thunderbird, 168
MPL (Mozilla Public License), 124
MTAs (Mail Transfer Agents), 163
Mutt, 167
mvnForum, 180
MySQL desktop DBMS, 156
    helpful knowledge to have about, 61

N

narrowness of commercial software,
    measuring, 74
Naughton, Patrick, 62
NetBSD license, 121
Netscape Public License (NPL), 124
networking with open source developers, 63
nightmares created by open source,
    preventing, 46–48
Novell and SCO lawsuit, 128–130
Novell Evolution, 166, 167

Novell Open Exchange, 161
NPL (Netscape Public License), 124

O

"one throat to choke", lack of, with open
source, 137
online forums as evaluation factor, 35
online publications, 190
online publishing solutions, 190
Open AMF project, 40
Open Office productivity suite, 156
open source
architecture of program as evaluation
factor, 38
benefits/responsibilities of, 2
code quality as evaluation factor, 37
commercial conflicts as evaluation
factor, 40
community vitality as evaluation
factor, 34, 36
corporate commitment as evaluation
factor, 40
culture factor when evaluating, 33
debate about, 3
definition of, 7–12
documentation as evaluation factor, 35
email and, 159–173
end-user support as evaluation
factor, 34
evaluating, 6
how it dies, 15–16
how it grows, 14
installation packaging as evaluation
factor, 36
interdependencies as evaluation
factor, 39
leadership factor when evaluating, 32
leadership in life cycle of, 16
maturity of (see maturity of open
source)
nature of, exploring, 6–8
origins of, 12–13
release frequency as evaluation
factor, 37
risks of (see risks)
second-generation trends in, 18
selling/marketing, 8
site design as evaluation factor, 39
skill levels, 48–57

standards support as evaluation
factor, 39
support for, 95–104
testing facilities as evaluation factor, 38
traps to avoid during evaluation, 30
understanding your readiness for, 4–6
Open Source Definition (OSD), 8, 9
Open Source Initiative (OSI), 8
open source licenses, 9
costs of, 71
types of, 40
Open Source Maturity model, 5, 23, 41–44
open source nightmares, preventing, 46–48
open source platforms, 148–150
assembling, 150
Open Source Policy Document (HP), 93
Open Source Review Process (HP), 93
Open Source Risk Management, 133, 135
Open Source Skills and Risk Tolerance
model, 5, 23, 26, 48
OpenACS (Open Architecture Community
System), 208
OpenBSD license, 121
OpenCms, 198
OpenLDAP, 161, 165
OpenOffice.org, 1
operational routines, reducing skills gap
with, 110
operational systems and risks, 65
operations and open source, 59
operations costs for open source/commercial
software, 74
elements of, 78
OSD (Open Source Definition), 8, 9
OSI (Open Source Initiative), 8
Outlook (Microsoft), 159–162

P

packaging installation as evaluation
factor, 36
page templates for web sites, 196
patents as threats to open source, 135
PEAR (PHP Extension and Application
Repository), 207
Perl application servers, 206
Perl Artistic license, 123
Perl programming language, 62
Perl-centric systems, 58
Peterson, Christine, 10

PHP Nuke project, 16
PHP scripting language, 62
PHP systems, 58
PHP-based application servers, 207
phpBB, 180
PKZIP program, 8
Plan 9 operating system, 126
platforms, 148
    for application development, 149
    for applications, 150
    for infrastructure, 149
Plone, 19, 198
portals, 180–182
portlets, 180
Postfix, 160, 164
presentation management facilities, 204
preventing open source nightmares, 46–48
problems with open source
    preventing, 46–48
    uncovering during evaluation, 30
process-based workflow on web sites, 195
product criteria, assessing maturity
    using, 41
product information, 190
product roadmap for commercial
    software, 20
productivity software, 154
productivity suites for desktop, 156
productization, 105–115
    of commercial software, 21
    lack of, when using open source, 23
    of Linux distributions, 153
    making projects easy to use, 109
    overcoming lack of, 105–107
    risk of, commercial software versus
        open source, 27
programming languages and open
    source, 61
projects, managing with intranets, 177
publishing
    basic online solutions, 190
    systems for weblogs, 201
purchasing commercial software, issues
    with, 138–140
Python scripting language, 62
Python-based systems, 58

Q

Qmail, 164
quality of code as evaluation factor, 37
quality risks, commercial software versus
    open source, 26
question-and-answer archive for
    projects, 108

R

Rational Unified Process, 143
Raymond, Eric, 10, 130, 133
RBLs (real-time blackhole lists), 170
release frequency as evaluation factor, 37
repository, content, 194
requirements gap, closing, 140
requirements gathering for commercial
    software, 20
risks
    adopting open source the low-risk
        way, 81
    of commercial and open source
        software, 24–28
    in open source lawsuits, 135
    skills and, 64
    (see also Open Source Skills and Risk
        Tolerance model)
ROI (return on investment)
    open source versus commercial
        software, 69–75
ROI analysis spreadsheet, creating, 75
Ruby scripting language, 62

S

sales process, commercial software versus
    open source, 24
sample code, accelerating learning with, 110
Santa Cruz Operation, 128
SCO Group lawsuit, 127–136
SCOsource, 129
scratching a developer's personal itch, 12
SCRUM, 143
search capabilities on the Web, 195
Searles, Doc, 141
Secure Web Server for OpenVMS, 2
security in web content management
    systems, 196

self-service sites for customers, 191
selling/marketing open source, 8
Sendmail, 162–165
Service Oriented Architectures (SOAs), 203
session management facilities, 204
Shared Source Initiative (Microsoft), 13
shareware, 8
Sheridan, Mike, 62
SISSL (Sun Industry Standards Source
   License), 125
site administration for web content
   management systems, 195
site design as evaluation factor, 39
skill building
  opportunities for, 115
  throughout the institution, 88
  using commercial open source support
   providers, 103
skill levels
  advanced, 53–55
  as part of evaluating costs, 70
  beginner, 51
  defined, 48–50
  expert, 55–57
  intermediate, 52–53
  risks and, 64
skill set for open source, 45–66
skills gap, reducing using automation, 109
skills versus money, 78
Smarty application server, 207
SOAs (Service Oriented Architectures), 203
Software Cost and Risk model, 5, 23
software development process, managing
   with intranets, 177
software, buying versus building, 138–140
Solaris, open source version of, 134
solutions for desktop space, 152–154
SourceForge, 15
SourceLabs, 99
SpamAssassin, 160, 171
SpamBayes, 171
SpamBayes Outlook plug-in, 160
SpikeSource, 99
stable IT systems, applying open source
   to, 89, 139
stages of open source projects, 98
Stallman, Richard, 9, 57, 117–120, 132
standards support as evaluation factor, 39
state-based workflow on web sites, 195

Stein, Greg, 57
strategic investments, 68
strategies, crafting for
  adopting open source, 80–89
  applying open source, 89–91
  managing open source, 91–93
strong engineering practices and open
   source projects, 143
Stroustrup, Bjarne, 62
structured content types, 194
submarine patents, 135
subscription model of open source
   support, 98
SugarCRM, 101
Sun Industry Standards Source License
   (SISSL), 125
Sun Microsystems and open source
   Solaris, 134
support costs for open source/commercial
   software, 74
  elements of, 78
support for open source, 95–104
  Linux distributions and, 153
  productization and, 105–107
  using forums and weblogs, 178
support issues, commercial software versus
   open source, 27
supporting commercial software, 22
system administration and open source, 59
systems integrators, 101
  creating custom features using, 103

T

takeover risks, commercial software versus
   open source, 27
task scheduling systems for web sites, 196
taxonomy of IT systems, 89–91
technical support sites, 191
templates for web pages, 196
testing facilities as evaluation factor, 38
TEX program, license for, 123
Thoeny, Peter, 112–114
Thunderbird (Mozilla), 168
Tigris.org, 6
Tikiwiki, 181
Tomcat application server, 35, 206
toolkits for content management
   systems, 202

tools for developers, creating using open
        source, 57
Torvalds, Linus, 12, 57, 133, 139
training/e-learning sites, 192
transparency of products, commercial
        software versus open source, 25
traps to avoid when choosing open
        source, 30
trends in open source, 18
Trillian, 186
TWiki project, 112–114, 147, 183

U
Ultimate Bulletin Board, 179
use criteria, assessing maturity using, 41
user interface design on web sites, 196
users, managing
        with open source groupware, 179
        with Wikis, 183

V
van Rossum, Guido, 62
vBulletin, 179
vendor lock-in, reducing, 145
versioning/change logs for web sites, 194
viral licensing, 119
virtual folders, 165

W
Wall, Larry, 57, 62
waterfall development methodology, 143
web browsing, 154
        with Firefox, 157
web publishing, 189
        capabilities of, 193–198
WebDAV protocol, 198
weblogs, 190
        providing product support with, 178
        publishing systems for, 201
Wikis, 112, 182
Wild Open Source, 99
Wind River Systems, 112
window managers and resource usage, 153
workflow management on web sites, 195
working examples of projects, 108

X
XFCE4 window manager, 153

Z
Zope application server, 11, 208
        Plone, built on, 198

About the Authors

DAN WOODS, a seasoned CTO, has built technology for companies ranging from Time Inc. New Media to TheStreet.com. He has managed the product development cycle from initial requirements through sales for web sites and software products designed for the publishing and financial services industries. Dan has also navigated all phases of the business cycle: crafting strategy and budgets, building and managing large development teams, writing patent applications, negotiating large vendor agreements, operating data centers, communicating with board members, raising money, and selling and marketing a product. Dan is the author of two books and a frequent contributor to InfoWorld and other publications.

GAUTAM GULIANI is a software architect and developer with over 10 years of experience in designing and developing enterprise grade to business problems in publishing, finance and education areas. He currently works as Director of Software Architecture at Kaplan Test Prep and Admissions, a Washington Post company.

Colophon

SARAH SHERMAN was the production editor and proofreader for *Open Source for the Enterprise*. Audrey Doyle was the copyeditor. Marlowe Shaeffer and Darren Kelly provided quality control. Judy Hoer wrote the index. Lydia Onofrei provided production assistance.

MIKE KOHNKE designed the cover of this book. Karen Montgomery produced the cover layout in Adove InDesign CS.

Phyllis McKee designed the interior layout and the template. This book was converted by Keith Fahlgren to FrameMaker 5.5.6 with a format conversion tool created by Erik Ray, Jason McIntosh, Neil Walls, and Mike Sierra that uses Perl and XML technnologies. The text font is Adobe's Berkley Book; the heading font is Trade Gothic. The illustrations that appear in the book were produced by Robert Romano, Jessamyn Read, and Lesley Borash using Macromedia FreeHand MX and Adobe Photoshop CS and using the ORA hand font.

Better than e-books

Buy *Open Source for the Enterprise* and access
the digital edition FREE on Safari for 45 days.

Go to www.oreilly.com/go/safarienabled
and type in coupon code NQEL-G8AG-3AY3-MWFM-65C9

Search → over 2000 top
tech books

Download → whole chapters

Cut and Paste → code examples

Find → answers fast

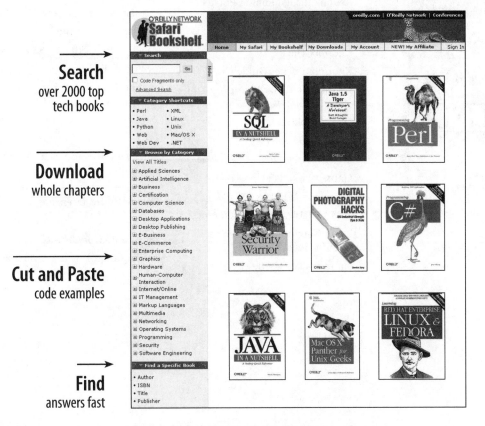

Search Safari! The premier electronic reference
library for programmers and IT professionals

Related Titles from O'Reilly

Linux

Building Embedded Linux Systems

Building Secure Servers with Linux

The Complete FreeBSD, *4th Edition*

Even Grues Get Full

Exploring the JDS Linux Desktop

Extreme Programming Pocket Guide

GDB Pocket Reference

Knoppix Hacks

Knoppix Pocket Guide

Learning Red Hat Enterprise Linux and Fedora, *4th Edition*

Linux Cookbook

Linux Desktop Hacks

Linux Device Drivers, *3rd Edition*

Linux in a Nutshell, *5th Edition*

Linux in a Windows World

Linux iptables Pocket Reference

Linux Network Administrator's Guide, *3rd Edition*

Linux Pocket Guide

Linux Security Cookbook

Linux Server Hacks

Linux Unwired

Linux Web Server CD Bookshelf, *Version 2.0*

LPI Linux Certification in a Nutshell, *2nd Edition*

Managing RAID on Linux

More Linux Server Hacks

OpenOffice.org Writer

Programming with Qt, *2nd Edition*

Root of all Evil

Running Linux, *4th Edition*

Samba Pocket Reference, *2nd Edition*

Test Driving Linux

Understanding the Linux Kernel, *2nd Edition*

Understanding Open Source & Free Software Licensing

User Friendly

Using Samba, *3rd Edition*

Version Control with Subversion

O'REILLY®

Our books are available at most retail and online bookstores.

To order direct: 1-800-998-9938 • *order@oreilly.com* • *www.oreilly.com*

Online editions of most O'Reilly titles are available by subscription at *safari.oreilly.com*

Keep in touch with O'Reilly

Download examples from our books

To find example files from a book, go to: *www.oreilly.com/catalog* select the book, and follow the "Examples" link.

Register your O'Reilly books

Register your book at *register.oreilly.com* Why register your books? Once you've registered your O'Reilly books you can:

- Win O'Reilly books, T-shirts or discount coupons in our monthly drawing.
- Get special offers available only to registered O'Reilly customers.
- Get catalogs announcing new books (US and UK only).
- Get email notification of new editions of the O'Reilly books you own.

Join our email lists

Sign up to get topic-specific email announcements of new books and conferences, special offers, and O'Reilly Network technology newsletters at:

elists.oreilly.com

It's easy to customize your free elists subscription so you'll get exactly the O'Reilly news you want.

Get the latest news, tips, and tools

www.oreilly.com

- "Top 100 Sites on the Web"—PC Magazine
- CIO Magazine's Web Business 50 Awards

Our web site contains a library of comprehensive product information (including book excerpts and tables of contents), downloadable software, background articles, interviews with technology leaders, links to relevant sites, book cover art, and more.

Work for O'Reilly

Check out our web site for current employment opportunities:

jobs.oreilly.com

Contact us

O'Reilly Media, Inc.
1005 Gravenstein Hwy North
Sebastopol, CA 95472 USA
Tel: 707-827-7000 or 800-998-9938
    (6am to 5pm PST)
Fax: 707-829-0104

Contact us by email

For answers to problems regarding your order or our products:
order@oreilly.com

To request a copy of our latest catalog:
catalog@oreilly.com

For book content technical questions or corrections: **booktech@oreilly.com**

For educational, library, government, and corporate sales: **corporate@oreilly.com**

To submit new book proposals to our editors and product managers:
proposals@oreilly.com

For information about our international distributors or translation queries:
international@oreilly.com

For information about academic use of O'Reilly books:
adoption@oreilly.com
or visit:
academic.oreilly.com

For a list of our distributors outside of North America check out:
international.oreilly.com/distributors.html

Order a book online

www.oreilly.com/order_new

Our books are available at most retail and online bookstores.
To order direct: 1-800-998-9938 • *order@oreilly.com* • *www.oreilly.com*
Online editions of most O'Reilly titles are available by subscription at *safari.oreilly.com*